The 1945 Burma Campaign and the Transformation of the British Indian Army

The 1945 Burma Campaign and the Transformation of the British Indian Army

Raymond A. Callahan and
Daniel Marston

University Press of Kansas

All art courtesy of the Imperial War Museum, unless otherwise noted.

Published by the University Press of Kansas (Lawrence, Kansas 66045), which was organized by the Kansas Board of Regents and is operated and funded by Emporia State University, Fort Hays State University, Kansas State University, Pittsburg State University, the University of Kansas, and Wichita State University.

Library of Congress Cataloging-in-Publication Data

Names: Callahan, Raymond A., author. | Marston, Daniel, author.
Title: The 1945 Burma Campaign and the transformation of the British Indian Army / Raymond A. Callahan and Daniel Marston.
Description: Lawrence : University Press of Kansas, [2021] | Series: Modern war studies | Includes bibliographical references and index.
Identifiers: LCCN 2020018384
ISBN 9780700630417 (cloth)
ISBN 9780700630424 (epub)
Subjects: LCSH: World War, 1939–1945—Campaigns—Burma. | India. Army—History—World War, 1939–1945. | Great Britain. Army. Army, XIV. | World War, 1939–1945—Japan. | World War, 1939–1945—Great Britain. | World War, 1939–1945—India.
Classification: LCC D767.6 .C289 2021 | DDC 940.54/2591—dc23
LC record available at https://lccn.loc.gov/2020018384.

British Library Cataloguing-in-Publication Data is available.

Printed in the United States of America

10 9 8 7 6 5 4 3 2 1

The paper used in this publication is recycled and contains 30 percent postconsumer waste. It is acid free and meets the minimum requirements of the American National Standard for Permanence of Paper for Printed Library Materials Z39.48–1992.

To my daughter Sarah, for her never failing support—and with thanks to Dan who invited me to join in writing this book.

To Nancy and Bronwen who the make the journey worthwhile—and to Ray who shared the idea and the endeavor. Finally, to all my AoW/STP alumni who have made me a better historian.

Contents

A photo gallery follows page 128.

Preface

In December 1944, the commander of the British XIV Army, Lt. Gen. Sir William Slim, revisited a site on the east bank of the river Chindwin recently cleared of the Japanese by his advancing army. Schwegyin was the place where, in May 1942, Slim, then an acting lieutenant general commanding the hastily improvised Burma Corps (Burcorps), had destroyed its remaining wheeled and tracked vehicles, as well as its artillery pieces, which he lacked the means of getting across the Chindwin. It was the last act in the long retreat of Burcorps—the longest in British military history, in fact. As Slim walked among the rusting wreckage of Burcorps's equipment he reflected on the transformation that had occurred in the two and a half years since that dark May: "Some of what we owed we had paid back. Now we were going to pay back the rest—with interest."[1] This book is the story of that payback.

Of course, the "forgotten" XIV Army of World War II has subsequently received considerable attention, scholarly and popular, and Slim, little known in 1944, is now regarded as one of Britain's finest generals. But there are aspects of the final act in the longest land campaign that Britain (or the United States) would fight in World War II that make it worthy of further attention.

There is Slim's remarkable career—the lower-middle-class boy who became an officer only because the First World War opened the door for him to become a "temporary gentleman." The unfashionable Indian Army allowed him to transform himself into a regular after 1918.

After leading Burcorps out of Burma in 1942, he played a crucial role in the remarkable military renaissance that transformed the Indian Army and then, with that reborn army, won two defensive battles in 1944 that fatally damaged the Imperial Japanese Army in Burma. In his campaign of 1945, the most brilliant feat of operational maneuver by any British general in World War II, he reconquered Burma, shredding his Japanese opponents. Then, in the moment of victory (won by an overwhelmingly Indian "British" XIV Army, whose African component outnumbered its British), he was sacked by his British Army superior, whom, in the aftermath, Slim replaced.

Behind this dramatic story was another. The war marked the effective end of the Raj—what happened in the last two years of its existence was, fundamentally, a protracted argument on when to vacate the premises and whom to hand the keys to. The end of the British Raj in India, entailing, as it did, the speedy demise of "British Asia," is one of the central facts of twentieth-century history. This great transformation was, of course, brought about by many factors but not the least of them was the "Indianization" of the Indian Army's officer corps under the pressure of war. As Slim's great victory signposted the change from the army Kipling knew to a modern army with a growing number of Indian officers, the praetorian guard of the Raj evaporated. "Every Indian officer worth his salt is a nationalist," the Indian Army's commander-in-chief, Claude Auchinleck, said as the XIV Army took Rangoon. That was a sign that the curtain was coming down on the Raj.

The Burma campaign may not have contributed in a major fashion to the final defeat of Japan—as a recent popular historian has pointed out—but was of first-rate importance in the transformation of South Asia, as well as underlining the continuing importance of inspired leadership in complex human endeavors.[2]

The 1945 Burma Campaign and the Transformation of the British Indian Army

Introduction

Early on 20 January 1942, Japanese forces advancing from recently occupied Siam (Thailand) clashed with a company of the 1/7th Gurkha Rifles, deployed near the Burmese frontier with Siam some fifty miles east of Moulmein. It was the opening encounter in a very long war that ended only with Japan's surrender, forty-four months later.[1] The first two years of that war were, for the British Raj and its army, a tale of unmitigated failure. Burma's defenses, hastily cobbled together at the last minute because Burma was not supposed to be at risk (until it was), were utterly inadequate and rested largely on the new, only partially trained the 17th Indian Infantry Division, commanded by a World War I Victoria Cross winner now too ill to be fully effective.[2] There was little air cover. The 17th Indian was forced steadily back until, at the Sittang River (the last barrier before Rangoon and its vital port), aggressive Japanese tactics, the growing weariness and disorganization of the division (the RAF, making a rare appearance, had bombed them), and their commander's debility produced catastrophe. The bridge over the Sittang was blown with two-thirds of the division on the wrong side. In the aftermath, the 17th Indian mustered less than a brigade—and only half of the survivors had rifles. The road to Rangoon was open and once Rangoon fell there was no possibility of holding Burma, even if enough trained troops and air support were available—and neither was. It was now a matter of whether the remnants of Burma's defenders could be successfully withdrawn to India (with which Burma had neither road nor rail connections). Into this gloomy picture two new commanders were introduced. The commander-in-chief, India, responsible for Burma, descended upon the scene and sacked the commander of the 17th Indian (he was subsequently reduced in rank and compulsorily retired). In his place, the assistant division commander, D. C. T. "Punch" Cowan, took over the etiolated division. He would command it, brilliantly, for the rest of the war. Even more important, to bring more coherence to the forces in Burma (in addition to the 17th Indian, there was the 1st Burma Division, most of whose Burmese troops had already deserted) a small corps headquarters (Burcorps) was created, without much of the equipment and personnel such a headquarters usually had. To command it Maj. Gen. William Slim, bumped up to acting lieutenant general, was brought from Iraq, where he had successfully commanded the 10th Indian Infantry Division. Slim took over on 19 March 1942. Over the next two months he would lead Burcorps, attenuated but intact, out of Burma and into the bordering Indian province of Assam. He was assisted by Cowan's success in breathing life into what remained of the 17th Indian and by the British 7th Armoured Brigade (landed just before Rangoon fell). With their long experience of the desert war against Rommel, the 7th brought not only a veteran presence, but firepower and a signals net that Burcorps desperately needed. But most of all, what got Burcorps back to India was Slim. He had taken over in the midst of disaster and Burcorps would several times teeter on the edge of further disaster as it trekked toward Assam and safety. Slim's determination, his refusal to panic, his tactical skill, and that intangible quality that already clung to him like a cloak and that we call leadership brought it through. Slim learned a lot on that long retreat and he formed a resolve to use that knowledge to expunge the debacles and defeats of 1942 with a victory that would recover all that had been lost.

The opportunity to craft that victory was long in coming—and at times it seemed as if Slim would have no part in it.[3] If 1942 saw the low point in Britain's war with the spectacular capitulations at Singapore in February and Tobruk in June—"defeat is one thing, disgrace another," Churchill remarked—the Indian Army had yet to hit bottom. That happened in mid-1943—by which time the victory at El Alamein in November 1942 had allowed Churchill to proclaim the "end of the beginning" in the war against Germany. The ugly defeat of the Indian Army in the first Arakan offensive in early 1943 nearly ended Slim's career but he survived to become instrumental in the Indian Army's rebirth. By the end of 1943 he was commanding the newly created the XIV Army and playing a key role in the Indian military renaissance that produced in February 1944 the Indian Army's El Alamein, the "Battle of the Admin Box."[4]

In the aftermath of the retreat from Burma a number of initiatives began to rebuild and restructure the Indian Army for its new war. Their efforts were not yet however systematic and army-wide. The Indian Army was

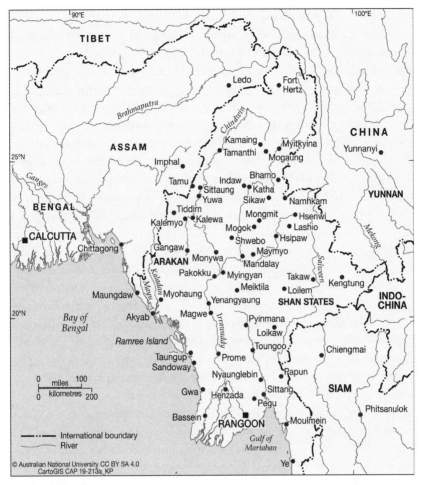

Burma, 1941–1945

still in the throes of open-ended expansion mandated by London after the fall of France, largely to support the imperial war effort in the Middle East. This expansion prioritized numbers over quality (producing half-ready divisions like 17th Indian) and made the task of reshaping the training of the army nearly impossible, as its officers realized. Nonetheless, beginnings were made, especially at the 15th Corps, Slim's next command, where ideas that would be central to the XIV Army's success were incubated.

But the whole complex business of recovering from defeat and retraining for victory was derailed by London in the autumn of 1942. Churchill was under pressure from the Americans, whose access to China had been barred by the loss of Rangoon, where the long rail and road connection known as the Burma Road originated. The Americans wanted that link restored. Alliance politics meant Churchill had to show willingness. Thus was born the first Arakan campaign, a crawl down that pestilential coastal strip of Burma aiming to take the island of Akyab as a jumping off place for an attack (someday) on Rangoon. The troops involved were, if anything, less prepared than the 17th Indian had been. The result was a debacle when the Japanese launched a counterstroke. The offensive had been conducted by Lt. Gen. Noel Irwin, a British Army officer who combined a disdain for the Indian Army (a trait far from rare among British Army regulars) with a bad temper and mediocre professional skills. He involved Slim at the last minute to save what could be saved—and to be available as a scapegoat. Irwin's message sacking Slim was only negated by one from the commander-in-chief, India, Gen. Sir Archibald Wavell, sacking Irwin. Slim had been saved by the fallout from an explosion in faraway London.

Winston Churchill's attitude to the Raj and its army is difficult to untangle and hard to explain—for that reason his admirers have rarely tried. Famous for his doughty defense of the British Empire, and his "die-hard" defense of British control of India, he in fact knew little of the Raj (despite having been stationed there as a young subaltern) and rather disdained what he thought he knew. He described the Raj machine as a "welter of lassitude and inefficiency." That was flattering compared to his view of the Indian Army. In August 1941 he asked Gen. Sir Claude Auchinleck, a career Indian Army officer who was pleading that army's case, as it expanded, for larger allocations of modern equipment, whether he was sure the Indian Army, with modern weapons in its hands, would point their guns in the right direction. Clearly the mutiny in 1857 in the East India Company's Bengal Army remained very vivid to Churchill, born only seventeen years after that event. But however deficient his understanding of the Raj and its army, he understood very clearly the impact of the debacle in the Arakan on alliance politics.

The Americans wanted a restored overland link to China (meanwhile they were mounting a very costly airlift from India to keep a trickle of American supplies flowing to China). They had imposed a US Army theater command (CBI—China, Burma, India) onto Britain's India Command. CBI's commanding general, Lt. Gen. Joseph Stilwell, might have been selected to personify the realities of the Anglo-American alliance in

South and East Asia. A toxic Anglophobe, he was retraining several Chinese divisions on American lines at Ramgarh in north India. With them he would mount a drive from Ledo in far northeast Assam into Burma. Behind his Americanized Chinese formations would come road builders cutting a new highway through jungles and across mountains to tie into the old Burma Road and make possible a flood of American supplies that would—together with American advisors—remake the manpower-rich but equipment-poor Chinese armies into a formidable fighting force. It was a beguiling vision—or, more properly, fantasy—that however required the Indian Army to reconquer at least northern Burma. The fiasco in the Arakan was not a good advertisement for its ability to do so.[5]

Success in Burma was important for Anglo-American amity—especially since Franklin Roosevelt was a strong supporter of the vision of an Americanized China. Between the end of the Arakan campaign in May and the Anglo-American summit conference at Quebec in September, Churchill reshaped the structure and strategy of the Burma campaign in order to ensure it did not have an adverse impact on Anglo-American relations. The prime minister intended to marginalize the Raj and its army, which he disliked and distrusted. India would continue to raise and train troops and provide logistic support but the war in Burma would be run by the new South East Asia Command (SEAC). The choice of a young, charming, glamorous (and moderately talented as well as overpromoted) relative of the royal family, Vice Admiral Lord Louis Mountbatten, as SEAC's supreme commander signaled Churchill's real long-term plan—an amphibious strategy, leaping from the Indian base across the Bay of Bengal to retake Malaya, rehoist the Union Jack at Singapore, and restore the imperial prestige shattered by the disasters of 1942. Burma would be dealt with—and the Americans satisfied—by embracing a new, unorthodox, and totally unproven approach to defeating the Japanese. This was Brig. Orde Wingate's theory of "long-range penetration."

Orde Wingate owed his career to Wavell, who met him in Palestine, where he served as GOC (general officer commanding) in 1937–1938 during the Arab revolt against the British Mandate. Wavell allowed the eccentric young gunner officer to run a highly unorthodox counterterrorism operation. A few years later, as commander-in-chief, Middle East, Wavell used Wingate to raise and lead Ethiopian guerrillas against the disintegrating Italian occupiers. Finally as commander-in-chief, India, he extracted Wingate from a dead-end posting in Britain (Wingate had few friends among conventional soldiers) and brought him to India to put his talent for the unconventional to work against the Japanese. Wingate's ideas were relatively simple: breaking an infantry battalion into its component companies (christened "columns"), he planned to infiltrate them into Burma through the porous Japanese front, coordinate their operations by radio, and resupply them by air as they struck deep behind Japanese lines, disrupting communications. Wavell gave him a brigade to retrain in his methods and, in February 1943, allowed him to lead it into Burma to field test his theories. Slim, who had met Wingate during the campaign in East Africa that destroyed the Italian empire there, doubted that tactics based on fighting Arab raiders in Palestine and demoralized Italian-led local troops in Ethiopia would work against the Japanese. Nor did they. Some easily repairable damage was done to railway lines, but the "Chindits" were cornered by the Japanese and forced to break into small escape parties to make their way back from Burma. They lost a third of their number and all their equipment in the process.[6] By the time they reached India, Wavell, Wingate's patron and protector, was on his way back to London, recalled by Churchill for "consultations" (in this case a euphemism for removal from command). The Wingate experiment seemed over, but Wingate was about to prove how right Napoleon had been when he said that luck was an essential ingredient of a general's career.

The returning Chindits reached India just as the Arakan operations drew to a dismal close. Desperate for something, anything, that looked like a victory, public relations officers in Delhi were unleashed to "write up" the Chindits. In very short order, what Slim had reckoned a cavalry raid in modern guise with few results became a brilliant feat of arms, heralding an entirely new way of making war, one that offered the key to defeating the hitherto-invincible Imperial Japanese Army in Burma's forbidding jungles. Winston Churchill, furious at the Raj and its army for creating a major problem in alliance politics, suddenly saw a possible solution to that problem and grabbed it with both hands.

Wingate was whisked back to London and dined with the prime minister on the eve of his departure for the Anglo-American summit, christened Quadrant, at Quebec. A dinnertime's worth of conversation convinced Churchill that Wingate was the answer to his Burma problem and he was immediately added to the prime minister's traveling party. The chief of the Imperial General Staff, Gen. Sir Alan Brooke, who had met Wingate before his dinner date at Number Ten and decided that his ideas, within strict limits, might have some uses, immediately recognized what Churchill was doing: Wingate was to be a "trick pony" to dazzle the Americans. And dazzle them he did. Wingate was always at his best when selling his ideas to those civilians whose support he needed (with the important exception of Wavell, senior professional soldiers were a harder sell). Wingate arrived in Quebec a lieutenant colonel and acting brigadier. He left an acting major general and was promised a much-expanded Chindit force—christened Special Force—whose creation would cause havoc in India Command. Gen. H. H. "Hap" Arnold, the commanding general of the US Army Air Force, excited by the idea of demonstrating the importance of air power in a new arena, gifted Wingate with a private air force to match his corps-size private army. It was a remarkable performance by both Churchill and Wingate. American suspicions, heightened by Stilwell's venomous commentaries (that the British lacked the competence and courage to tackle the Japanese in Burma), had been allayed, at least temporarily, and a strategy for clearing the Japanese out of the path of Stilwell's road builders had been shaped and agreed on. When the 1943 monsoon season ended in the autumn and the campaigning season arrived, Special Force, striking in numbers deep into the Japanese rear, would lever them out of north Burma, Stilwell's construction units would surge forward, overland communications with China would be restored, and American supplies would rejuvenate Chiang's armies. And what of the Indian Army? One of the points of agreement between Wingate and Churchill was that the Indian Army was a second-rate force, suitable only to follow Special Force, mopping up and garrisoning rewon Burmese territory.

While Churchill trumped American concerns over the British commitment to reopening their road to China by producing Wingate, in India a remarkable transformation was underway that would ultimately do more to shape the way the war in Burma played out than either the prime minister or the military visionary. Wavell, as he left India for the "consultations" in London that ended his tenure as commander-in-chief—and saw him elevated to viceroy (a job no politician of rank in Britain wanted to touch)—not only sacked Irwin but appointed a committee to recommend how to upgrade the Indian Army's infantry, which had performed poorly in Malaya, in Burma, and, most recently, in the Arakan. The committee included Maj. Gen. "Taffy" Davies, who had been Slim's chief of staff in Burcorps and was familiar with the ideas Slim had developed on the training and tactics needed to combat the Japanese. In London, coincidentally, a decision was taken as the committee assembled that greatly facilitated its work. Open-ended expansion, decreed by London in 1940, had been the driver of declining quality. A cabinet committee, sitting in Churchill's absence and chaired by Clement Attlee (always more reasonable on Indian matters than the prime minister), decided to end breakneck expansion and cap the size of the Indian Army. Thus when the Infantry Committee adopted a series of recommendations for reform they could do so with the assurance that the stabilization of the army's size would allow those recommendations to actually have an effect.

A series of personnel changes during the summer of 1943 consolidated the changes set in motion by the Infantry Committee. Churchill had never quite felt comfortable with Wavell (who he once characterized as reminding him of the chairman of a suburban golf club). When he relieved him as commander-in-chief, Middle East, in June 1941, he sent him to India because it was a convenient way to fill the gap in India opened by his naming the commander-in-chief there, Gen. Sir Claude Auchinleck, to succeed Wavell in Cairo. Auchinleck, in turn, was removed by Churchill in August 1942—like Wavell, he had failed to beat Rommel. He had been unemployed ever since. Now Churchill (who respected Auchinleck personally) sent him back to Delhi, as commander-in-chief, for the second time. Auchinleck, an Indian Army officer, would be the driver of a great transformation in his service. He summoned Maj. Gen. Reginald Savory from divisional command to become director of infantry at army headquarters. With Auchinleck at his back Savory would drive a remarkably rapid change in the battered Indian Army. As the new SEAC headquarters took shape, another key player appeared on the scene. The SEAC command structure called for Mountbatten to have three service commanders under him. The SEAC land forces commander would be Gen. Sir George Giffard, one of the war's important but forgotten figures. Giffard came to India from West Africa, where he had presided over the explosive growth of the colonial light infantry units there into field force divisions, two of which would fight in Burma. Giffard's headquarters, the 11th Army Group, would have as its principal fighting formation a new XIV Army, formed out of the Indian Army's Eastern Army. To command the new army, Slim was summoned from his 15th Corps headquarters, where he had been stabilizing the situation created by Irwin in the Arakan. As he was driven from Calcutta's airport to his new headquarters in suburban Barrackpore he looked at the new army commander's flag flying on the car's bonnet and, as he recalled in his memoirs, "wondered where I was going." He was heading into history—and it would be the Indian Army that took him there.

The makeover of the Indian Army set in motion by the debacle in the Arakan gathered steam very quickly. Driven by Auchinleck and Savory in Delhi, and the tireless energy with which the army's Directorate of Training cranked out instructional guidance culminating in a new jungle warfare manual (promptly christened "The Jungle Book"), training establishments across the subcontinent changed gears rapidly, and in the eight months between the end of the Arakan battle and the XIV Army's first battlefield test, in February 1944, a new army was forged.[7]

But the real test of any army—or any commander—is combat. And until February 1944 no one was sure how the new Indian Army would fare against the battle-hardened Imperial Japanese Army—or how Slim would handle his new role as an army commander. When he became the XIV Army commander, he made the conclusions he had drawn from Burcorps's retreat and the fiasco of the first Arakan offensive the operating instructions for his army: tough physical and weapons training for everyone; aggressive patrolling to avoid surprise; cut-off and encircled units were to stand fast, await aerial resupply, and provide the anvil against which counterattacking forces could shatter the Japanese attackers. One crucial element in the formula was not, however, under Slim's control: aerial resupply. That depended on the single-most important piece of equipment in the Burma campaign: the American-built Douglas DC-3, the "Dakota" to the British, destined to be the pivot of Slim's campaign. Aerial resupply was not a new idea in 1943. There had been experiments with it during World War I and Slim, as a young staff officer at Indian Army headquarters in the 1920s, had explored its possibilities. Wingate's first Chindit venture had helped refine techniques. But it had never been tried on a large scale and the transport squadrons necessary to do so did not belong to the RAF—or SEAC. They were owned by the American transport command that ran the "Hump" airlift to China. And that command answered to Stilwell and, ultimately, Washington. When SEAC had been created, Mountbatten was told that in an emergency he could draw on the American Hump squadrons but the only air transport assets SEAC directly controlled were two RAF Dakota squadrons.

In February 1944 the Japanese gave the new Indian Army, Slim and his new headquarters, and the Dakota-based air supply organization a stress test. In the autumn of 1943, Lt. Gen. Mutaguchi Renya had assumed command of the Japanese 15th Army in Burma. Since conquering the country in 1942 the Japanese had stood on the defensive. Burma was the western anchor of the Greater East Asia Co-Prosperity Sphere. Mutaguchi argued for a switch to an offensive stance. Wingate's raid had led Mutaguchi to doubt whether the river Chindwin—the Indo-Burmese border—really was a good defensive line. Better, he argued, to cross the Chindwin and take the large British base area on the Imphal plain in eastern Assam, the jumping off point for Wingate—and for any future British counteroffensive into Burma. With the Imphal plain in their possession the western frontier of Japan's empire would be secure.[8] As a preliminary to the capture of Imphal, a subsidiary offensive would be mounted against Slim's old 15th Corps in the Arakan to draw in and tie down British reserves. This set the stage for the XIV Army's debut.

The XIV Army expected a Japanese forward move in the Arakan but the actual launching of the attack, on the morning of 4 February 1944, came as a tactical surprise. The attacking Japanese brigade quickly penetrated to the rear of the 7th Indian Infantry Division and surrounded its principal maintenance base. For two years this had guaranteed victory for the Japanese but now they faced a new army. The miscellany of units that formed the garrison of what became known as the "Admin Box" stood fast in a new version of the legendary British square. Slim's insistence that everybody, down to cooks and mule drivers, be able to double, in an emergency, as infantry bore fruit. So did his plan for resupply of cut-off units. The Dakotas came, dropping from treetop height and ignoring ground fire, to be sure of hitting the small drop zone. The Japanese had expected to resupply themselves from captured British dumps (which they christened "Churchill supplies"). Balked by the unyielding defense of the Admin Box and the refusal of Slim's units to conform to their expectations by retreating in disorder, the relentless commitment to tactical aggressiveness baked into the Imperial Japanese Army's ethos became a death warrant. Shredded by the XIV Army firepower, the Japanese, starving, broke off their attack on 24 February. The British counted five thousand dead (and many more doubtless lay undiscovered in the jungle). For the first time since December 1941, the Indian Army had decisively beaten the Imperial

Japanese Army on the battlefield. It was the turning point of the war in Burma—the Indian Army would never lose again.

Years before, as a student at the Indian Army's staff college at Quetta, a tactical solution Slim offered to a problem set had been critiqued by an instructor as using a pile driver to crush a walnut. "Sir," Slim responded, "have you ever seen a walnut that's been crushed by a pile driver?" The Admin Box battle was the first example of what that clever retort would look like in practice. Slim and his army were about to produce a second. As the Japanese offensive in the Arakan petered out, Mutaguchi's main attack opened several hundred miles to the north as the three divisions of his 15th Army hurled themselves at Slim's 4th Corps, holding the Imphal plain.

Lt. Gen. Geoffrey Scoones's 4th Corps was as strong as the Japanese 15th Army but was sprawled over a vast area, exposed to defeat in detail. The 17th Indian Infantry Division (the Black Cats) was 130 miles south of Imphal at the end of a road the division had built largely by itself with minimal road-building equipment. The division, and its road, had as their object the Chindwin River port of Kalewa. Douglas Gracey's 20th Indian Infantry Division was some seventy miles southeast of the Imphal plain also trailing a road. Its objective was the river port of Tamu. Kalewa and Tamu would be the crossing points into Burma when the XIV Army launched—someday—the offensive that would redeem 1942. Only Scoones's corps reserve, the 23rd Indian Infantry Division, was actually on the plain.[9]

Mutaguchi's plan was quite straightforward. Taking advantage of the dispersion of 4th Corps, he planned for two of his divisions to isolate and destroy the 17th and 20th Indian while the third, crossing the Chindwin north of Imphal, struck across the wild, partially unmapped Naga Hills, aiming at the small town of Kohima on the road from Imphal to the major supply base at Dimapur, whose capture would complete the isolation of Imphal. Then, with the 17th and 20th Indian destroyed, all three Japanese divisions would close in on Imphal, crushing Scoones's remaining division and reaping a harvest of "Churchill supplies." So certain was Mutaguchi of victory that his men carried only three weeks' supplies. He would present Imphal to his emperor as a birthday present. He seems not to have noticed the spectacular failure of a similar plan to isolate and destroy an Indian division in the Arakan.

Slim's plan was equally simple but much more realistic. Scoones's two divisions would withdraw in the face of the 15th Army's offensive—until they reached the "gates" of the plain, the points where the roads entered it. There they would stand fast and a concentrated 4th Corps, backed by artillery, armor, and tactical airpower, would shred Mutaguchi's divisions, committed as they would be to a relentless offensive. To support his plan Slim reorganized the sprawling base complex that had grown up on the Imphal plain. Some surplus personnel were flown back to India; the rest were gathered in defended boxes covering the Imphal plain's two all-weather airstrips. Those airfields, which were expected to remain operational in monsoon conditions, were the key to everything—along with the Dakotas. The 4th Corps would allow itself to be besieged. A Dakota "air bridge" would sustain the three Indian divisions while they methodically pulverized the attacking Japanese: Have you ever seen a walnut crushed by a pile driver? The only weak point in Slim's design was in fact the indispensible Dakotas—there were still not enough RAF Dakota squadrons and so the Americans would have to loan the XIV Army Dakota squadrons from the Hump airlift. Dakota availability and the alliance politics that swirled around it would be one of Slim's major concerns during the three-and-a-half-month struggle that opened in mid-March.

At first, Mutaguchi's design seemed to be working. A key part of Slim's plan was the timing of the withdrawal of Scoones's divisions to the gates of the Imphal plain. Scoones's headquarters waited almost too long to order his most-exposed division, the 17th Indian, back and, as a result, the Japanese were already across its line of retreat. But the Black Cat division, under Cowan, had become perhaps the best division in the XIV Army. Cowan turned his division around and sixteen thousand men, twenty-five hundred vehicles, and thirty-five hundred mules started back to the Imphal plain, 130 miles away. The Japanese had lost none of their skill in building roadblocks or any of their tenacity in defending them. Such road-blocks had time and again proved fatal to Indian formations in Malaya and Burma in 1941–1942. Now the 17th Indian punched its way through them and, fed by Dakota air drops, marched up the road to a rendezvous with brigades from Roberts's 23rd Indian, which had hammered through more roadblocks to link up with the 17th Division. When the united force reached the plain, its southern gate was firmly shut in the face of the already-rather-battered Japanese 33rd Division (whose commander told Mutaguchi that the offensive had already failed and was sacked for his candor).

Another gate, the eastern, was also sealed when Gracey skillfully withdrew his 20th Indian Division. But north of the plain several crises erupted in the opening stages of the battle. The deployment of most of the 23rd Indian to help the 17th Indian's withdrawal left the Imphal plain unscreened on the north and northeast. The Japanese 15th Division might have had a clear run at the plain—and one of the crucial airfields—but for a desperate stand at Sangshak by the enormously outnumbered the 50th Indian Parachute Brigade, deployed at the last minute to seal the last gate to the plain. The delay the brigade expensively imposed on the Japanese bought the time necessary for the first decisive intervention by the Dakotas. Slim switched Maj. Gen. Harold Briggs's veteran 5th Indian Infantry Division by air from the Arakan. Its leading brigade deplaned as the parachute brigade was making its Rorke's Drift stand a few dozen miles to the northeast. With the plain secure, attention shifted to Kohima, a small civil administration "hill station" and cluster of military depots sprawling across a series of ridges around which the road from Imphal to the major supply base at Dimapur in the Brahmaputra Valley wound. The XIV Army believed that if the Japanese struck at Kohima, a brigade was the largest unit they could maintain across the rugged Naga hills. Mutaguchi, however, committed his entire 31st Division.

The defense of Kohima was complicated by some confusion as to who was responsible for it. In succession, the 4th Corps at Imphal, a Line of Communications command at Dimapur, and then Lt. Gen. Montague Stopford's 33rd Corps, transferred to Slim across the breadth of India by rail and Dakota, took control. But again a heroic delaying action, by a battalion of the newly raised Assam Regiment, bought time. Kohima's garrison, improvised from what personnel were available there, as well as the survivors of the Assam Regiment battalion and the 4th Royal West Kents, pushed into Kohima at the last minute, just before the Japanese 31st Division laid siege to it, and held for ten dramatic days before they were relieved, inflicting considerable punishment on the Japanese 31st Division.

Slim would later write that battles he was involved in seldom went according to plan.

The opening phases of the Imphal battle certainly didn't. But errors and mistaken assessments—by Scoones about the timing of the 17th Indian's withdrawal, by Slim and Stopford about where to place the responsibility for Kohima—were redeemed by the fighting qualities of his reborn army.

Cowan's Black Cats blasted their way back to the plain, as did Gracey's division. The stand of the parachute brigade at Songshak bought the time needed to secure the north gate of the plain. The Assam Regiment performed the same role for Kohima's improvised garrison. The ten-day siege that followed has drawn more attention than any other part of the sprawling three-month battle—perhaps because British historians were drawn to the role of the Royal West Kents, a British unit reprising the desperate defense against long odds theme so common in the military history of the British Empire. This has rather distorted the picture—these anxious weeks when the XIV Army, faced with unexpected situations, rallied and held their assailants were overwhelmingly the work of the rebuilt Indian Army. Cowan's two brigades had one British battalion; the 23rd Division's three brigades had no British units; the 50th Indian Parachute Brigade had none either; the Assam Regiment was both new and all Indian, and the stubborn defenders of Kohima in the epic ten-day siege were mostly Indian and Gurkha. Without the staunchness and fighting power of the Indian Army, Mutaguchi might well have given the emperor Imphal for his birthday.[10]

With the Imphal plain and its airfields secure and Kohima relieved by the advance from Dimapur of Stopford's corps (the 2nd British and 7th Indian Divisions) Slim could now begin the "pile driver" phase of his plan. He would remark in his memoirs that the Imphal battle was not easy to follow. But, while the detail is bewilderingly complex, the outline is clear. From mid-April until Mutaguchi's army, reduced to a thing of shreds and tatters, finally began to retreat in late June, the Imphal battle was in fact a series of separate battles—the 17th Indian at the plain's southern gate, the 20th Indian at the eastern, and the 5th and 23rd Indian in the north. Slim had invited the Japanese 15th Army to besiege XIV army, in a setting where his firepower—artillery, armor, tactical airpower—would be most effective. When he ordered the XIV Army to take the offensive in mid-April, he did so knowing that the relentless Japanese commitment to the offensive would force them to counterattack repeatedly, offering more targets for the XIV Army firepower. The refusal of the Imperial Japanese Army to yield ground, their death before withdrawal tactical doctrine, meant they would nail themselves in place while the XIV Army remorselessly pulverized them. Meanwhile, as the fighting power and vastly improved tactical skills of Slim's infantry turned the approaches to the plain into a killing ground, 33rd Corps began to grind its way south—the descending pile driver. Stopford moved slowly. The terrain the Japanese 31st

Division dug itself into was fiendishly difficult and one of his divisions, the 2nd British, although dourly determined, was learning on the job (for the past year it had been training in south India for amphibious operations). At Mountbatten's SEAC headquarters and in faraway London the situation gave rise to uneasiness—Would besieged Imphal be able to hold out? This seems remarkable since Slim had always been quite clear about his plan: the 4th Corps was the anvil upon which the advancing 33rd Corps would crush the Japanese. Slim's immediate superior, Giffard, understood Slim's design and supported it, but either because Giffard's own relations with Mountbatten (who was scheming to replace him) were poor or because the SEAC hierarchy and London were not paying close enough attention, the feeling grew in the command stratosphere that Imphal was in danger of falling. Slim had always expected Stopford to reach Scoones by the third week of June (the actual date the siege was lifted was 21 June), but at least concerns at the top helped focus attention on the one thing Slim needed above all from his superiors—Dakotas.

The Admin Box fight had depended on the Dakotas. Imphal-Kohima much more so. They fed the 17th Indian on its anabasis, and once the deliberately courted siege of Imphal locked into place they were crucial to the XIV Army. Slim needed more Dakotas than the RAF owned in the theater and that meant borrowing from the American Hump airlift and ultimately drawing in squadrons from the Mediterranean theater. The negotiations were complex and difficult but Mountbatten fought relentlessly for Slim to be given enough Dakotas—his major contribution to the XIV Army's victory. Even the prime minister, who generally ignored Burma after foisting Wingate onto the campaign, weighed in powerfully in support of what he saw as "Mountbatten's battle"—a British victory, wherever gained, was to be cherished.

In the end Slim got his Dakotas even if the process was intensely nerve-wracking. His air bridge, Operation Stamina, would deliver eighteen thousand tons of supplies and 12,250 reinforcements, while evacuating thirteen thousand sick and wounded plus removing forty-three thousand noncombatants and rear-area personnel. The Dakotas did this in the teeth of the monsoon, which heralded its arrival with increasingly heavy showers from late April on and broke in full fury in May. All but one of Imphal's airfields were washed out. The flying weather was horrendous. Ground crews worked in downpours to load, unload, and service the planes but the Dakotas always arrived. Stalingrad was a disaster for the Wehrmacht because the Luftwaffe could not supply the 6th Army. The XIV Army won at Imphal because RAF and USAAF Dakotas could sustain the 4th Corps. When the 33rd Corps linked up with the defenders of the plain, the supply situation there was actually better than it had been at the beginning of the battle. Slim designed the battle; the rebuilt Indian Army fought it. But the Dakotas and the men who flew and serviced them made it all possible.[11]

Victory, classical military theory held, was consolidated by an aggressive pursuit of the beaten enemy to see that he never had the opportunity to catch his breath and rally. Slim's pursuit of Mutaguchi's shattered army must be reckoned to be in a class by itself. Slim intended to drive ahead during the monsoon season, which lasts from May to late summer or early autumn—a season when drenching downpours made movement difficult as whole hillsides slid away, carrying roads with them. Watercourses rose in spate, flying was difficult and often extremely hazardous, and tropical diseases ran riot. Not surprisingly, military operations were usually suspended during the monsoon. The Japanese were falling back on two different routes: down the track that led to Kalewa on the Chindwin—up which they had vainly pursued the 17th Indian—and down the Kabaw Valley to the east. (The division that had attacked Kohima was returning along its route of advance across the Naga Hills in such a state of disintegration as to be hardly worth pursuing.) On the road that led via Tiddim to Kalewa, the veteran 5th Indian slogged forward, making as little as two miles a day, maintained by Dakota as the monsoon washed the road away behind it. By the end of the monsoon pursuit, it was on its third commander, the other two having been forced to go on leave due to illness and exhaustion. But it was the drive down the sodden, pestilential Kabaw Valley that wrote the most remarkable chapter in the monsoon pursuit. It was the work of the 11th East African Division, one of three African divisions in XIV Army (whose neglected stories make them the truly forgotten army of the Burma campaign). The 11th East African was chosen for the Kabaw drive because of what the official history later coyly called (in a footnote to an appendix) its "supposed higher resistance" to malaria. Slim himself, in his memoir, sounded slightly defensive about the Kabaw, arguing it was chosen as the best route to the objective—securing the crossings of the Chindwin. He added that he had been told the East Africans had fewer malaria cases—he does not specify the source of that briefing. The Kabaw was a nightmare. Nothing wheeled or tracked could move. The East African division's porters (a feature of all the African divisions and one of which

Slim disapproved) got artillery pieces forward by disassembling them and moving them as head loads. Monsoon-generated atmospherics blotted out radio communications from time to time. Even the Dakotas had serious difficulties getting through. But Maj. Gen. "Fluffy" Fowkes's division kept squelching ahead. On 13 November 1944, as the monsoon faded, African and Indian troops entered Kalewa and a bridgehead across the Chindwin was secured. The monsoon pursuit was over. The XIV Army stood poised on the edge of the north Burma plains, ready to launch the dry-season offensive that would reclaim Burma. The 33rd Corps, which had conducted the monsoon pursuit, had fifty thousand casualties, 55 percent of its average daily strength. Ninety percent of those casualties were due to sickness. Slim's ruthless determination to push the monsoon pursuit at a very high cost (more casualties than the Imphal-Kohima battle) was, as he argued in his memoirs, based on his determination to see that the Japanese were given no breather and that the XIV Army was ready to launch its offensive the minute the monsoon ended. But there may have been another motive as well. Slim's plans for 1944–1945 were for an offensive that his hierarchy of superiors were not interested in launching and any pause in operational tempo might mean the sidetracking of the XIV Army, something that Slim intended to preclude.

As the Imphal-Kohima battle was won and the monsoon pursuit launched, a furious, protracted argument was taking place in London between Churchill and the British Chiefs of Staff about the future shape of Britain's contribution to the war against Japan. SEAC had been created with two missions: to satisfy the Americans that their desire for a restored road to China was being properly supported by the British in north Burma and—of greater importance to Churchill—that plans were developed and preparations made for a future in which, with Germany defeated, Britain's military strength could be redeployed eastward to reclaim Singapore and, in the prime minister's words, erase "the shame of our disaster at Singapore."[12] Churchill had never liked the Burma campaign, memorably likening it to going into the water to fight a shark. Indeed once Stilwell's Chinese-American force was in sight of capturing Myitkyina, the last obstacle to the completion of the road, he decreed that "our operations in Burma should be reduced to defensive operations."[13] The prime minister and SEAC both wanted a maritime amphibious strategy, aimed at seizing a foothold in northern Sumatra, a first stop on the way back to Singapore (Operation Culverin). It was in hopes of such an operation that 2nd British

Division had trained for a year in south India. The British Chiefs of Staff also had little interest in the Burma campaign, something reflected in the paucity of references to it in the contemporary diary entries of the powerful chief of the Imperial General Staff, Gen. Sir Alan Brooke. What they wanted, however, was to play a role in the American trans-Pacific drive by introducing a British Pacific Fleet to US admiral Chester Nimitz's central Pacific drive or a British task force, based in Australia, to operate on the left flank of MacArthur's Southwest Pacific theater, whose thrust was aimed at the Philippines. Both proposed British strategies were cloud castles. The British would not have the resources for either until Germany was beaten and even then would need extensive American help. The Americans, however, neither needed nor wanted a British presence in "their" war against Japan (nor were the Australians very enthusiastic). But much of 1944 was taken up wrangling over these competing strategies in London—unreal arguments between tired and increasingly rancorous men over a strategy for which Britain totally lacked the resources. Slim and the XIV Army were unlikely beneficiaries of this futile debate. Until London made up its mind, SEAC could not be given a new directive so its mission remained clearing north Burma, protecting Stilwell's new road—and hoping for a very different future. All the while, the XIV Army drove remorselessly toward the Chindwin and the prospect of a major victory in the 1944–1945 dry season, and Slim knew that it is hard to put the brakes on an army accumulating victories. As the monsoon pursuit played out, Slim's XIV Army staff was already working on Operation Capital, a plan to bring the Japanese Burma Area Army to battle on the plains to the west of the Irrawaddy, on terrain where the XIV Army's armor, tactical air support, and battle-hardened divisions could most advantageously operate. There the Burma Area Army would be destroyed, after which the XIV Army would descend on Rangoon, taking it before the next monsoon.[14]

But, as the monsoon pursuit concluded and the XIV Army readied itself for its next campaign, a small cloud appeared on the horizon, no bigger than a man's hand, but one that would grow until in May 1945 it burst, bringing the final crisis of the XIV Army's campaign. It was born out of problems in the SEAC command structure. Mountbatten had a trinity of service commanders under him. His ground force commander, Gen. Sir George Giffard, was immensely senior to the supreme commander, who was a substantive Royal Navy captain holding acting higher rank. Giffard therefore outranked him and was repelled by his self-aggrandizing

personality. (Similar problems, rooted in rank and personality, bedev-
iled Mountbatten's relations with his naval commander, Adm. Sir James
Somerville.) Mountbatten very quickly decided to remove Giffard, but
that could not be done until October. Slim liked Giffard, and the XIV
Army and the 11th Army Group worked smoothly together. Giffard un-
stintingly backed Slim from the Admin Box fight through the lengthy,
often fraught Imphal-Kohima battle. When he finally went in the autumn, his replacement could not have been worse chosen. Lt. Gen. Sir
Oliver Leese, Bt., was a Guards officer and a Montgomery protégé. After
commanding a corps under Monty in North Africa and Italy, he succeeded him at the 8th Army when Monty returned to Britain to prepare
for Overlord. His handling of the 8th Army in the Italian campaign was
none too deft, but he was nonetheless the War Office choice to succeed
Giffard as commander of Allied Land Forces, South East Asia (or ALFSEA,
as the 11th Army Group was renamed). Leese was overpromoted, which
would have been bad enough but he made a decision about the staffing of
his headquarters that made matters worse. The commander of the allied
armies in Italy, Gen. Sir Harold Alexander (who knew Slim from the
retreat from Burma in 1942, when he was the theater commander under
whom Burcorps served), warned Leese that taking his 8th Army staff with
him was unwise. Leese ignored the caution. He made a nearly clean sweep
of Giffard's headquarters, installing his 8th Army team. In his memoirs
Slim said pleasant things about Leese but then pointedly remarked on the
"desert sand" in the newcomers' shoes and their tendency to shove the 8th
Army practices and procedures down the XIV Army's throat. Slim noted
that this was annoying because he and his staff thought the XIV Army had
proved itself "quite something." ALFSEA was largely British Army; the
XIV Army largely Indian Army. The historic British Army condescension
to the Indian service henceforth hovered over the scene. To Leese Slim's
belief that the XIV Army was quite as good as the 8th Army (with its
corollary that Slim was as good a general as Monty) was simply *lese majeste*.

Sir William Slim—knighted for his victories in 1944—therefore entered the campaign of 1945 with multiple uncertainties hanging over him.
Would his masters, at SEAC and in London, shut down his campaign in
favor of the maritime strategy they had always wanted? Would the crucial American Dakotas still be there for him now that Washington had
its coveted road to China? Could he depend on Leese and his 8th Army
staff to have his back at crucial moments as Giffard had done? Seldom

has a general embarked on a major campaign with so many uncertainties hovering over him.

Appendix 1: The XIV Army behind the Scenes

Assam was never expected to be the scene of a huge military campaign. Added to the Raj in bits and pieces in the nineteenth century, much of it was wild, mountainous, and jungle-covered. Its principal industry was tea cultivation. Separated by the rest of India by the unbridged Brahmaputra River, its communications, both internal and with the rest of India, were scanty.

There were steamers on the Brahmaputra and a narrow-gauge railway whose freight had to be ferried across the river and then reloaded on rolling stock suitable for India's broad gauge system. The roads were mostly fair weather. When the monsoon broke they were impassible. The few all-weather roads—along with their bridges—were often washed out or closed by landslides during the monsoon season. Suddenly this sleepy Raj backwater was in the front lines and soon enough hosting first a division, then a corps, and then much of the XIV Army plus the American Hump airlift and Stilwell's Chinese American force building the Ledo Road, which was, someday, supposed to tie into the old Burma Road and open China to massive American aid.

The construction, operation, and maintenance of the Assam line of communications are one of the great logistic feats of World War II and remain virtually unknown. When the Western allies invaded Europe in 1944, they had as a base a highly industrialized, completely mobilized Britain. In 1942, as Burcorps staggered to safety in Assam, India, whose agricultural economy was only slowly modernizing, was already struggling to mobilize for a war no one ever expected to arrive on its doorstep, and from the most unlikely direction. Behind the logistic success of supporting the XIV Army was an even bigger story: the mobilization of the Raj to fight its last great war.[15]

This brief note cannot begin to do justice to that effort. But it is crucial to understand just what was involved to grasp the full extent of the XIV Army's accomplishments in 1944–1945. Most of the personnel of a modern army function in support roles (something Churchill had occasional difficulties with). In India numerous truck companies were being raised. Recruits to the Indian Army were largely illiterate; few had ever seen the sort of vehicles they had now to learn to operate and maintain. Communications are the nervous system of modern forces. As the signals branch of the Indian Army ballooned, recruits had to be taught English (the signals language) before being taught signaling. In 1941 as the Indian Army's Middle Eastern commitment deepened, locomotives, rolling stock, and even fifteen hundred miles of rails were given up to strengthen the infrastructure of Iraq and Iran. Replacement locomotives from the United Kingdom failed to arrive as the tonnage hauled on Indian railways inexorably increased. Much of the Brahmaputra river fleet moved to the Tigris-Euphrates. *Then* came Japan's conquest of Burma. The river fleet had to be rebuilt. The single-track meter-gauge Bengal and Assam railway, built largely to serve the tea industry, had to be dramatically improved and its hauling capacity increased in the face of a shortage of everything except problems.[16] Roads had to be vastly improved despite the almost complete lack of modern road-building equipment (the US Army engineers working on the new road to China alone had reasonably adequate machinery). Then a large number of new airfields had to be constructed for the RAF and, above all, the American Hump airlift to China. Then pipelines had to be built to carry fuel to those fields. All this in the face of the annual monsoon, which could erase in a day the work of weeks. If necessity is the mother of invention, the XIV Army became a case study in the truth of that proverb. Tea estate labor became road-builders (completing just in time the track Burcorps took from the Chindwin to Imphal). Because they lacked materials and equipment to hard surface roads and airfields "bithess" was invented—bitumen (asphalt) coated jute sacking (Eastern India grew most of the world's jute, the raw material for sacking). The XIV Army also used jute for cargo parachutes when a silk shortage developed. In 1944, when the Chindwin was reached, the XIV Army would build and run its own fleet of inland water transport. Much of this work was handled for Slim by two very talented staff officers whom he found and kept, because he understood that only sound logistics could produce operational success: Maj. Gen. Alfred Snelling ("Grocer Alf"), Major General Administration, the XIV Army (whom Slim had "pinched" from another formation when he was commanding the 10th Indian Infantry Division in Iraq); and Maj. Gen. Bill Hasted, the XIV Army's chief engineer. But behind this trio stood the machinery of the Indian Army under its commander-in-chief, Gen. Sir Claude Auchinleck, and his director of infantry, Maj. Gen. Reginald Savory, who raised and trained the troops and created the vast Indian base. And behind the army was the Raj administrative machinery, largely Indian by 1944–1945, which, although derided by Churchill in 1943 as a "welter of lassitude and inefficiency," did a remarkable job of conjuring out of a largely agricultural economy a huge, modern war effort.[17]

Last but far from least, there was the Dakota. They were American-built and, in Burma, largely American-controlled, and Slim's grip on this vital part of his logistic structure was always precarious and yet it was the key to his victories in 1944–1945. Without the Dakota—its pilots flying in terrible weather and its ground crews working flat out in dry-season heat and dust or monsoon torrents—the XIV Army would never have reached Rangoon.

The "forgotten" XIV Army was in fact splendidly memorialized by Slim in his memoir, *Defeat into Victory*, which has never been out of print since its publication in 1956. Slim acknowledged what he owed to the hidden part of the iceberg, of course, but the full treatment it deserves still awaits its historian.

Appendix 2: The Wingate Phenomenon

Much of the writing about the campaigns in 1943 and 1944 in Burma has focused on Wingate and his Chindits (officially, in 1944, "Special Force"). Because this book focuses on 1945, there is little need to plunge into the Chindit issue beyond noting a few points relevant to understanding how the Burma campaign developed. When Churchill seized on Orde Wingate as the answer to his problem of convincing the Americans that the British were serious about clearing the way to China for them, the impact in India was drastic. The XIV Army lost the British 70th Division, one of only two full-strength British divisions in India. It had trained with Slim's 15th Corps and Slim remained convinced that, committed as an all-arms division to the XIV Army, it would have paid much greater dividends than it would broken into Chindit light infantry "columns." The 70th was not enough to satisfy Wingate's demands for British infantry—other units were broken up and swept into Special Force. Wingate would not use Indian troops, except Gurkhas, and the XIV Army lost four battalions of those elite infantry as well. When Slim finally put his foot down, Wingate agreed to take Nigerian troops to garrison his defended airheads ("strongholds" in Wingate-speak). The shortage of British infantry in the

XIV Army, which became acute in 1944–1945, was due in part to the Chindit experiment. Special Force casualties were high. They were kept in the field far longer than originally intended, and battle casualties, disease, and exhaustion decimated them, and when they were finally withdrawn, few were fit for further active service. (Special Force was disbanded early in 1945.)

It is often argued that Special Force opened eyes to the potentiality of air mobility. This is a huge exaggeration. The possibilities of air supply and mobility had been apparent from World War I onward. Indeed during a tour at Indian Army headquarters before the war Slim had been involved in studying the subject. Chindit 1 certainly acted as a laboratory for the development of techniques but it is questionable whether the lessons it taught needed to be learned quite so expensively.

Finally, what did the Chindits accomplish? The Americans had embraced Wingate, and had expensively supported him, in the expectation that his Chindits would operate against the communications of the Japanese forces opposing Stilwell in North Burma, which they did effectively but at horrendous cost (and the Japanese held on to the key position of Myitkyina until August 1944 anyway). The impact of Special Force on Imphal-Kohima was slight (Slim was given one of Wingate's reserve brigades, which did good work under the XIV Army). The British official history labeled Special Force a "military misfit"—too heavy to be effective as raiders but too light to confront Japanese regular formations brought against it. In the end, Special Force composed its own Iliad of courage and endurance but made surprisingly little difference to the XIV Army's victory in 1944. The verdict of the Indian official history was withering: Special Force paid about a 5 percent return on the huge investment it represented.[18]

Appendix 3: The Prime Minister and Burma

The publication of the twentieth volume of *The Churchill Documents* allows us to track the prime minister's thinking about the Burma campaign during the months when Capital was planned and launched.[19] There are no great new revelations but quite a lot that underlines the prime minister's distaste for the Indian Army, eagerness to do the least possible (and to stop doing it at the earliest possible moment) in north Burma, and determination to focus the empire's war effort in SEAC on reclaiming Singapore.

The documents also make clear that he was very concerned about the willingness of British troops, conscripts in a citizen army, to support a continuing war in the East once Germany was beaten.

On 7 May 1944 Churchill sent a note to Maj. Gen. Leslie Hollis of his staff: "the fact that India, with 2 million men on her ration strength, can only support the equivalent of ten divisions on the Burma frontier . . . is indeed a disgrace."[20] This shows his usual archaic concentration on ration strength, and a total failure to grasp the logistic issues that made the "teeth to tail" ratio so great in the XIV Army's war—or the fact that Indian logistic and administrative units underpinned the imperial war effort in the Middle East as well. While describing the Indian war effort as "feeble," the prime minister seems to have missed the fact that, even as he dictated his note, Slim's overwhelmingly Indian XIV Army was demonstrating on the battlefield one of the war's most remarkable transformations.

As the summer of 1944 wore on, and the XIV Army carried out its monsoon pursuit and began to plan the 1944–1945 dry-season campaign, in London the interminable argument between Churchill and the British Chiefs of Staff over what British strategy in the war against Japan should be ground on—an argument that grew so bitter even Churchill's ever-loyal chief of staff, "Pug" Ismay, thought of resignation. Churchill made very plain that, now that the Americans had their road to China, he saw no further point in the XIV Army's operations: "our operations in Burma should be reduced to defensive operations," he told the chiefs of staff. At the same meeting he made the basis of his argument for an Indian Ocean–centered strategy for SEAC unmistakably clear: "The shame of our disaster at Singapore could, in his opinion, only be wiped out by our recapture of that fortress."[21] In August, reality began to break in and it became clear that major amphibious operations would not be possible until after the end of the European war, which pushed them back to, at the earliest, late 1945 after that year's monsoon. The prime minister was still unenthusiastic about the XIV Army's campaign, complaining that "we were committed to the laborious reconquest of Burma, swamp by swamp."[22] By that time Slim's planners were beginning to elaborate the design that became "Capital," the crossing of the Irrawaddy and the return to Mandalay. At year's end, writing privately to his trusted confidant, Field Marshal Jan Smuts, the prime minister of South Africa, Churchill lamented that "we have been compelled to work downward from the north, through the jungles I had hoped to avoid. . . . We seem condemned to wallow at half-speed through these jungles."[23] As he wrote, the XIV Army was well into "Capital," with its 33rd Corps preparing to cross the Irrawaddy and its 4th Corps readying itself for the great outflanking sweep, Slim's masterstroke, which would crush the Japanese Burma Area Army. It is clear that, whatever was being discussed at SEAC headquarters at Kandy or in London, Slim was driving ahead, leaving his layers of superiors to catch up as best they could.[24]

One other concern surfaces in these papers: the prime minister worried about the reaction of British troops to having to carry on the war in the East after the end of the German war. Richard Casey, the Australian diplomat who was serving as governor of Bengal, had summed up for the prime minister, in late May, the sense that British personnel, civil and military, had of being in a strategic backwater: "We all realise that, as soon as the advance into Western Europe starts, the Burma front news will be relegated to the classified advertisement columns."[25] This sense of being in an uncomfortable and dangerous exile unredeemed by any real strategic significance would power both the desire for a quick return home by British personnel once the war in Europe was over and a corresponding reluctance to go East to finish the Japanese war by the soldiers (and sailors and airmen) who had survived the German war. At a meeting of the Chiefs of Staff Committee on 8 August 1944, Clement Attlee, the deputy prime minister and leader of the Labour party, pointed out that "We should undoubtedly experience difficulty in keeping men in the forces for the Far East war, despite any inducement we might offer."[26] The Cabinet's attention quickly turned to what these inducements might be and by 6 September the chancellor of the Exchequer, Sir John Anderson, was submitting to Churchill a paper on "further benefits for service in the Far Eastern Theatre."[27] Several Cabinet meetings discussed the "amenities" available to British service personnel in India and SEAC. This concern over those serving there would produce first the Python repatriation plan of September 1944 for the return home of those with three years and eight months of "Eastern" service and then its extension in June 1945 (during Britain's general election campaign), which gutted many of SEAC's remaining British units. The recognition that British participation in the final stages of the war against Japan would require a British manpower commitment that would be politically problematic (and quite expensive) underscored the importance of Indian manpower, which, of course, Churchill assumed would continue to be available.

Through all this high-level discussion of strategy (designed to, among other things, close down the XIV Army) and concern about the morale of British troops in the East and the likely reaction of other British service personnel ordered out to replace them (and, perhaps, invade Japan), Slim's army carried on, winning a spectacular victory. Seldom has any army, or commander, carried on as complex a campaign against such a background of high-level attempts to truncate it. But perhaps that was one of the keys to Slim's success: everyone was so busy trying to find an alternative to what the XIV Army was doing that it was left to get on with its own plans. The only senior commander involved in the Burma campaign whose plans invariably worked out was Slim.

1

A Professional Force

The XIV Army at the End of 1944

In most of the literature on the Burma campaign, General Slim is seen as the main architect and embodiment of the victories of 1945. While Slim and his commanders have much to be proud of, and had an important role in the final victories, the XIV Army as an institution was the true instrument of the Imperial Japanese Burma Area Army's defeat.

The XIV Army's victories of 1945 were underpinned by a series of reforms across its own home base, GHQ India, and the Indian Army as a whole. Those foundational reforms occurred during the Second World War, and the introduction summarizes some of the key tactical reforms that occurred from 1942 to 1944. This chapter will cover some other key reforms, such as recruitment and officer expansion, as well as the tactical and organizational changes that occurred in the autumn of 1944.[1] Without these reforms, including recruiting enough volunteers from South Asia to create the largest all-volunteer army in history, and the need and desire for Indian officers to fill command and leadership positions, the outcome in 1945 could have been very different. With the reforms, Slim and the XIV Army command created a strongly forged sword with which to strike the Japanese Burma Area Army.

It would be difficult to overstate how far-reaching and fundamental were the changes to the Indian Army in the Second World War. By the end of 1944, it had become a highly professional and modern force that included in its ranks representatives of ethnic groups that had traditionally been ignored as "nonmartial." Indian commissioned officers (ICOs) and emergency Indian commissioned officers (EICOs) were in positions of command on the battlefield, units were integrated and cohesive, and the army as a whole had played the leading role in the destruction of the Imperial Japanese Army in Burma. In almost every way, the Indian Army of late 1944—battle-seasoned, imbued with regimental esprit de corps, and above all victorious—was a different force from the one that suffered crippling defeats in the difficult early days of the Second World War in Burma and Malaya.

Through all the upheaval of the war years, the XIV Army's officers and men kept focused on the need to learn from the mistakes that were inevitable for any force finding itself in new situations and environments with inexperienced personnel. The XIV Army had a number of teething troubles as it grew in strength and experience, but it was always able to point with pride to its ability to learn from mistakes and adapt to conditions. Postbattlefield assessment was one of its hallmarks.

By the end of 1944, the Indian Army had reached a level of performance characterized by consistent and reliable professionalism in an impressive variety of types and theaters of warfare.[2] This success, particularly in contrast to earlier defeats in Malaya and Burma, reinforced the army's perceptions of itself as a truly professional force, and bolstered esprit de corps throughout the war.[3] The Burma campaign, which had begun as the longest retreat in British military history, ended in July 1945 as the Imperial Japanese Army's most conclusive defeat, with the XIV Army playing the central role. It was a spectacular reversal of the events of 1942. The reforms of recruitment and officer expansion went hand in hand with the tactical- and operational-level reforms that occurred on the battlefields of Assam and Burma. The main engine for such radical changes was ultimately senior Indian Army leadership, led by officers such as Auchinleck, Slim, and Savory. As Raymond Callahan noted:

> The rebuilding of the Indian Army and Slim's Arakan and Imphal
> victories were demonstrations of the aggressive determination
> and imaginative leadership Churchill had always called for and so
> frequently lamented. But those qualities were being displayed by an
> army he had always undervalued and in a campaign he had never
> wanted to fight. . . . It [the Indian Army] had remade itself by
> 1944 and 1945, perhaps in some ways aided by the quasi autonomy
> that allowed Auchinleck, Savory, Slim, and many others to get
> on with the business of forging a battleworthy weapon, with few
> interventions from above. . . . The war in Burma was the war the
> Indian Army had, and it got on with preparing to win it, accepting
> whatever new structures or doctrines were necessary. It seems safe

to predict that Slim's campaigns will be deemed examples of the military art far longer than of Monty's victories.[4]

Recruitment and Indianization of the Army during the Second World War

The XIV Army that reentered Burma in late 1944 was fundamentally different from its 1939 counterpart. The Second World War precipitated a period of unprecedented expansion for the Indian Army. Between 1939 and 1945, the army expanded from two hundred thousand to more than 2.5 million men and officers, even though conscription was never imposed.[5]

Throughout the Second World War the Indian Army also faced fundamental questions about its existence, size, and composition.[6] The Indianization of the officer corps reached new heights during this period, signaling the end of the traditional all-British officer corps. Recruitment also expanded to include South Asian ethnic groups that had long been dismissed as being "nonmartial."[7] The army's rapid expansion in response to the needs of the war raised additional questions concerning the quality of troops and officers.

Recruitment

The rapid expansion of the Indian Army placed a significant strain on the areas from which recruits were traditionally drawn in northern India, chiefly the province of the Punjab. By 1943, the Punjab was providing 36 percent of all soldiers recruited into the army.[8] Rapid expansion placed noticeable strain upon the resources of the traditional recruitment areas, and GHQ India headquarters realized that recruitment must be broadened to other areas and groups. This decision was undertaken tentatively at first, by taking Madrassis and others into the expanding service corps of the army. Following Lt. Gen. Claude Auchinleck's appointment as commander-in-chief, recruitment reform became more focused. Auchinleck stated that "as regards to recruitment of the rank and file I have no doubt at all that apart from political considerations we must broaden our basis and this was already in hand before I arrived. I propose to continue and hasten the process. There is plenty of good untouched material which we can and should use."[9]

Auchinleck intended to broaden the recruitment from nonmartial races beyond the service corps. He specifically suggested that the old 3rd Madras Regiment should be reraised, and that new infantry units should be raised to represent the other provinces.[10] He asserted that these units were not to be for show only, but would be used alongside other units in fighting the war.[11] Leo Amery, secretary of state for India, recognized and accepted these proposals, and was disappointed when Auchinleck was chosen as commander-in-chief of the Middle East in June 1941, taking him away from the opportunity to implement the recruitment reforms personally.[12]

The recruitment of nonmartial races had been stepped up from 1940 to 1942, but there was still a faction in GHQ India that doubted their potential as fighting troops. Many of the new recruits were sent to noninfantry or cavalry services within the army, as well as to the Indian Army Service Corps, signals, engineers, and artillery.[13] A report published in February 1942 documents thirty-eight thousand recruits from nonmartial races enlisted, of whom thirty-three thousand were stationed in India. Meanwhile, "martial races" such as Jat Sikhs and Punjabi Musalmans (PMs) reported numbers at 50 percent stationed in India and 50 percent overseas.[14]

A report by the Indian Army's Adjutant General's office in late 1942 argued for recruitment from nonmartial races by making the claim that the performance of PMs, Dogras, and Jat Sikhs in the field was declining. The report stated that "the general quality of the recruit [prewar classes] is tending to decline both physically and in terms of intelligence and this is when guts and brains are needed."[15] The report by the Adjutant General's office also documented how many of the units, including both the Madras and newly raised Sikh Light Infantry, were lacking in junior leaders, and recommended that this be remedied quickly, noting, however, that "foreign" VCOs or British NCOs were not the answer.[16] On the other hand, at least one witness considered that the Madras Regiment's turnout and abilities improved when it received British Guardsmen as drill instructors.[17]

In a War Staff communiqué to London, GHQ India formally announced that "the former distinction of martial and non-martial race has been removed."[18] By mid-1943 there were still those within the Indian Army who were willing to concede that the recruitment of nonmartial races was necessary but continued to assert that it should not be done too quickly.[19]

The arrival of Auchinleck as commander-in-chief, India, for a second stint in late June 1943 brought new energy for expanding recruitment and training of nonmartial race troops for battle. His arrival coincided with the aftermath of the First Arakan defeat in 1943.[20] The nonmartial race units had all been stationed in India or near the front on lines of communication duties. During the summer of 1943, the British Government called upon the Indian Army to reduce the numbers of units and formations. Auchinleck viewed this as a signal that the British Government had lost confidence in the Indian Army and that this loss was partly due to the expanded recruitment of nonmartial races. In a letter of response to the viceroy, Field Marshal Archibald Wavell, Auchinleck described in some detail his thoughts and feelings on the topic of nonmartial races and the British Government's attitude. He bluntly stated: "the idea underlying the demand for reduction seems to be based upon the idea that the Indian Army is now composed to a large extent of men who because they belong to classes previously untried as soldiers are unreliable and unsuitable."[21] This was untrue.

Auchinleck went on to comment that the Madrassis comprised about half of the new recruits and noted that "from all accounts the Madrassis are doing very well." He further stressed that "the recruitment of the old classes has been pushed to such lengths that the recruits now coming forward are often of poor quality and it is time to say that it is preferable to secure good specimens of new classes which can be maintained."[22] A speech given in the Indian Assembly in November 1943 highlighted GHQ India's attempts to deal with the issues of recruitment. The officer speaking stated that the Indian Army was open to all of the classes of India. The only parameters for officers and other ranks were sufficient education and physical attributes. The officer ended his speech by stating: "Sir I assure the house that there is no discrimination at present against scheduled classes and there will be none."[23]

Auchinleck's commitment resulted in two significant achievements. First, he was able to forestall the vast cuts proposed to the numbers of the Indian Army, which was sorely needed on the battlefields of Asia and Europe.[24] Some units were disbanded, but this was because units stationed on the Northwest Frontier and Paiforce were brought back to serve in the Burma campaign.[25] Second, he had some of the nonmartial race infantry units committed to battle to gain experience and, if possible, to make a name for themselves and dispel critics.[26] Some of these units, such as the 1st Sikh Light Infantry, would fight particularly well in the final battles in Burma in 1945. The new classes also provided significant numbers of men and officers for the supporting combatant and noncombatant services. Failure to expand recruitment would have resulted in a shortage of supplies for the forward units, brought on by a shortage of troops in the Indian Army Services Corps. The supporting services provided by the engineers and artillery paid huge dividends for the army during the final operations in Burma.

The Indian Army's recruitment in the traditional infantry and cavalry regiments had also undergone a shift in terms of recruits during the Second World War. A famous elite cavalry regiment, the 5th Probyn's Horse, saw a drop in the numbers of available Dogra Rajputs early in the war; as a result, the regiment was ordered to accept Dogra Hindus for the Dogra Squadron. The 5th Probyn's would be a spearhead unit during the fighting in central and southern Burma. The battalions of the 13th Frontier Force Rifles (FFRifles), who also saw a drop in their traditional pool of recruits, introduced two additional classes, one of which was a new class. The problems of securing enough Jat Sikhs for the Sikh Company led to the recruitment of Jat Hindus, including VCOs.[27] The FFRifles also recruited Ahirs to bring their battalions up to strength.[28] The FFRifles were not alone in broadening their base of recruitment. Low numbers drove the 1st Punjab Regiment to open up its recruitment to include Jat Hindus for the Sikh companies. The Baluch Regiment began accepting Brahmins from non-Dogra areas to bring the Dogra companies up to strength. The 12th Frontier Force Regiment (FFR) accepted Kumaonis into its battalions to fill up the spaces created by the drop in Dogras and Jat Sikhs.[29] Officers from various units noted that recruits from the new classes performed as well as the prewar classes already serving in the battalions.[30] The battlefield performances of the Indian Army in the final battles of Burma demonstrated the ability of the various battalions and regiments and "new" classes to mesh and perform as cohesive units. Replacements were needed for all the various units and the new and expanded recruitment practices allowed the Indian Army to maintain the momentum of the offensive in 1945.

Indianization of the Officer Corps

With the expansion of the Indian Army in April/May 1940, the Indianization of the officer corps took on a new importance, since the army would need more officers to serve in the new units and formations.[31] By 1945, there were 7546 ICOs in the combatant arms of the Indian Army. Counting the noncombatant arms, the number was closer to thirteen thousand officers. The total, British and Indian, for the Indian Army, including all arms and services, was close to forty thousand officers. Indian officers in the combatant arms represented 20 percent of the number, compared with 10 percent in 1939.[32] Without the Indian officers, serving in leadership and command positions within the units and formations of the XIV Army, it would not have been able to march and defeat the Imperial Japanese Army in 1944 and 1945.

In 1939 there were 577 Indian officers serving in the Indian Army.[33] As early as 22 September of that year, Army Headquarters in India contacted London about the possible need to expand the Indian officer corps, noting that many Indians had asked to join up as officers but that under current conditions they were barred from doing so. The Army Headquarters had been contemplating emergency commissions for Indians,[34] but it is unclear who in the headquarters actually began the process of expanding the Indian officer corps. Auchinleck was still the deputy chief of the General Staff when war broke out. His relationship with the then commander-in-chief, General Sir Cassels, was very good. Cassels may have shared Auchinleck's views or eventually been swayed by him when the need presented itself with the outbreak of war.[35] General Auchinleck did, however, send a letter to the secretary of state for India, Leopold Amery, in October 1940, which was very critical of the prewar system of Indianization.[36] He specifically stated that "we have been playing a losing hand from the start in this matter of Indianization . . . and held the following views for many years." He even raised the issue of pay discrepancies, stating that "pay of all officers British and Indian should be the same and the present invidious distinctions should be removed." He commented that British regulars and ECOs could be part of the expanding Indian Army "provided they refuse to acquire the racial prejudices which have soured the whole course of Indianization." Finally, he stated that "the only logical corollary is equal treatment, regardless of color."[37] This last statement made clear his intention that all new British emergency commissioned officers were to be posted throughout the army, with the possibility that they would be commanded by ICOs. Auchinleck was aware that his opinions were not widely shared; he made clear that his views were personal and that at the time "they [were] far from being accepted widely in India . . . [and] some may look on them as dangerous and unworkable."[38] As units expanded, many ICOs were posted to new units where British officers might serve under them.[39] Others in Headquarters took it upon themselves to help change the system, but Auchinleck spent most of the war attempting to destroy any barriers left in the prewar system. The war and the need for expansion of the officer corps offered a chance to end the prewar system of Indianization, and the Indian Army took the lead. When Auchinleck was commander-in-chief in 1941, and later in 1943, he made it clear that he intended to overcome any obstacles to placing Indian officers on par with their British counterparts.

A press communiqué dated 17 June 1940, sent from the Government of India Defence Department at Simla to the secretary of state for India, signaled the end to the prewar Indianization process. Due to expansion, the Defence Department stated that all units of the Indian Army would be opened to ICOs.[40] This communiqué meant that from then on all emergency commissioned Indian officers could be posted anywhere in the army, not just to designated prewar Indianized battalions and regiments. The old VCO rank structure was brought back to the Indianized units.[41] There were teething problems during the expansion of the Indian officer corps,[42] but the commander-in-chief, Gen. Sir Robert Cassels, and the Indian Army opened the door in the summer of 1940. It is interesting to note that Amery may have taken an interest in Auchinleck's opinions. A month after his communications with Amery, Auchinleck was appointed commander-in-chief, Indian Army,[43] for the first of two tenures, partly due to the fact that Amery believed that Auchinleck could mobilize the war effort in India.[44]

While Auchinleck was commander-in-chief in 1941, the order ending the old Indianized system was formally listed.[45] The last group of regular ICOs graduated in June 1941, and the Indian Military Academy (IMA), Dehra Dun, was reopened as an "emergency" Officer Training School (OTS), initially for Indian cadets. Officer cadets had been coming out from the United Kingdom to take up positions in the Indian Army; however, Auchinleck did not want to see the numbers of British Emergency Commissions stay high while the numbers of Indians dropped. Further on in the letter to Amery, Auchinleck went on to say that while good officer material was coming out from the United Kingdom, "all the same we must at our end see that we get an adequate supply of Indians both as regards quantity and quality."[46] By the end of 1941, the ratio of Indian officers to British officers had risen by 4 percent,[47] an upward trend that continued throughout the war.[48]

The prewar Indianization process officially came to an end in 1941. This did not mean that prewar prejudices disappeared overnight among officers, and the important question is when and how the prejudices were for the most part eradicated.[49] From January 1940, all Indian and British officer candidates who joined the Indian Army were ECOs or EICOs.[50] The first batch of EICOs was sent to Dehra Dun for a shortened emergency commission course, while an OTS was set up at Belgaum to accept British cadets only. By summer 1940, two more OTS units were set up at Bangalore (British) and Mhow (Indian/British).[51] During this early period, many British cadets and other ranks were sought for commissions, and by January 1941, the ratio of British to Indian officers had risen from 10:1 to 12:1. The trend peaked there, however; from 1941 on, the numbers of British cadets dropped significantly, while the numbers of Indian cadets rose.[52] By January 1945, the rate was 4.2 British officers for every one Indian officer throughout the Indian Army.[53] By 1945, there were 36,438 British officers and 15,747 Indian officers (again including medical officers).[54] Additionally, by the end of the war, all of the OTS, except Bangalore, were accepting both British and Indian cadets, including the IMA. Mixing training companies of Indian and British officer cadets had been happening since 1943, and many of the officers who participated in this, both Indian and British, felt that this integration had helped to break down any remaining barriers.[55]

A pamphlet listed as "Lectures for Officers Joining the Indian Army," intended for British officers from the United Kingdom joining the Indian Army, was published in 1942. The pamphlet discussed the various fighting "classes" targeted for recruitment into the army, including the new ones, and made clear that there were already ICOs in the Indian Army. Old designations, such as KCIO and ICO, were to be done away with. All officers were to be classified as BOs, British officers. The pamphlet stresses that the British must "get to know" their fellow Indian officers and "pull together," and points out that, in an expansion, there will be good and bad officers, both Indian and British. The author, a brigadier, stressed the equality of all officers by commenting, "one of my ICOs I could not wish for a better leader British or Indian."[56] Another pamphlet, "Notes for Guidance of Commanding Officers, Staff and Regimental Officers," published in January 1943, also highlighted an important point regarding Indian officers. It still divided the Indian officers into KCIOs, ICOs, and VCOs. In discussing ICOs, which included the emergency commissioned Indian officers, it stated that "they wear the same badges of ranks as British officer and should be treated in exactly the same way."[57]

Necessity was initially the prime motivation for the rapid expansion of the Indian officer corps, due to the expansion of the army from two hundred thousand to 2.5 million by 1944. When Auchinleck returned for his second stint as commander-in-chief of the Indian Army in the summer of 1943, he took on the role of champion of the abilities of the Indian officers and their capacity for command. Auchinleck had inherited an army that had been soundly defeated in two campaigns, in Burma as well as Malaya. The report produced by the Infantry Committee, India, in June 1943 also considered the caliber of officers serving in the Indian Army, noting that leadership in the Indian battalions left much to be desired, and that both British and Indian officers were lacking in this respect.[58] The report also made reference to what were apparently unresolved issues between Indian and British officers, stressing that "no discrimination must be allowed" by or among officers.[59]

General Auchinleck brought Lieutenant Colonel (later Major General) Rudra to GHQ India in the autumn of 1943, in part to "keep in touch with promotions and appointments for Indian officers." Auchinleck had heard reports that Indian officers believed they were being denied access to higher command.[60] In August 1943 there were ninety-seven Indian lieutenant colonels, of which only six were in command of fighting units. The vast majority were in the Indian Medical Services, with a few in staff positions. There were six lieutenant colonels at General Staff Officer (GSO) 1 level, nine majors at GSO 2, and three captains at GSO 3,[61] so obviously Indian officers were underrepresented at high levels of command at this juncture. However, to be fair, the casualty rates of 1940–1943 were not that high, so many COs had not been replaced and one cannot rapidly promote officers who have not been trained and educated for their positions. This would happen later, in 1944 and 1945, and as a result more Indians took command at the company, battalion, and even brigade levels. Nevertheless, Rudra stated that Auchinleck "was determined to do something to redress the grievances."[62] The numbers of Indian COs of regiments and battalions had risen by late 1944 and 1945, and three Indian brigadiers had been rewarded for their service with the Distinguished Service Order (DSO).

In December 1944, Auchinleck clearly stated his intentions for the future of the Indian Army: "I propose as a principle that the three services [Indian Army, Air Force, and Navy] after the war shall be officered entirely by Indian officers so far as this is possible and that the number of European officers shall be limited to that required to fill positions which cannot be held by Indians owing to their lack or experience or training."[63] Auchinleck's intent in formulating this proposal was partially to determine the postwar demand for British personnel. By the end of 1944 there was only a handful of Indians capable of brigade-level commands. It was improbable to believe that senior Indian officers would be able to hold command positions at the division or corps level by the end of 1945, due to natural wastage and the need for proper training and education for senior command. Officers, both British and Indian, would not be promoted without the necessary battlefield experience and attendance at the Indian Staff College at Quetta. Auchinleck had set the system in motion: one need only look at the attendance figures at the Staff College to see this.

Attendance at Quetta was the precursor to higher command positions during the prewar and war period, and during Auchinleck's tenure, the admission of Indian officers increased significantly. The Staff College class of 1940 at Quetta listed sixty-two officers, of whom four were Indian. The staff of this period included eleven instructors, of whom none was Indian.[64] The last time that students were listed by name at the Staff College was January 1942; in this class, there were 140 officers, of whom twenty-one were Indians. The staff of twenty-three instructors included only one Indian.[65] For the remainder of the war, students were not listed, only instructors. The 1944 list showed twenty-five instructors, including three Indian officers,[66] indicating a slow but steady trend.

The trend outlasted the end of the war. The first peacetime Staff College course at Quetta was set for 1947. The number of students was established at two hundred, of which sixty-two were Indian officers. Additionally, another nine Indian officers were selected to complete the course at the British Army Staff College, Camberley. Auchinleck was still the commander-in-chief of the Indian Army when these plans were made.[67]

In the spring of 1945,[68] Auchinleck, Wavell, and Amery began the process of full Indianization of the Indian Army.[69] Anticipating that either Dominion status or outright independence was imminent for India, the three men agreed on the need for planning ahead. In one of the first memoranda written on this topic, Wavell outlined three areas of focus. First, the need to maintain the efficiency of the army during whatever transition period would be necessary. Second, the need to convince Indian political leaders and the population that the intent was ultimately to hand over full control of the Indian Army to them. Third, the need to safeguard the interests of British officers who would remain during the interim period.

To attain these goals it was understood that many ECIOs would need to be offered regular commissions. The Government of India began the final process of Indianization with this document.[70] Further deliberations continued; the War Cabinet (as well as others) was aware that British officers would need to remain in some positions, especially at the highest levels, due to the lack of Indian officers at or above the brigadier rank. It was estimated that it would take a decade for the Indian Army to educate and train enough senior Indian officers to take over the higher levels of command from British officers and twenty years for complete Indianization to occur.[71]

Auchinleck, as he had done previously with the expansion of the recruitment base, had steadily expanded the role of Indian officers within the army, throughout his two tenures as commander-in-chief, India. He recognized that the slow and conservative Indianization of the prewar period was not sustainable for the war period. With the rapid expansion of both the British and Indian armies in the Second World War, there was a need for quality officers to fill the leadership and command positions within the armies. He clearly understood that India had the reserves of potential officer material to fill positions within the Indian Army and hence the XIV Army. As the XIV Army reorganized and focused on the final campaign of 1945, it had numbers of recruits and officers that would not have been accepted in 1939 as a core element for the victories of 1945. As author and Indian Army officer John Masters noted:

> As the [XIV Army] tanks burst away down the road to
> Rangoon . . . it took possession of the empire we had
> built. . . . Twenty races, a dozen religions, a score of languages
> passed in those trucks and tanks. When my great-great-grandfather
> first went to India there had been as many nations; now there was
> one—India. . . . It was all summed up in the voice of an Indian
> colonel of artillery. Now the Indian, bending close to an English
> colonel over a map, straightened and said with a smile, "O.K.,
> George. Thanks. I've got it. We'll take over all tasks at 1800. What
> about a beer?"[72]

Tactical and Organizational Reform

Even with the recent successes in the Arakan and Imphal Plain, the XIV Army and GHQ India did not sit idle, but set out to make sure that lessons were identified, absorbed, and distributed throughout the command. It also came to realize that with the planned operations of fighting on the central plains of Burma, there were needs for further adaptation. As General Slim noted: "For two years our formations had fought in the jungles and amongst the hills; they were now about to break into open country with unobstructed views and freedom of movement away from tracks. Not only would the laborious tactics of the jungle have to be replaced by speed, mechanization, and mobility, but commanders and troops would have to adjust their mentality to the changed conditions."[73] Throughout the late summer and autumn of 1944, the units and formations of the XIV Army assessed, analyzed, and applied lessons from recent fighting, and implemented this knowledge in the changing conditions of the battlefields of central Burma. This was an army that never rested on its laurels; it knew it needed to constantly critically analyze itself and seek for better resolutions.

Lessons Identified and Retraining

As stated above, even with successes in both the Arakan and Assam, commanders in the XIV Army and India Command felt that room for improvement remained in both tactical training and organization. As Maj. Gen. Douglas Gracey, 20th Indian Division, GOC, noted: "Our doctrine has proved to be sound but we have learnt many lessons. . . . The fact that these instructions contain a good many criticisms must not be taken to mean that the division did not fight well or very well. . . . There cannot, there, have been much wrong with our doctrine or training, but don't think we have nothing to learn."[74]

This section will detail the organizational changes implemented within the divisions of SEAC, based upon the 220 Military Mission, tactical changes made at the India Command level, and the retraining that occurred in some of the units and formations. The tactical lessons outlined in the various doctrinal manuals, *Army in India Training Memoranda* (AITM), will be briefly discussed. Some of the XIV Army's units and formation training periods in late 1944 and early 1945 will also be described.

One of the first recommendations that were made as a result of the fighting in the Arakan and Assam was to regularize the organization of the infantry divisions in SEAC to create the "standard division," based upon the findings of the 220 Military Mission published report of 1 April 1944.[75] Between 1942 and early 1944, there were five different divisional organizations in SEAC: two kinds of Animal and Motorized and Transport divisions (A & MT), the one with a high level of MT,[76] the other with fewer vehicles;[77] a light division;[78] and two kinds of amphibious divisions, one with two brigades of four battalions,[79] and the other with three brigades of three battalions.[80]

Gen. Sir George Giffard and Maj. Gen. J. S. Lethbridge were principally responsible for overseeing reorganization.[81] Lethbridge had formed and headed the 220 Military Mission from the War Office, London, to liaise with and report on the jungle fighting practices of the Allies and British/Indian forces, including the United States, Australia, New Guinea, the Solomon Islands, New Caledonia, Burma, and India. The exhaustive report was intended to develop a training program for British units sent to the Pacific theater as the war in Europe ended.[82] The 220 Military Mission set out in June 1943, comprising twenty-seven officers from all services, ordered to visit training areas and operational units in the jungle to assess the organizational needs of future units. Its report, submitted in March 1944, documented the requirements for units to become jungle-oriented and adopt the various A & MT organizational charts.[83] A series of four meetings was held during the month of March,[84] although Lethbridge did not participate, having returned to India to join the HQ of the XIV Army.[85] The report, although sent to London, influenced the reorganization of all Indian formations.[86] While some initially thought it was a document to handle future "jungle warfare" environments, upon further reflection it was all about better combined-arms fighting abilities and needs. The roles of artillery, engineers, tanks, and other supporting elements in a combined-arms effort were clearly analyzed and outlined based upon the experiences of all the allies in the Pacific and Southeast Asia region.

A conference was held on 26–27 May 1944 at the XIV Army HQ to discuss various topics, including the findings of the 220 Military Mission. Senior officers[87] from the HQs of India Command, the 11th Army Group, the XIV Army, and the 4th, 15th, and 33rd corps were present.[88] They decided that an infantry division should be capable of normal jungle fighting, open-style warfare, being transported by air, and amphibious landings. Lethbridge proposed a four-battalion brigade, with one battalion used to protect the Brigade HQ and three rifle battalions to move forward, but manpower shortages forced this idea to be dropped.[89] The findings of the meeting were to be implemented over time; as each division was pulled out of the fighting, it would refit according to the new organizational structures.

It was also decided that "all"[90] divisions would require a Divisional HQ Protection battalion,[91] as previous fighting had shown their worth in protecting divisional and brigade HQs. Divisions would also have a reconnaissance battalion. Each division was to be allocated a medium machine gun (MMG) battalion. The experiences of the 2nd Battalion, the Manchester Regiment[92] with the 2nd British Division in the Kohima fighting, had highlighted the need for each division to have an MMG battalion attached.[93] Three infantry brigades would consist of three battalions each.[94] The artillery of the divisions was to be standardized as well, with two field regiments of three batteries of twenty-five-pounders and one mountain regiment of three batteries of 3.7-inch howitzers. An antitank regiment of three batteries of six-pounders was also added.[95]

Each Indian battalion would have 866 men. Within the infantry battalion, the Bren gun carrier platoon was abolished and replaced by an HQ protection platoon.[96] An additional meeting was held at the XIV Army HQ on 30 June to deal with the organization of tank forces. The recent fighting had highlighted the need for protection of tanks by infantry and the breakdown of mutual support. Debates led to a simplified system in which there was to be only a brigade structure for tanks. The 44th Armoured Division had already been disbanded in early March 1944, and it was decided that each brigade[97] would consist of two medium regiments[98] and one light regiment.[99] The meeting also highlighted the need for serious training involving tank, artillery, and infantry units; the recent fighting had indicated a poor level of coordination among units in the field.[100] Combined-arms training needed to be revamped and stepped up across the Army. This last criticism would be dealt with heavily by all the units and formations throughout the end of the summer and autumn of 1944. The units and formations of the XIV Army were formally restructured, based upon clear lessons identified and analyzed from the recent fighting, not just in Burma, but across the Pacific. This was just one element of the overall reform package that was set in motion in late summer 1944.

Army in India Training Memorandum (AITM) and Director of Military Training

An American officer from the 4/8th Gurkha Rifles, 7th Indian Division, highlighted the state of the XIV Army and its view on doctrine in the summer of 1944, when he stated: "we read the manuals, which by now were thick on the table, packed with advice won by two years of campaigning in Burma."[101] The first AITM, which focused closely on the actions of 1944, was No. 24, March 1944, under the heading "Words of Wisdom from the Front." The manual is subheaded with topics such as siting posts, preparation of posts, camouflage and track discipline, digging, wiring, and so on. These points, originally the notes of the GOC, Maj. Gen. Frank Messervy, 7th Indian Division, were reproduced not only in AITM No. 24 but also in the *Jungle Omnibus*.[102] AITM No. 24 also includes lessons from the "Arakan" and "Chindwin," and stressed that it was crucial for all units to "PATROL, PATROL, PATROL," commenting that while HQ protection battalions were an excellent innovation, there was still the need for the HQs to be situated within the boxes.[103] The manual also reiterates the critical need for units to dig in immediately after seizing a position, since the likelihood of a Japanese counterattack or at least a mortar attack was assessed as high.[104]

AITM No. 25 went into more detail about lessons learned from the fighting in both the Arakan and Assam. The text noted that "operations in ASSAM and the ARAKAN have demonstrated that a formal frontal infantry attack supported by a barrage and made against organized Japanese positions is rarely effective and often costly." It also made the contention that one reason for the defeats tended to be the loss of the element of surprise, with an artillery bombardment indicating the direction from which the attack would come. The manual recommended a two-phase approach.[105] First, active patrols were to be used to locate and discover the extent of the enemy's positions and pinpoint any gaps in his defense, which would be infiltrated by units and subunits.[106] Firm bases in both the rear and flanks of the Japanese position would also be established in this phase. Second, steps were to be taken to deal with the possible repercussions of the infiltration. The Japanese might attack from outside the position to relieve pressure on their position, or from inside to open their lines of communication. The position could be attacked by British/Indian troops from any side, or from all sides at once. The manual further reiterated that all firm bases had to employ an all-round defense. It also noted that artillery and air support could be used to pound the Japanese positions, to smoke the area for an attack or to lay down deception fire on a specific area to make the Japanese think an attack was imminent in that area.[107]

AITM No. 25 also commented on other issues, including the need for proper training in minor tactics. The war in most cases was a platoon commander's war, and this meant that minor tactics played a very important role. Junior leadership was very important and all moves had to have a plan. Another point raised was fire discipline, which continued to be a problem. Not only was the loss of ammunition in arbitrary firing wasteful, but more importantly, it gave away positions to the enemy.[108] A further suggestion was for all administration units to be trained to fight as infantrymen, to be able to carry out patrols, to dig slit trenches, and to undertake wiring.[109] This in turn raised another point, namely that it was necessary for commanders and troops to pay more attention to wire. It was important for the wire to be placed outside the range of Japanese attempts to throw grenades. Finally, the need for a stand-to order was noted, and recommended to be given effect before dawn, as this was the most likely time of a Japanese attack.[110] The remaining AITM dealt with other items, such as lessons from the Australian and American forces in the Southwest Pacific regions. This last point is important to note. There was a series of crossover communications between the various theaters and commands, in a time of no computers and emails. The various militaries were able to collect, analyze, synthesize, and then disseminate important lessons across thousands of miles and multiple commands.

The Director of Infantry, India,[111] Monthly Pamphlets[112] also highlighted lessons learned from the fighting in 1944. The first mention of the fighting appeared in the May 1944 pamphlet, under the heading "Officer Notes from the Arakan." As with AITM No. 25, it mentioned that fire discipline was still an issue for some units, and concurred that units were not sufficiently concerned with wiring. On a positive note, it commented that the divisional HQ protection battalion system was working well. The June 1944 pamphlet reproduced a reconnaissance and fighting patrol and highlighted the positives to be learned from the example. The rest of the monthly pamphlets went into more detail regarding lessons learned from tank/infantry cooperation and organizational plans for the future.[113]

One other central organization analyzed the lessons of 1944. The Infantry Committee, India, published a series of letters that were distributed to commands throughout the world, as well as to the infantry training schools in India. A total of ten were published during 1944, all highlighting various lessons by specifically describing tactical problems or citing reports from the front. Focal points included fire discipline, patrolling, and tank/infantry cooperation lessons. The issues of tank/infantry cooperation became a major focus, after the 220 Military Mission Report was published and the various meetings in May.[114] A team of trainers and experienced XIV Army officers traveled to the United Kingdom in late 1944. Their mission was to meet with the various commands across the United Kingdom and lecture on the character of the war in Burma and the latest lessons and thinking on how to wage against the Japanese.[115]

Unit and Formation Retraining

Each battalion, regiment, brigade, and division that was withdrawn from the line in mid- to late 1944 and sent into reserve took with it not only a wealth of knowledge based upon the personal experiences of the officers and men, but also records that documented and made accessible that knowledge. Each unit and formation carried out some level of retraining during the autumn of 1944 and the winter of 1944/45 before returning to battle. All units were by this point capable of jungle fighting and airmobile and amphibious operations if necessary,[116] and during this period many units and formations received their first sizeable installments of reinforcements, both men and officers, from the training divisions.[117]

This section of the chapter will show evidence of this reform and professionalism by looking at various units and formations. These units and formations would play key roles in the fighting in central and southern Burma in 1945. The formations that will be discussed are the 5th, 7th, 17th, 19th, and 20th Indian divisions, and the 255th Armoured Brigade.

The 5th Indian Division had been pulled back to milestone eighty on the Dimapur-Imphal road at the beginning of December 1944 after its difficult monsoon fighting along the Tiddim Road. The division set out to reorganize and train up the many replacements that were arriving in the division. The division was now structured with two motorized brigades and one air-landing brigade. Over two thousand vehicles arrived and drivers were trained up; the various units also worked with the new organizational tables and worked out tactical deployment practices.[118] The experience of one of the units, the 2/1st Punjab, highlights what occurred within the division throughout this training and reorganization phase.

The 2/1st Punjab carried out a period of refitting and retraining,[119] centered mostly on jungle warfare tactics. It was principally a period of completing the training of new reinforcements from the training division.[120] The strategic situation in Burma was changing rapidly, and in early January 1945, the division was moved north to the Jorhat area, where it established a new camp and began a new style of training, focusing on the need for boxes, open-style warfare, and attack on the flanks. The No. 15 training instruction noted: "units will always operate from a firm base. . . . This is the first and greatest principle. . . . Deep patrolling in all directions is still needed. Frontal attacks on Japanese positions are seldom successful. Experience shows a hook combined with surprise, when possible, produces results. Therefore aim at maneuver and surprise."[121] The 5th had adopted a new divisional structure. Two of the brigades, the 123rd and 161st, were to be completely motorized, while the 9th Indian Brigade was to be air portable.[122] The animal transport disappeared and was replaced by jeeps and fifteen-cwt trucks.[123] February and early March 1945 were spent in reorganization and training in a motorized role. The men were learning to drive and how to mount and dismount from trucks, but there was still an emphasis on the need, at least sometimes, for foot patrols.[124] Additionally, even while motorized, the practice of all-round defense was still to be followed for all vehicles. Linear tactics would not reemerge.[125] The lessons of the recent past were to be incorporated even as the units' roles and surroundings changed.

The 7th Indian Division as with its sister formation, the 5th, had been commended for its battlefield performance in both the Arakan and on the Imphal Plain in 1944. While the division was one of the strongest and most experienced, it did not rest on its laurels. It recognized potential future shortcomings. The GOC, Maj. Gen. Frank Messervy, stated in July 1944: "Although we have now behind us 10 months of operational experience [it] does NOT mean that [we] are by any means perfect in battle. On the contrary, the wastage in junior leaders and the absorption of a large number of reinforcements has decreased our battle efficiency. But, with that experience to guide us, we can now in a comparatively short time not only regain the efficiency of last autumn but greatly surpass it."[126] Frank Messervy published another series of "operational notes" throughout the year. His operational notes, No. 13, dealt in detail with the use and deployment of tanks with infantry, based upon the lessons identified in battle. He was clear that all branches, artillery, infantry, and tanks needed to understand the advantages and disadvantages of their respective services in destroying the Japanese. Messervy's operational notes on "Japanese Air Threat," in early 1945, highlight once again the attempts of the army to come to terms with any aspect of the battlefield in 1945. His notes were highly detailed and distributed throughout the division.[127]

The 4/8th Gurkhas remained attached to the 89th Indian Brigade,[128] 7th Indian Division.[129] In late summer 1944, the entire division was sent north of Imphal to build training and rest camps. The 4/8th Gurkhas, at this point commanded by Lt. Col. W. C. Walker,[130] spent the months of October through December undertaking further retraining in jungle warfare.[131] As with most training,[132] this began with individual exercises, leading to battalion and later brigade movements.[133] During the month of November, a series of officers and men were detailed with 255th Armoured Brigade for tank/infantry TEWTs (tactical exercises without troops) and exercises.[134] Training also included an introduction to loading trucks and using trucks during movement, as well as river-crossing exercises.[135] Lt. Patrick Davis, 4/8th Gurkhas, discussed the retraining and reform in great detail in his book *Child at Arms*: "Walter Walker drove us hard. During his long period of recuperation and re-training he caused much heart-ache, much grumbling, sometimes feelings for which grumbling is a polite euphemism. He was strict. He insisted on high standards. . . . For myself, I was in awe of him, but committed to his way of running things. I thought it right that he was tough and hard on us. We were not playing a game."[136] The 17th Indian Division was ordered to proceed to Ranchi on 23 July 1944. There it was scheduled to meet up with the 99th Indian Brigade, which would form the third brigade of the division. It was to adopt the new organizational structure of XIV Army divisions.[137] The 1st Sikh Light Infantry (SLI) formed part of the 99th Indian Brigade; the battalion had been ordered to Raiwala Bara Jungle Warfare Training Centre to begin jungle training in February 1944.[138] It spent five weeks learning the basics of jungle warfare, patrol activities, and all-round defense, and putting them into practice.[139] The battalion was then ordered to proceed to Ranchi during May 1944, and spent June and July engaged in countless TEWTs and intercompany and battalion exercises.[140] When the rest of the 17th Indian Division joined the brigade, the exercises and training became steadily more intense.[141] With the 255th Armoured Brigade stationed in Ranchi, the 1st SLI carried out joint infantry and tank exercises.[142] Reinforcements for the SLI were sent to the 39th Training Division and put under the charge of Major Baldwin of the 7/9th Jat Regiment, who had served as the training major for all reinforcements to the Jat Regiment. Baldwin set out to train the reinforcements in all aspects of jungle lore and tactics, beginning with individual training and then progressing to section, platoon, and company level. He noted that the men and officers adapted to the needs of the jungle very quickly.[143] The 1st SLI was part of the 99th Indian (air portable) Brigade. The battalion had only two jeeps for transport, and expected for the remainder of its transport needs to rely upon the local population's bullock carts, or any extra divisional transport that might become available. The 1st SLI spent January and part of February exercising with C-46s and C-47s getting men and materiel onto the planes.[144]

The 7/10th Baluch began the retraining process in earnest in mid-July 1944, when it was put into reserve and ordered to Imphal. As the unit was shifting back, the HQ held a conference on 27 July to discuss recent operations and ways to deal with issues that had arisen. The battalion also outfitted itself to follow an ordinary infantry battalion organization that had been selected at the XIV Army HQ. The battalion HQ drew up and distributed training instructions while in Ranchi,[145] highlighting the need for better patrolling activities and wire placement.[146] Feedback on the lessons presented was sought from officers and VCOs.[147] The battalion carried out individual training and then higher-level battalion exercises during August and September. In November, the battalion was earmarked to serve in the 63rd Indian Brigade, and continued with interbrigade exercises.[148]

The 4/12th FFR followed a similar process to the 7/10th Baluch, holding small conferences where lessons were conveyed to all officers within the battalion. As with all units, retraining began with individual training and led to more advanced interlevel training. The 4/12th FFR adopted the new war establishment for ordinary infantry battalions, and was attached to the 48th Indian Brigade.[149] It continued training with other units of the 48th Indian Brigade until December 1944. The HQ then distributed all of the relevant information to the company officers, both in verbal and in written form.[150]

In mid-December 1944, the 17th Indian Division received orders to proceed to Imphal. When the division arrived in early January, it adopted a new divisional structure. This came about as a result of the changing strategic conditions in the advance into Burma, which caused the XIV Army to adopt a new divisional structure for both the 17th and 5th Indian divisions. Two of the three brigades became completely motorized, using jeeps and fifteen-cwt trucks. The third brigade became air portable. The scale of ammunition was drastically reduced and the units were expected to be completely mobile.[151] News of this development did not reach units until they were in Imphal. On 22 January, all the units that were to be motorized were given jeeps and trucks and instructed to give up all animal transport. The 48th and 63rd Indian Brigades were among those chosen for the motorized role, and both the 4/12th FFR and the 7/10th Baluch were required to send men on driving courses and learn the specific aspects of loading and unloading materiel and men with motorized transport. Units were given just short of one month of training before being ordered forward into Burma, but both brigades managed time to carry out further tank/infantry cooperation training with the 255th Armoured Brigade.[152] Officers from both the 7/10th Baluch and the 4/12th FFR noted that even in training men for the motorized role, jungle tactics were still evident, especially the use of boxes, planning for air resupply, and organizing foot patrols.[153] The divisional GOC, Major General Cowan, noted: "all round defense is just as important out of the jungle as it is in it. . . . Our basic training [jungle warfare] has stood the test now we have to adapt it to the new situation."[154]

The 8/12th FFR, the 98th Indian Brigade,[155] and the rest of the 19th Indian Division continued to train for operations in Burma throughout 1944. By the time the division reached Burma in December, it was the most highly trained division in SEAC, but still lacked active service. The months of January through April 1944 had been spent training as a "combined operations and open warfare division," and by the middle of May, it was again training for jungle warfare. From June 1944 the battalion, and the rest of the 19th Indian Division, focused on all aspects of jungle warfare, including animal transport and movement in the jungle.[156] As 1944 was drawing to a close, the division reorganized according to the 220 Military Mission's recommendations and began to deal with tighter combined-arms training in open terrain. An officer from the 4/4th Gurkha Rifles, Lt. Col. Hamilton Stevenson, highlighted in his papers the many lessons and the debates regarding how to disseminate the lessons from the recent fighting and how best to contend with the future. His papers highlight the key roles of artillery and tanks and how best to destroy the Imperial Japanese Army in a war of movement. The papers do not just highlight assessments of the XIV Army; they include many discussions on Japanese tactics and procedures.[157] A COY commander in the 2nd Royal Berkshire Regiment, Maj. John Hill, discussed the levels of training and the readjustments within the unit and formation as the division arrived in Assam. He specifically stated the 19th Indian Division was the most highly trained division, but still had something to learn. By late November 1944, "our preparation was complete. We were ready to go."[158]

The GOC of the 20th Indian Division, Major General Gracey, was direct to his units in his division regarding tactical and leadership lessons. He stated: "COs and 2 i/cs must concentrate their energies on [officers] and NCOs [training]. Lessons learnt, mistakes made, Japanese methods and tactics, leadership on patrol co-ordination of fire, new methods and weapons . . . must all be discussed in these cadres and sound practical leadership inculcated."[159] Units of the 20th Indian Division were pulled back into reserve in August 1944.[160] The 14/13th FFRifles carried out intense retraining during this period,[161] beginning with the arrival of reinforcements from the training division. As with the 7th Indian Division, the program began with individual training and led to interbattalion and brigade exercises. Some officers were posted away for tank/infantry cooperation training, and in October, the records mention training in emplaning and deplaning from airplanes (C-46 and C-47s) with men and supplies, as well as exercises in river crossing.[162] By November, the battalion was carrying out exercise with tanks.[163] Throughout this period, dialogue was ongoing among the officers about the problems and lessons presented in the previous months of fighting, especially the operations near the Ukhrul road, which had brought the battalion up against dense Japanese hill defenses. An officer noted that the flanking attack instructions described in AITM No. 25 were practiced a few times, and commented that the officers' awareness of the need for further retraining was an essential component of making the program successful.[164]

The 5th Probyn's Horse, under the command of Lt. Col. Miles Smeeton, arrived at Ranchi in August of 1944,[165] and joined the 255th Armoured Brigade.[166] Prior to the move, the regiment had been, over the course of the first half of 1944, outfitted with Sherman tanks[167] in Secunderabad.[168] The time in Ranchi was spent on the more basic aspects of operating Sherman tanks in the field and their problems in close country,[169] incorporating some of the lessons from the Imphal fighting that had begun to filter through to regimental HQ.[170] In early September, the regiment, along with the rest of the brigade, received orders to proceed to Imphal.[171] The commanding officer of the 255th Armoured Brigade, Brig. C. E. Pert, drew up a brigade training instruction for tank/infantry cooperation in the jungle and open country of Burma. Brigadier Pert, as well as many other officers, embraced the need for constant assessment and tough training based upon important lessons from battle. He also clearly understood the needs to deal with the spectrum of geography as the XIV

Army moved into Burma.[172] He listed two principal roles for tanks in this theater: first, assault with attacking infantry and, second, close fire support to an attacking infantry force. He pointed out that previous operations had demonstrated that tanks could be used effectively in hills, in thick jungle, in villages in open clearings, and on roads and tracks in hilly and jungle terrain. He further divided his plans into five parts, specifically outlining both the appropriate and the inappropriate use of tanks in a joint tank/ infantry engagement. The fifth part focused particularly on units operating together in open country and plans of attack.[173] The brigade HQ sent out thirteen training instructions to the various units during the months of October through December.[174] It was made clear to all within the 5th Probyn's that "all training will be based upon BDE training pamphlets which will be known in detail by all."[175]

When the 5th Probyn's arrived at Imphal, the daily training instruction had been set. The procedure for the regiment covered individual and troop training (protection of fighting unit) and squadron training with infantry to assess the abilities of both units as well as potential problems. Specific training instructions were also developed for the establishment of boxes (harbors) for the regiment. As future operations would demonstrate, these included instructions on the size of the harbor, based upon the terrain and the size of force requiring protection. The 5th Probyn's dismounted some of their machine guns and added them to the perimeter to bolster defense. Tanks were stationed at different vantage points to give covering fire to the whole box. Instructions included emphasis on the need for slit trenches to be dug by all men and officers.[176] During this period, as time permitted, officers and men carried out training as infantry in jungle conditions, preparing for the possibility that reconnaissance patrols with attached infantry might be necessary at some point. Officers and men also visited the various battlefields in and around Imphal to see how tanks performed.[177] By December, the regiment received orders to move forward,[178] and Lt. Col. Smeeton noted: "I felt that no commanding officer could be as lucky as I was, in his men and in his officers and in the time; for it was the beginning of a new campaign, we had a good tank to fight with, and of training we had almost more than enough."[179]

As 1944 came to an end, the XIV Army was ready to inflict more pain upon the Imperial Japanese Army. It was a professional force, born of battle. It was reformed across many lines of effort, recruitment, command and leadership, and tactical abilities. Many previous notions had been over-turned and questioned. The XIV Army now sought the complete destruction of its foe, the Imperial Japanese Burma Area Army. Payback was now in the offing, and it would come with a lightning speed that the Burma Area Army would never recover from.

2

Endless Frustration
The Arakan

Writing about the monsoon pursuit Slim remarked that, given a choice, he would have fought the Japanese in a healthy, not a disease-ridden, setting. The 11th East African Division's drive down the Kabaw Valley consumed several months. The Arakan operations lasted from late 1942 until the spring of 1945—almost thirty months. The Arakan was as inhospitable as the Kabaw Valley and its Japanese defenders were not small, exhausted rear guards but intact units, tenacious defenders of country that might well have been designed to give such defenders every advantage. The Burma campaign was not of course decided in the Arakan but at Imphal and then on the plains on either side of the Irrawaddy. It is true that the curtain raiser for the XIV Army's great campaign, the Admin Box battle, took place in the Arakan but thereafter history's attention focused on the decisive clashes that shattered first the Japanese 15th Army and then the entire Burma Area Army—the largest Japanese formation ever to face a Western army on the battlefield. To fully understand, however, the climax of the XIV Army's great campaign, it is necessary to follow the story of Slim's old command, the 15th Corps, which carried the burden of months of frustrating campaigning and then, just when he needed it most, handed him a vital piece for the great design that carried the XIV Army to Rangoon. That part of the Arakan where most of the campaign took place was the Mayu peninsula, a long, tapering finger of land running north-south, with the Bay of Bengal on the western side, and the Mayu River on the east. Its forty-five-mile length is neatly bisected by a two-thousand-foot range of jungle-covered hills, the Mayu Range. East-west communication across the hills was virtually nonexistent apart from one road at the top of the peninsula. On either side of the hilly spine of the peninsula there were numerous streams flowing from it, called chaungs. They ran at right angles to any north–south advance and none was bridged. Since they were tidal they were impassible when the tide rose; in monsoon season they were simply impassible. The strips of flat land on either side of the Mayu Range were mostly given over to rice cultivation. The paddies would be under three feet of water during the May–November monsoon; the bunds between them were an obstacle to the movement of anything wheeled or tracked during the December–May dry season. The monsoon also meant malaria, the loathsome elephant leech, prickly heat, and ringworm; in the dry season the leeches vanished but the jungle tick arrived, bringing scrub typhus. There were also poisonous centipedes.

Before Japanese defenders could be overcome, it was necessary to find a way to move troops forward, supply them, and protect them from diseases and insects as formidable as the Imperial Japanese Army. Churchill kept up a drizzle of complaint throughout the war about the disparity between the Indian Army's "ration strength" (an obsolete metric of which he was inordinately fond) and the number of fighting units available. The Arakan, had he investigated the matter, would have explained it to him. The XIV Army was not fighting in Western Europe. Without the huge number of support units building roads, bridging chaungs, moving supplies by every known method of conveyance from Dakotas to sampans, and dealing with the casualties inflicted by weather and disease, a campaign in the Arakan would have been impossible (this statement, in fact, applies to the XIV Army's entire campaign).

It was into this very grim physical environment (and logistician's nightmare) that the Indian Army was sent in the autumn of 1942 in the first British counteroffensive against the Imperial Japanese Army. The driving force behind the first Arakan offensive was the high politics of coalition warfare, as pointed out in the introduction. Indeed, throughout the Burma campaign the prime minister's interest in it was solely as a means of satisfying his increasingly powerful, demanding—and indispensible—American allies. This premature offensive, which collapsed in the spring of 1943, was the low point in the Indian Army's war. Perhaps the most mismanaged British military operation of the war, it almost numbered Slim among its casualties when Lt. Gen. Noel Irwin, who was responsible for the debacle, tried to pin the blame on Slim, whom he disliked. Slim survived—and so did the Indian Army.

The ensuing months saw dramatic changes both in the command structure for Britain's war against Japan and in the organization of the Indian
Army, changes described in chapter 1. The first field test of the new XIV
Army and its commander took place, appropriately, in the Arakan—the
"Admin Box" battle in February 1944.[1] After that victory, the XIV Army's
attention swung to the Central Front in Assam: the epic Imphal-Kohima
battle. But the Arakan front remained. Slim's old 15th Corps, now commanded by Lt. Gen. A. F. P. Christison, Bt., would fight there for the
remainder of the Burma campaign. However, its role would be now a
supporting one. The decisive point was the Central Front, where Slim,
having decimated the Japanese 15th Army in the Imphal-Kohima battle,
was preparing to launch Capital, the offensive into the north Burma plain
that was to carry the XIV Army to the Irrawaddy and on to Mandalay. The
role of the 15th Corps in Slim's design was twofold: to hold in place the
divisions of the Japanese 28th Army that might otherwise be drawn upon
to support the Japanese 15th and 33rd armies facing him, and to get to Akyab. Whether Rangoon was retaken overland from the north (Slim's plan)
or by amphibious assault (Operation Dracula)—SEAC's preferred option
(because it was London's)—Akyab's airfields would play a crucial role.

To carry out his tasks, Christison had a rapidly changing assortment of
units. Soon after the Admin Box fight Christison's two most experienced
divisions (and division commanders), Harold Briggs's 5th Indian and Frank
Messervy's 7th Indian, left for the Central Front, where they would play
a major role in the Imphal-Kohima victory. Christison kept the 25th and
26th Indian and the hybrid 36th Indian, which was, in fact, a two-brigade
division, British in composition and soon to become British in name, and
which would leave the 15th Corps in May on its way to north Burma and
the thankless job of collaborating with Stilwell's Northern Combat Area
Command. Christison also had the 3rd Special Service Brigade, made up
of two battalion-sized "Commandos." They were present because the Arakan was expected to provide scope for amphibious operations, although
shortage of amphibious craft meant they were fated to serve as regular
infantry (and they would soon rotate back to India). Finally, there was the
81st West African Division, the first of three African divisions (plus two
independent brigades) to serve in Burma.[2]

For the balance of the 1944 campaigning season, the 15th Corps both
reestablished itself in a position that would be a platform for postmonsoon
operations and, at the same time, pulled a number of units back from

locations where logistic support would be impossible once the monsoon broke. This complicated rebalancing—as units continually departed for the Central Front—was most marked in the case of the 81st West African Division, the first African division to join the XIV Army, whose star-crossed debut may have shaped Slim's views of African troops.

Raised from units recruited in Gambia, Sierra Leone, the Gold Coast (now Ghana), and Nigeria the division was ready for action with the XIV Army by December 1943, commanded by Maj. Gen. Christopher ("Kit") Woolner, a Royal Engineer who had been general officer commanding in Gambia and Sierra Leone when the African empire began to mobilize. The expansion of the colonial forces in Africa was an even more remarkable story in many ways than the expansion of the Indian Army. That army had fought major campaigns in a modern war in 1914–1918. Its prewar plans called for it to play a significant role in any future imperial war. The resources to modernize its equipment were late in arriving and open-ended expansion complicated everything, but the Indian Army had always known it would be called upon to play a major role "the next time." The local forces raised in Britain's African colonies were in a very different position. Essentially light infantry without the heavy weapons, motorized mobility, experience in operating in formations larger than a battalion, or air mobility, they suddenly graduated from being a colonial constabulary force to facing the extremely formidable Imperial Japanese Army. Moreover, Woolner's West Africans had several additional handicaps. One of the division's brigades was handed over to Wingate, who needed troops to garrison the airheads he planned to establish deep inside Burma (he had tried to grab Indian Army units for this role but had been stopped cold by Slim). Then 81st West African had been given a role that would have challenged much more experienced units. East of the Mayu River lay the rugged Arakan Hill Tracts, whose tangled, jungle-covered summits rose to three thousand feet. East of them lay the valley of the Kaladan River, which ultimately empties into the Bay of Bengal, opposite Akyab Island.

So remote was the Kaladan that Woolner's men had to cut a jeep track through the Arakan Hill Tracts (subsequently known as the "African Way") to even reach its area of operations. Once there, the division, understrength and new to combat, would operate, remote from the rest of the 15th Corps and maintained by air supply—something else it had no experience with. It was the first division ever to be supplied solely by air. Finally the 81st West African—in common with the other African units serving in XIV Army—had the handicap of being viewed critically by Slim, who visited the 81st while it trained near Bombay. He was impressed with its spirit and how comfortable the troops seemed in the jungle. All the African units, however, seemed to him to have too many European officers. Slim felt this limited the development of leadership skills and initiative on the part of the African NCOs (unlike in the Indian Army, where the number of European officers was limited and much depended on VCOs and NCOs). All the African units had, as an integral part of their organization, columns of unarmed porters. Slim was dubious about this as well—unarmed support units could so easily become a liability in combat. (Although in the "monsoon pursuit" the 11th East African Division's porters could move supplies when nothing else could.) One additional peculiarity of the African divisions Slim did not remark on: no African brigade contained a British battalion, as every Indian Army brigade did, at least in theory. In the brief life of the African forces, of course, there had never been anything like the mutiny of 1857 in the East India Company's Bengal Army. Still it is striking that no one ever expressed the sort of doubts about the loyalty of African askaris that Churchill did on occasion about Indian jawans.

The role initially assigned to the 81st West African shifted when, in February 1944, the Japanese launched the offensive that culminated in the Admin Box battle. From covering the open eastern flank of the 15th Corps, the division was ordered to take the offensive, pushing down the Kaladan toward its lower reaches, threatening the right flank, rear, and communications of the Japanese force engaging the rest of the 15th Corps. This was an error. Far from support, an inexperienced division was courting a Japanese riposte that was not long in coming. Woolner's left flank, east of the Kaladan, was covered by the 11th East African Scouts—until suddenly radio communication with them ceased. A Japanese brigade-size force had swept around Woolner's left, seizing a dominating position threatening his line of communications (and retreat) as well as one of the Dakota airstrips that the 81st West African had built during its advance and that were the division's logistic lifeline. Woolner began to rapidly retreat. The 81st West African successfully extricated itself, although Slim noted that its units, dashing in attack, did less well in defense (a Gambian battalion had lost a key position). Although it might be thought that, for a raw, understrength division given a demanding assignment, it had performed, if not brilliantly, at least as well as could reasonably be expected, clearly

Slim was not satisfied. During the monsoon lull, Woolner was replaced by Maj. Gen. Frederick Loftus-Tottenham, an Indian Army officer who had commanded a brigade in Messervy's 7th Indian Division. Like Slim, and so many XIV Army senior officers, he came from the Gurkha Rifles.

As the monsoon rains faded and floods subsided in the late autumn, the Arakan front again came to life. Its operations during the 1944–1945 dry season, however, would take place in a different context. Imphal-Kohima had been won; Slim's vanguards were across the Chindwin and he was preparing to launch "Capital," the offensive that would crush the Burma Area Army on the plains around Shwebo, with its back to the wide, bridgeless Irrawaddy. Then, the XIV Army would cross the Irrawaddy and take Mandalay. The XIV Army staff was already thinking out the final step, "Extended Capital" (ultimately known as SOB—"Sea or Bust"), the drive on Rangoon from the north. London, of course, still hoped to shut down Slim's campaign in favor of an amphibious assault, Dracula, on Rangoon, a first step toward Singapore, and SEAC was actively planning for Dracula. SEAC itself had changed. Mountbatten had rid himself of Giffard, whose antipathy to the supreme commander had been marked—when SEAC headquarters moved to Kandy in Ceylon (Sri Lanka), Giffard had refused to go along. Mountbatten had him, and the XI Army Group, replaced in November 1944 by a new headquarters, Allied Land Forces, South East Asia (ALFSEA), under Lt. Gen. Sir Oliver Leese, Bt.

Amid all this, the 15th Corps operations seemed to have been reduced to a sideshow. However, on the eve of his replacement, Giffard held a conference in Delhi where Slim said that airfields at Akyab and on the large island of Ramree (over a hundred miles south of Akyab and off the southern Arakan coast) were necessary for his drive on Rangoon. The effective range of Dakotas based on Imphal would not allow aerial resupply much south of Mandalay. Giffard thereupon told Christison that the 15th Corps should clear the Mayu peninsula, hold the Japanese 28th Army away from the Central Front, and take Akyab. Ramree would be the next step. Giffard also, recognizing that Slim was about to launch a complex offensive operation and that the 15th Corps was conducting its operations over three hundred miles from the Central Front, detached it from the XIV Army. Henceforth it would be directly subordinate to the 11th Army Group and, soon enough, to ALFSEA.

To do this Christison had four divisions (the 25th and 26th Indian, the 81st and 82nd West African) and two independent brigades (the 22nd East

African and the 3rd Commando). This might seem a handsome superiority over Lt. Gen. Sakurai Shozo's 28th Army, which had lost one of its
divisions, recalled to face the XIV Army on the Central Front. Sakurai's
remaining force, the 54th Division and a brigade-sized independent detachment, were tasked now not with a die-in-place defense of existing
Japanese positions but with fighting a delaying action to keep the 15th
Corps from crossing the mountains known as the Arakan Yomas that separated the Arakan's narrow coastal strip from the Irrawaddy Valley, where
Burma Area Army expected the decisive clash with the XIV Army to take
place.

However, the disparity was, perhaps, less than it seemed. Christison's
two Indian divisions were experienced units.[3] The 81st West African had,
as noted, a mixed record in the previous dry season fighting; the 82nd West
African was making its combat debut. Both Indian divisions had their full
complement of artillery while the African divisions had fewer guns, and
those they had were light pieces. The 22nd East African Brigade had no
artillery at all. The terrain of the Arakan still favored the defense and, even
fighting a delaying action, the Japanese could be very hard to evict from a
position they wanted to hold.

However, when the 15th Corps began to move forward—the 25th Indian west of the Mayu Range, the 82nd West African east of it, and the 81st
West African again pushing down the Kaladan Valley—it quickly became
apparent that the Japanese were retiring. Christison and his commanders
had expected the Japanese to make a stand near the southern tip of the
Mayu peninsula, where they had stopped the 14th Indian Division in late
1942. But the Japanese continued to fall back—only the 81st West African
in the Kaladan was encountering significant opposition. On 27 December
the 25th Indian reached Foul Point, the tip of the Mayu peninsula, and
Christison ordered the preparations for an attack on Akyab, scheduled for
March, to be speeded up. The assault (Operation Romulus) was set for
3 January but on the preceding day an artillery spotter in a light aircraft
reconnoitering Akyab saw no sign of the Japanese but noticed the local
inhabitants waving—something that guaranteed that the Japanese were
gone. He thereupon landed on the airfield and recaptured Akyab. The
assault landing went ahead as a training exercise.

The explanation for the relative ease of the 15th Corps clearance of the
Mayu peninsula and seizure of Akyab was the impact on Japanese plans
of what was happening in central Burma. The Japanese had elected not

to fight west of the Irrawaddy, falling back behind the river and facing Slim with an assault crossing of the often mile-wide river. Slim promptly changed his plans. His 33rd Corps closed up to the river while the 4th Corps, masked by Operation Cloak, one of the war's most successful deception schemes, swung south, then east, crossing the Irrawaddy well below Burma Area Army's prepared defenses and then striking for the Japanese communications node at Meiktila. The Japanese, mesmerized by the threat to Mandalay and believing the 33rd Corps, now with bridgeheads on the Irrawaddy's east bank, was Slim's entire army, began to concentrate against it. One division of the 28th Army had, as noted, already left the Arakan for the Irrawaddy Valley. Now the remaining division had as its mission blocking the two passes over the Arakan Yomas to keep the 15th Corps out of the Irrawaddy Valley—an objective the 15th Corps actually did not have. By yielding Akyab, and later Ramree and the adjacent island of Cheduba (occupied on 21 January), so easily, the Japanese command showed that despite Imphal-Kohima it had not yet properly appreciated how important the Dakotas were to the XIV Army. The airfields Christison immediately began to build were to be crucial to the maintenance of Slim's drive on Rangoon. Lengthening the reach of the Dakotas was the most important thing that the 15th Corps did in the 1944–1945 campaign.

The last chapter in the long Arakan saga is quickly told. South of Akyab, the Arakan Yomas swing close to the coast. Only a narrow strip of flatter terrain borders the Bay of Bengal, along which a track ran south to Tangup, where it swung east over a pass that led to the Irrawaddy Valley. About halfway between Akyab and Tangup another pass, the An pass, also linked the coastal strip to the Irrawaddy Valley. The Japanese intention was to hold these passes, preventing the 15th Corps from reaching the Irrawaddy Valley behind the two Japanese armies battling the XIV Army in central Burma. The Japanese did this successfully, largely because the 15th Corps had no intention of driving through the passes. Its role, once Akyab and Ramree were secured, was, first, to try to cut off and destroy as much of the Japanese rearguard as possible and then to pose enough of a threat to the passes to hold the remnants of the Japanese 28th Army in place, defending the barrier of the Arakan Yomas and away from the decisive clash in central Burma. Christison's divisions failed to trap Sakurai's rearguards, although a series of vicious small-scale encounters certainly reduced their numbers. The official historians would later claim that more of the Japanesefacing 15th Corps could have been cut off had the 82nd

West African Division's "advance not have been so hesitant."[4] This seems rather unfair. The 82nd was committed, new to combat, to moving south along the difficult coastal track against veteran Japanese formations. In the midst of this operation its commanding officer, whose behavior had gotten erratic, was evacuated sick and a new commander took over.[5] Then the air supply the division had learned to work with was withdrawn, as it was necessary to concentrate every available Dakota on supporting the XIV Army's campaign. The official historians opined that the West African troops regarded the disappearance of the Dakotas "to mean that something had gone wrong and their morale suffered in consequence." They added a footnote to this judgment to remind their readers that "West African troops had previously shown that any setback quickly affected their morale and fighting value."[6] This seems to underrate the difficulty of the role assigned to the West Africans in their first campaign and the logistic problems posed by the switch from Dakotas to supplies delivered by sea and then moved forward over difficult land communications—it may reflect as well a systematic undervaluing of African troops.

The Arakan campaign had begun badly in 1942, a bad plan leading to disaster, and then became the setting for the first great victory of Slim, the XIV Army, and the reborn Indian Army. Thereafter it reverted to secondary status, but in December–January 1945 it yielded an absolutely crucial success—Akyab and Ramree, whose airfields would host the Dakotas that powered Slim's drive on Rangoon. In the dark days of 1942 Wavell had launched the Arakan campaign to take Akyab, whose airfields would cover an attack on Rangoon when the resources came to hand. In the 1944–1945 dry weather campaign, the 15th Corps success (aided by the curious lack of interest of the Japanese in denying airfields to the XIV Army) made the final stages of "SOB"—Sea or Bust, Slim's final dash to Rangoon—possible. The official historians' verdict—that the Arakan campaign "dragged on to a frustrating and inclusive end"—seems both ungenerous and imperceptive.[7]

Appendix 1: The Truly Forgotten Army

Churchill talked and wrote of Britain standing alone in 1940–1941 and posterity has accepted that description. But it was not, of course, totally accurate. Britain stood at the center of the largest empire in recorded history,

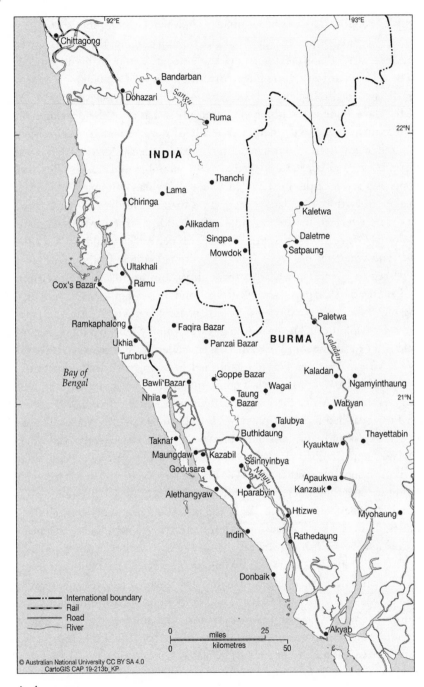

Arakan, 1945

which brought to its assistance finance, industrial output, foodstuffs, raw materials, and manpower. The huge British imperial mobilization is one of the Second World War's most remarkable stories, and one only beginning to be told.[8] In 1939 Britain's huge African empire was a much more recent creation than the Indian Raj. In West Africa coastal enclaves, remnants of the slave-trade era, had morphed into, first, bases for the development of legitimate trade and, then, as a result of the late-nineteenth-century "scramble for Africa," substantial territories. In East Africa, Kenya and Uganda were also products of that wild scramble and Tanganyika had come as a result of the First World War—a German colony turned into a League of Nations mandate conferred on Britain. All the African territories were overseen by the Colonial Office and governed by the standard Colonial Office guidelines: minimal British personnel would work whenever and wherever possible through traditional rulers. Every colony was expected to cover its own costs through various forms of local taxation, and application for grants-in-aid from London was not a career-enhancing move for governors (who were otherwise given wide latitude in running their colonies). The provision of local security reflected these ground rules. The local forces in West Africa were collectively known as the Royal West African Frontier Force, established in 1900, with individual regiments based in Gambia, Sierra Leone, the Gold Coast (now Ghana), and Nigeria. In East Africa the romantically named King's African Rifles, created in 1902, had units stationed in Uganda and Kenya, as well as Tanganyika, Nyasaland, and Northern Rhodesia (now, respectively, Tanzania, Malawi, and Zambia). Because colonies were supposed to pay for their own local security neither the RWAFF nor the KAR was very large—in 1939 the former numbered forty-four hundred and the latter twenty-nine hundred. They were basically light infantry with essentially constabulary duties. They did not have, as did the Indian Army, a permanent European officer corps—British regular officers were seconded to them for tours of duty. This colonial police force was never intended to deal with anything more serious than tribal unrest. The inspector general of African Colonial Forces, Maj. Gen. George Giffard, had worked very hard in the last years before the war to lay the foundations for a wartime expansion of these colonial constabularies into units able to play a battlefield role in a future conflict. He was handicapped both by lack of funds and by local belief that a major war could not come to Africa. His seldom remarked work, however, laid a foundation for the growth, very rapidly, of the African forces into a massive contributor to the imperial war effort—one that sent units all over Africa and added three divisions plus two independent brigades to the war in Burma.[9]

There had never been any intention to deploy African units outside the continent. The expansion in West Africa (presided over by Giffard, who had returned as general officer commanding there) was intended to protect the British colonies from the possibility of attack from the Vichy-controlled French possessions that surrounded them on every side. In East Africa, Kenya and British Somaliland had to be defended against the impressively large army that Italy maintained in its East African empire. Then, when the British, having realized the torpidity of that force, mounted the offensive that eradicated Italian East Africa with incredible speed, two hastily improvised African divisions containing both East and West African units played a significant role and performed well.[10] The commander-in-chief, Middle East, Gen. Sir Archibald Wavell, who bore overall responsibility for that campaign, would, two years later, draw African troops into the Burma campaign.

In the emergency created by the fall of Malaya and Burma and then the eruption of the Japanese fleet into the Indian Ocean, Ceylon seemed at risk and reinforcements were rushed to the island, including an East African brigade. Then, in the autumn of 1942, Wavell, now commander-in-chief, India, suggested the use of African troops on a large scale in Burma. He felt that African units would bring a familiarity with operating in the jungle while their organization, using porters rather than mechanical transport, would give them greater flexibility and ease of movement in the dense forests of the region. The East African brigade in Ceylon swelled into the 11th East African division and by early 1943 the 81st West African Division was readying itself for shipment to India (the 82nd West African would follow in 1944). The East and West Africans would play a significant role both on the Central Front and in the Arakan in 1944–1945, but wherever they were deployed, their contribution would be treated rather critically by Slim, whose widely read memoir shaped subsequent views. Slim was critical of many of the organizational features of the African divisions—too many European officers (and NCOs), leading to lack of selectivity in choosing them and a dampening effect on African initiative, as well as "hordes" of unarmed porters.[11] His accounts of their performance in the field always mixed praise with criticism—the West Africans were dashing in attack but not staunch in defense; the 11th East African, which conducted the dreadful monsoon pursuit down the Kabaw Valley, had performed a remarkable feat of arms, but, if it had moved a bit faster (!), the Japanese rearguards might have been cut off. Where Slim led, the official histories seemed to follow. The *War against Japan* series had as its principal author Maj. Gen. Stanley Woodburn Kirby, a Royal Engineer who had been deputy chief of the General Staff in India in 1942–1943. He was assisted by an interservice team that prepared drafts for him. The army member of Kirby's team was Brig. Michael Roberts, an Indian Army officer from the Gurkha Rifles and close friend of Slim, for whom he had done research as Slim wrote his fine memoir, *Defeat into Victory*, which was published the year before the first of Kirby's volumes appeared. While Slim did offer some praise for the Africans, in the official histories it was faint praise indeed. The only thorough study to date of any of the African divisions has described the official history's errors as "staggering."[12] It is worth taking a closer look at the African story to try to assess how fairly both Slim and Kirby treated the men who by 1945 had made up a higher percentage of the victorious "British" XIV army in Burma than did ethnically British units.[13]

The East Africans (with one small exception) fought on the Central Front—the XIV Army's main front. The 11th East African division, commanded by Maj. Gen. C. C. ("Fluffy") Fowkes, a British Army regular who had served in East Africa since the mid-1930s, concentrated in Ceylon in 1943, then moved in stages to the Imphal plain, where it joined Lt. Gen. Montagu Stopford's 33rd Corps, which was conducting the "monsoon pursuit" phase of the Imphal-Kohima battle. It was tasked with pushing down the Kabaw Valley ("the Valley of Death"), with its ultimate goal being the Chindwin River port of Kaleymo. The valley's nickname was well merited. It housed a veritable library of tropical diseases, the most devastating being malaria, to which the Africans were "supposed" (in the carefully chosen phrasing of the official historians) to have higher resistance than British or Indian troops. It is not clear on what this assumption was based, but despite it—and the lavish use of mepacrine plus DDT—the 33rd Corps suffered 50,300 casualties in the monsoon pursuit, most of them in 11th East African Division. Only 372 were killed in action. Of the forty-seven thousand who went sick, half had to be evacuated back to India, and there were twenty thousand cases of malaria. The 11th East African's march down the Kabaw Valley was a minor epic, through knee-deep mud, with monsoon weather making air supply precarious and in conditions that made a mile a day a good advance. Of course there were as well "die-in-place" Japanese rearguards. Nonetheless, by mid-November they were at Kaleymo and bridging the Chindwin, carving out bridgeheads on the river's east bank. In his memoir, Slim, as noted, described the division's march down the Kabaw as a "great achievement" that would have been considered impossible only a year before. However, he also pointed out that, ideally, the 11th East African would have gotten to Kaleymo faster, trapping the Japanese rearguard between it and the other prong of the monsoon pursuit, the 5th Indian Division advancing down a parallel route further west. Quite how they could have gone faster in the conditions they faced, he did not say. It is an example of the ambivalence that he seems to have felt about his African divisions.[14]

When the 11th East African was flown back to India and a well-earned rest and rotation into the XIV Army reserve, its place in the XIV Army was taken by the 28th East African brigade, an independent brigade. It would play a significant role in Slim's great victory, Operation Capital. When the Japanese Burma Area Army decided to fall back behind the Irrawaddy rather than, as Slim expected, fighting in front of it, he quickly revised his plan. One corps continued to advance on the Irrawaddy, simulating (aided by a complex deception plan) the entire XIV Army. Slim's 4th Corps, meanwhile, moved in great secrecy down the Gangaw Valley, which ran parallel to the Irawaddy but well west of it. It would then turn east and cross the great river well below where the Japanese were massing to defend it. As part of Slim's deception plan, the 4th Corps was to be led by the 28th East African Brigade and the Lushai Brigade, an improvised Indian Army formation that had been part of the monsoon pursuit. The Japanese would be bound to notice that *something* was happening in the Gangaw Valley. But the 28th East African Brigade, all of its vehicles re-painted with the 11th East African Division's sign, and the Lushai Brigade were intended to give the Japanese the impression that Slim was sending only light forces down the Gangaw Valley. But behind them came the hammer blow, two of Slim's best Indian divisions and a tank brigade that would cross the Irrawaddy at an unexpected place, seizing the modal point in the Burma Area Army's communications at Meiktila and fatally un-hinging the Japanese. To further the deception, the 4th Corps only broke its radio silence to come on the air as the 11th East African Division. The 28th East African brigade played its role well. The Japanese never realized what was coming at them. Even when the 4th Corps reached the banks of the Irrawaddy, the 28th East African Brigade continued its deception role moving further down the west bank and simulating a crossing near the Burmese oil fields—an objective the Japanese expected the British to aim for. This had the effect of drawing troops away from the 4th Corps's crossing area. The Japanese, in fact, built up their forces on the west bank to meet 28th East African Brigade's "threat." The lightly equipped brigade then had to give some ground and was involved in significant fighting before rotating back to India in March 1945.

Important as were the services of the East Africans in the XIV Army, the heaviest commitment of African forces was in the Arakan (which, as noted, ceased to be a XIV Army responsibility in November 1944). The 81st and 82nd West African divisions plus the independent 22nd East African brigade fought there. The unit that fought longest (and whose role is best documented) is 81st West African, commanded by Maj. Gen. C. G. Woolner. It took the field early in 1944, given a difficult and complex task. The focus of the Arakan campaign was the Mayu peninsula. The 15th Corps (now commanded by Lt. Gen. Sir Philip Christison, Bt.) was to drive down the peninsula with its two Indian divisions (25th and 26th). The 81st West African was to operate in the Kaladan Valley, east of the Mayu river (the peninsula's eastern boundary), separated not only by the river but by a range of tangled, jungle-covered hills from the rest of the 15th Corps. Land communications with the Kaladan were nonexistent. To even reach their jumping-off point, the division had to hack out a seventy-three-mile jeep track (without any construction equipment or engineering assistance). Thereafter it would be entirely on air supply—the first major unit in the war to operate this way (months before Wingate's "Special Force" took the field). The division began its campaign of 1944 understrength—one of its brigades had been handed over to Wingate for his impending foray into Burma.[15] Furthermore the 15th Corps commander and his headquarters made the division's task more difficult by showering it with orders that contained contradictory elements: the 81st West African was to safeguard the 15th Corps's left flank (the direction from which the devastating Japanese counterstroke had come in the debacle of 1943) but at the same time push down the Kaladan as far and fast as possible so as to pose a threat to the communications of the Japanese 28th Army, facing the 15th Corps on the Mayu peninsula. This Woolner's division did very successfully, but as it drove ahead, it became very spread out and exposed its own line of communications—and retreat. The Japanese created an ad hoc task force, launched a counterattack, looping around the 81st West Africa's left and forcing a withdrawal. That withdrawal was far from a rout. The 81st West Africa withdrew up the Kaladan slowly, coming to rest at the outset of the monsoon in the hills on the India–Burma frontier. It had, in fact, carried out its mission—no threat from the Kaladan had disturbed Christison's main effort. But that was not how the story took shape afterward. What was, in fact, a tactical reverse became "disastrous" in Slim's memoirs and the reputation of West Africans was badly dented. This seems quite unfair. An understrength division, new to combat, built a road to get to its battlefield, adapted quickly to the technique of air supply, and though handicapped by unhelpful and contradictory orders did what it was supposed to do. The "Auxiliary Groups," far from being a "horde" of unarmed porters, were fully trained infantry, unarmed only initially. Over the course of the campaign about half acquired weapons, which allowed the "UAS" (unarmed soldiers, their technical designation) to supplement the firepower of the rifle companies. In fact the carriers with their head loads could move in terrain where nothing else could and in weather that bogged anything wheeled or tracked, baffled mules, and even shut down the Dakotas. They gave the 81st West African a mobility that, in the circumstances, nothing else could have—a greater mobility, in fact, than Wingate's Chindit columns enjoyed. Slim feared that the large numbers of British officers and NCOs in the West African units would cramp African initiative, but as British ranks were thinned by battle and disease, there was plenty of African initiative carefully listed by the division's meticulous historian.

The 81st West African settled for the monsoon in far from comfortable quarters intended to guard against Japanese infiltration from the Kaladan Valley over the Indo-Burmese frontier. A meaningless minor Japanese incursion, which higher headquarters regarded with great alarm, further blotted 81st West African's copybook. Almost inevitably there was a change of command. Woolner, a Royal Engineer, was replaced by Maj. Gen. F. J. Loftus-Tottenham, a Gurkha Rifles officer who had previously commanded a brigade in the XIV Army's 7th Indian Division.

The story of the 81st West African's second Kaladan campaign is quickly told. By the time the 1945 dry or campaigning season opened, the 82nd West African division had joined the 81st in the 15th Corps. The 81st West African still was only a two-brigade division, its 3rd Brigade not rejoining until Special Force was disbanded in March 1945. The 82nd West African was part of the 15th Corps's main effort down the Mayu peninsula, while the 81st West African again moved down the Kaladan, and this time the vastly more experienced division cleared it. The Japanese were falling back, much of the 28th Army being drawn off to reinforce Burma Area Army's attempt to contain Slim's offensive. Curiously the Japanese, despite having seen in 1944 what the Dakotas could do to them, yielded Akyab, whose airfields would be vital to Slim's drive on Rangoon, without a fight (and nearby Ramree Island almost as easily). The 15th Corps's role now was to try to contain as much as possible of the 28th Army in southern, coastal Arakan. This was very difficult because not only did terrain, as usual, favor defenders but the Japanese were not trying to hold positions to the bitter end. Their intention was to slowly fall back, covering the two passes through the coastal range—the Arakan Yomas—leading to the Irrawaddy Valley, passes through which, ironically, the 15th Corps had no intention of moving. What was left of the 28th Army managed to extricate itself—only to face final destruction by the XIV Army. The official history criticized the 82nd West African Division for contributing to the successful Japanese withdrawal by moving too slowly, although offering no evidence to establish that it could have moved more rapidly.

When the Burma campaign ended, some African units remained briefly in Burma as an occupation force but most were rotated back to India and then, as shipping was available (and their priority seems not to have been very high), returned to Africa and historical oblivion. Official histories of both the Royal West African Frontier Force and the King's African Rifles appeared toward the end of the colonial period in Africa, but their treatment of the Burma campaign was summary and in some cases inaccurate.[16] Slim's very influential memoir makes clear that he had reservations about his African divisions, although he always mixed praise with his criticism. Sir Philip Christison's unpublished memoir, completed in 1982, is much more critical (and much less accurate).[17] The official history reflects these attitudes. Most African soldiers—who were decorated sparingly—were illiterate, so there are no offsetting memoirs.[18] The British (and Polish) officers of the African units—unlike the Chindit officers—did not produce widely read memoirs and the newly independent African states of the

1960s, whose armies had their roots in either the RWAFF or the KAR, had little interest in (or resources to devote to) the soldiers who had served under the Union Jack. And so their role in the Burma campaign slid into the shadows. But historical fairness requires remembering that more African divisions than British helped Slim back to Rangoon.

3

Operation Capital to Operation Extended Capital

Following on from previous chapters, the decision making for the final campaigns in Burma began as the Imperial Japanese Army's operation, U-Go, was coming to an end in late July 1944. Lord Mountbatten recommended two different plans: Y, later named Capital; and Dracula. Capital was the plan for the conquest of northern and central Burma, while Dracula covered an amphibious and airborne operation to seize the Rangoon area. Neither plan was an obvious winner: the issue with Capital was the overland route from Assam, which was tenuous at best due to road conditions and supply system. The issue with Dracula was its need for adequate amphibious shipping and reinforcements from outside of SEAC—an unlikely prospect, as depleted British divisions still embroiled in campaigns in northern France and central Italy were likely to be a higher priority for any available reinforcements.[1]

It was also at this point that Mountbatten began to reorganize the SEAC and land forces command structures.[2] The XIV Army submitted the first draft operational plan for Capital to the 11th Army Group in late August 1944, and General Giffard forwarded the plan with his comments to SEAC in mid-September. The initial plan envisioned the destruction of the Imperial Japanese Army (IJA) and occupation of a defensive line along the Mandalay-Pakokku-Maymyo-Lashio corridor. The Chinese-American force, NCAC, would close up in support of the XIV Army, while operations by the 15th Corps would continue in the Arakan. The airstrips in the Arakan would provide air support for the fighting in Central Burma, and an airborne mission was listed to support the approaches to Mandalay.[3]

Mountbatten took the planning and comments from the XIV Army and the 11th Army Group with him to meet with the British Chiefs of Staff in mid-September. Mountbatten's deputy, Major General Wedemeyer, traveled to Washington, DC, to brief the Joint Chiefs of Staff on the planning. Both meetings went well; the British and the American chiefs agreed that northern and central Burma needed to be cleared before Operation Dracula could proceed. They also emphasized that the original planning was lacking an honest assessment of the reinforcing divisions that would be needed. They stated that at least six to seven British and Indian divisions from outside SEAC would be required, and made clear that these resources were unlikely to be available before mid-1945. The Germans had begun to reorganize and offer stiff opposition as the Allies closed in on the Rhine River in late September, and the Allies would be spending another winter in Italy.[4] In light of this information, Slim and his staff at the XIV Army decided to focus on the planning and execution of Capital and clearances of the Arakan, using the resources that were at hand in India and Burma, as SEAC debated and planned with the American and British Chiefs of Staff.

Decisions were finalized at the highest levels at both the Second Quebec Conference (Octagon) and the British Defence Committee in early October. After extensive discussions, the Combined Chiefs of Staff issued the following directive on 16 October:

> Your object is the destruction and expulsion of all Japanese
> forces in Burma at the earliest possible date. . . . Following
> are approved operations:—(a) the stages of Operation Capital
> necessary to the security of the air route and attainment of
> overland communications with China; (b) Operation Dracula. The
> Combined Chiefs of Staff attach the greatest importance to the
> effective discharge of the task . . . before the monsoon in 1945, with
> the target date of March 1945.[5]

Interestingly, the orders specifically stated that "If Dracula has to be postponed until after the monsoon of 1945, you will continue to exploit Operation Capital as far as may be possible, without prejudice to preparations for the execution of Op Dracula in November 1945."[6] Slim and the XIV Army proceeded with planning for Capital as the main offensive of 1945 and viewed Dracula as a subsidiary mission. As noted previously, Slim also understood that resources in the form of amphibious shipping and, most importantly, more British and Indian divisions from Europe were not going to ship in 1944 or early 1945. It was clear that the war in

Europe was not going to end by Christmas; the most recent estimates of a German surrender were set for late spring 1945. With this knowledge, the British divisions in the United Kingdom, which had been earmarked for Burma, were shifted to the 21st Army Group in northern France. The three Indian Divisions, the 4th, the 8th, and the 10th, stationed in Italy, were also to remain in Europe and fight the last German defenders in Italy and Greece.[7] SEAC, the 11th Army Group, and the XIV Army would continue to "make-do" with the resources that already existed. There were a few formations in India Command that had not been "blooded"; however, they were all that was left for the coming campaign in central Burma.[8]

Mountbatten issued the same plan that the XIV Army and the 11th Army Group had written up in September, confirming that operations would continue in the Arakan. The chief role in the Arakan was to secure airstrips to support Capital in central Burma. In central Burma, the XIV Army was to capture Kalewa and secure a bridgehead across the Chindwin River. They would follow this with capture of the Yeu–Shwebo area by land and airborne operations by mid-February 1945 and possibly exploit opportunities. Op Dracula was formally delayed until late 1945, due to resources and the war against Germany continuing. General Giffard then asked to strip the forces from the Dracula operation and place them at the disposal of the XIV Army and Operation Capital, and SEAC agreed to this proposal.

Mountbatten did add another layer of red tape: he specifically stated that he would need to give approval for further exploitation from central Burma to Rangoon. He feared that if the IJA was pushed back during Capital, it would be in a better position to oppose Dracula in Rangoon.[9] In the end, Slim and the XIV Army would not wait and would exploit. In mid-November, orders were given to the 15th Corps in the Arakan to clear the northern Arakan and seize the important island of Akyab.[10]

The XIV Army had not been idle over this period. As previously noted in Raymond Callahan's *Triumph at Imphal-Kohima: How the Indian Army Finally Stopped the Japanese Juggernaut*, the 11th East African and the 5th Indian divisions had followed and continued pressure on the retreating IJA 15th Army from the failed Operation U-Go.[11] By late November 1944, the XIV Army had established bridgeheads across the Chindwin in two locations: the 11th East African Division had seized Kalewa and sent a brigade across the Chindwin to establish a formal beachhead, and the 268th Indian Brigade had established a bridgehead in the Sittaung region.[12] The initial phase of Capital envisioned in August had been achieved by early December, and the second phase of Capital was ready for implementation.[13]

Slim and the XIV Army's planning for the second phase was clear. They were to destroy the remnants of the Japanese Burma Area Army, consisting of ten divisions of infantry (the 2nd, 15th, 18th, 31st, 33rd, 49th, 53rd, 54th, 55th, and 56th divisions), two INA divisions, and two mixed independent brigades. The three key Japanese armies in the Burma Area Army were the 28th (the 54th and 55th divisions) in the Arakan; the 15th Army (the 15th, 31st, and 33rd divisions) and the northern 33rd Army (the 18th, 56th, and 53rd divisions); and BAA level formations, the 2nd and 49th divisions.[14] Three of the divisions from the 15th Army—the 15th, 31st, and 33rd divisions—had been badly mauled during the campaigns in 1944, and the Japanese High Command in Tokyo sent reinforcements during the autumn. On average, each division, which numbered between five thousand and ten thousand men in total, received a further two thousand reinforcements.[15] In the late summer and early autumn of 1944, changes had been made in the Japanese command structures. On 30 August, Lt. Gen. Hyotaro Kimura was assigned as commander of the Burma Area Army, replacing Lieutenant General Kawabe. Lt. Gen. Shihachi Katamura was brought in to replace Lieutenant General Mutaguchi as the IJA 15th Army commander. Lt. Gen. Shinichi Tanaka was appointed chief of staff, Burma Area Army, and Maj. Gen. Gompachi Yoshida was appointed chief of staff, 15th Army.[16]

The Japanese Burma Area Army command had prepared three principal defensive plans, each contemplating an enemy offensive against the three army fronts. These plans were termed "Dan" (the 33rd Army in northern Burma), "Ban" (the 15th Army withdrawing from Assam), and "Kan" (the 28th Army in the Arakan). The appropriate operation would be activated when the British offensive was launched and Slim's objectives became clear. The British main offensive was expected to be launched either against the IJA 15th Army on the Irrawaddy River or against the 28th Army in the southwestern Burma seacoast area. The issue for the Burma Area Army HQ was that by the late autumn of 1944 it had no means of determining where the decisive battle would be fought. In any event, it was absolutely necessary to secure the area along the Irrawaddy from Mandalay to Rangoon.[17]

The combat strength of the IJA 15th Army was extremely low and would be even lower at the conclusion of the withdrawal operation. The army would be faced with directing an operation on a front extending approximately 125 miles, from the Monglong Range (north of Mandalay) to Pakokku, with three reduced-strength divisions facing a British-Indian army consisting of about eight divisions. The Japanese Burma Area Army commander, Lieutenant General Kimura, decided that the army would attempt to hold a defensive line along the Irrawaddy River, from Lashio to the Monglong Mountains to the northeast of Mandalay, with other units in reserve south of the Irrawaddy River.[18] In a postwar interview, Lieutenant General Kimura described the intention "to hold a line running SW from LASHIO and also along the entire IRRAWADDY axis." General Naka added more detail: "we were to hold the IRRAWDDAY line, with particular reference to MANDALAY, MYINGYAN, PAKKOKKU, YENANGYAUNG, PROME and at TAUNGUP."[19]

After a series of planning sessions in the 15th Army HQ, the final plans for the defense along the Irrawaddy River were laid out as follows:

1. The Army will build strong positions on the hill north of Madaya, around Mandalay, at Myinmu and Myingyan and in the delta area northwest of Myingyan. A series of covering positions will also be built north and west of Sagaing. Main positions will be concealed and will be covered by the 15th Division from its Singu defenses, the 31st Division in positions near Shwebo and the 33d Division advance positions near Monywa. Using the positions at Singu, Sagaing and Myinmu as key positions, raiding operations will be carried out against the enemy with a view to diminishing enemy combat strength and obstructing river crossing preparations. If the enemy should attempt a river crossing the front line units will make repeated counterattacks to defeat the enemy on the beach or while actually engaged in the crossing.

2. In anticipation of enemy airborne invasion forces, key counterattacking positions will be established in strategic positions around Meiktila and Maymyo.

3. The 15th Division, will occupy positions in depth along a line connecting Singu and a point slightly west of Mongmit, keeping in close contact with the 18th Division. A rear position will be established around the hill northeast of Madaya. Strong advance positions will be built near Kyaukmyaung (west bank of the Irrawaddy River opposite

Singu) and a strong element of the Division will occupy the positions in order to harass the enemy and obstruct river crossing preparations.

4. The 31st Division will occupy the bridgehead at Sagaing, the Mandalay perimeter, and the high ground south of Kyauktalon as well as the uplands across the river from Myinmu.

5. The 33d Division will occupy the vicinity of Sameikkon, the upland country around Myingyan, the delta at the confluence of the Irrawaddy and Chindwin Rivers and the key area around Pakokku. A strong advance unit will be deployed in the vicinity of Monywa.

6. The 53d Division will build counterattack positions to be utilized against any enemy airborne raiding force in the Meiktila area. The Main force of the Division will assemble in the Meiktila-Kyaukse sector and make preparations for movement to the Kyauktalon and Singu fronts when needed.

7. One regiment of the Indian National Army will cover both banks of the Irrawaddy River in the vicinity of Nyaungu. The Army artillery unit will emplace elements in the Sagaing area and its main force in the Kyauktalon sector to support the defense of the Sagaing and Myinmu fronts.

8. In the event of an offensive on the Kyauktalon-Myinmu fronts, the main forces of the 31st and 33d Divisions the entire 2d and 53d Divisions, the 14th Tank Regiment, elements of the 18th and 49th Divisions as well as elements of the Army artillery will participate. In the event of an offensive directed against the Singu front, the 15th and 53d Divisions, the 14th Tank Regiment and elements of the Army artillery will participate.

9. Guerrilla units will be deployed in the sectors northwest of Thabeikkyin (northeast of Shwebo) and east of Monywa.[20]

This second phase of Operation Capital envisioned a Japanese defensive position on the Shwebo Plain,[21] where Slim anticipated sending the 4th[22] and 33rd Corps,[23] hoping for a major decisive battle with Kimura. However, as noted previously, the Japanese had decided to pull back to the eastern side of the Irrawaddy River. The lines of communication for the XIV Army would become stretched at this point, as Dimapur was four hundred miles to the rear and the roads down to the Chindwin bridgeheads were of poor quality. There were only 150 miles of all-weather roads; the rest were fair-weather only. The supply system relied on a mixture of road transport and aircraft.

The second phase of Capital began on 3 December 1944. The 20th Indian Division crossed the Chindwin thirty miles north of Kalewa, followed by the 19th Indian Division the next day at Sittaung.[24] Meanwhile, the 33rd Corps shifted troops of the 20th Indian and 2nd British divisions over the Chindwin from various positions north and south of Kalewa.[25] By mid-December, the 19th Indian Division had moved nearly fifty miles toward the Irrawaddy River.[26] The Japanese offered some resistance, but Slim became increasingly convinced that the Japanese had left only rearguard units on the Shwebo Plain and had shifted their main efforts to defense of the Irrawaddy River area and the eastern bank.

As the units and formations of the 4th and 33rd Corps pushed forward and opposition was still slight, it was becoming more and more apparent that the IJA 15th Army had pulled back across the Irrawaddy River. Slim and his staff had correctly anticipated the plans for General Kimura and the 15th Army; on 16 December, Brigadier Lethbridge sent a telegram to Army Land Forces South East Asia (ALFSEA),[27] informing them that Capital was being scrapped and a new plan was to be issued—Operation Extended Capital.[28]

Slim sent a summary of the revised plan on the 17 December to ALF-SEA, and followed this on the 20 December with a more detailed plan. He briefed the revised plan on the 18 December to his corps commanders, before he received approval from higher command.[29] The revised plan had a new name, Extended Capital, but its overall goal remained the destruction of the Japanese Burma Area Army, with a new addition—the seizure of southern Burma ports between March and May.

Slim was aware that he would lack the aircraft to carry out an airborne operation on the south or eastern side of the Irrawaddy River, though he would still have an ability to have "air-landed" troops. The 17th Indian Division, the 5th Indian Division, and the 11th East African Division were still in reserve and were now tasked with supporting the new plan over the coming weeks. He then fundamentally shifted his formations within the various corps.[30]

Since the 19th Indian Division was the only 4th Corps formation on the eastern side of the Chindwin, Slim proposed to shift all units of 4th Corps to the south and to reassign the 19th Indian Division to the command of the 33rd Corps. The 33rd Corps, with the 19th, would proceed across the

Shwebo Plain and close up to the Irrawaddy River. The 19th would cross the Irrawaddy River north of Mandalay and attack south toward the city. This was intended to deceive the Japanese High Command into thinking that the 4th Corps was still north of Mandalay and that the 33rd Corps was in the south. In the meantime, 33rd Corps would cross the Irrawaddy River south of Mandalay and encircle the city. The Japanese High Command, it was hoped, would then throw most of its forces into destroying the 19th Division's and the rest of the 33rd Corps's bridgeheads north and south of the city. In the meantime, the 4th Corps would move south of Kalewa and cross the Irrawaddy River near Nyaungu. The Japanese would be surprised by the arrival of the 4th Corps so far south,[31] and the 4th Corps, with motorized and tank units, plus the 17th Indian Division, would then push toward, with the 255th Armoured Brigade, the valuable supply area in and around Meiktila and seize it.[32] This would force Lieutenant General Kimura to commit most of his reserves to attempting to dislodge the 4th Corps.[33] As Slim noted: "If we took Meiktila while Kimura was deeply engaged along the Irrawaddy about Mandalay, he would be compelled to detach large forces to clear his vital communications. This should give me not only the major battle I desired, but the chance to repeat our hammer and anvil tactics: XXXIII Corps the hammer from the north against the anvil of IV Corps at Meiktila and the Japanese between."[34]

The final version of the revised plan organized the corps in the following manner: the 33rd Corps now included the 19th and 20th Indian divisions, plus the 2nd British Division, the 254th Armoured Brigade, and the 268th Indian Brigade. The 4th Corps included the 7th Indian and the newly assigned 17th divisions and the 255th Armoured Brigade as well as the 28th East African Brigade. The 5th Indian Division would be assigned to the 4th Corps in February. The third phase of Extended Capital envisioned the 33rd Corps encircling Mandalay from the north and the south, while the 4th Corps would cross the Irrawaddy River further south and strike out toward the main rail and road junction at Meiktila. This would force the IJA Burma Area Army into a decisive battle on Slim's terms. The fourth phase would be a further exploitation to the south from the Irrawaddy River line toward a southern Burma port. The 5th Indian, 11th East African Division, and the Lushai Brigade were, in mid-December, the 14th Army reserve.[35]

Slim made it clear to the new commander of ALFSEA, General Oliver Leese, that

I am confident that, if these comparatively small extra resources
can be provided, there is every prospect of attaining the object
[destruction of the Burma Area Army and reoccupation of Burma].
The enemy is still disheartened and disorganized, and provided that
we can maintain the pressure, we may well inflict a major defeat
on him. If, however, he is given the time to recover, we may be
forced to employ greater forces after the 1945 monsoon to achieve
the same object.[36]

The corps commanders were given the new orders and by the 26 December, all forces east of the Chindwin fell under the command of the 33rd
Corps and the forces on the west side of the river were under the command
of the 4th Corps. It was during this period that the 4th Corps was ordered
to march under utmost secrecy. Only officers that needed to know within
the 4th Corps HQ were told where they were heading: 250 miles to the
south and then forcing a crossing of the Irrawaddy River and striking
toward Meiktila. To further maintain this level of secrecy, Slim ordered
that there was to be radio silence south of Kalemeyo. There would be a
landline communication set up and air letter service to communicate with
higher HQ. A dummy HQ was to remain in the Tamu area that would
transmit wireless communications between formations that had originally
been part of the 4th Corps, to mislead the IJA to the actual whereabouts
of the 4th Corps.[37]

This was a bold plan. As stated above, Slim and the XIV Army were
going to rely upon a very tenuous line of communications back to Assam.
For the plan to achieve success, the 15th Corps in the Arakan would need
to remain engaged in combat with IJA divisions in the area; airfields would
need to be rapidly developed in the Arakan as well as central Burma; and
finally, the Chinese/American NCAC would need to engage with the
IJA 18th Division in the north and not allow those forces to be shifted to
central plains.[38] In the end, the revised plan was approved in retrospect by
both Leese and Mountbatten. Mountbatten specifically stated in his post-
war Combined Chiefs of Staff Report:

I entirely approved, [it] was as brilliant in its conception as in its
subsequent successful execution; for it laid the foundation for the
complete destruction of the Japanese Army in Burma. It was a
bold plan, relying for its fulfilment on secrecy, on speed, and on

taking great administrative risks. Planning and execution had to be completed in rather less than two months and so that it should have the best chance of succeeding, our resources on land and in the air were to be strained to the utmost.[39]

In terms of airpower, a major debate erupted in terms of the transport wings. It was recognized that flying hours would need to be increased to supply the XIV Army as it drove across the central plains of Burma. After a series of meetings, Eastern Air Command agreed to two fundamental points to increase the lift of supplies. Flying hours were increased from one hundred to 125 hours a month for RAF pilots and from 120 to 125 hours for USAAF pilots. Eastern Air Command also diverted thirty-two Dakotas from training missions to work forward in support. With these increases, it was hoped that the XIV Army would be supplied with enough air-lifted assets. In terms of other air support, the RAF 221st Group would support the movement of both the 4th and 33rd Corps for close air support and provide protection for transport aircraft.[40] The USAAF would provide support in the form of 12th Bombardment Group, plus further support from the Strategic Air Force. The bombing targets ranged from close in support to long-range bombing missions against targets in southern Burma. Elements of the RAF 224th Group from the Arakan would also be able to support when called upon. Closer air and ground integration occurred in the previous months, based upon lessons from the battles of 1944. By mid-February, more air assets were placed in support; No. 1 and No. 2 Air Commandos were to support in the Meiktila region.[41]

As noted in the introduction, at the end of 1944 and the start of Operation Capital/Extended Capital, the XIV Army was a fine instrument of war. It recognized its limitations and had reformed accordingly. The reasons for the future successes of 1945 can be summed up best by Professor Raymond Callahan's assessment:

The rebuilding of the Indian Army and Slim's Arakan and Imphal victories [future success in 1945] were demonstrations of the aggressive determination and imaginative leadership Churchill had always called for and so frequently lamented. But those qualities were being displayed by an army he had always undervalued and in a campaign he had never wanted to fight. . . . It is doubtful if either man [Churchill and Chief of the Imperial General Staff (CIGS),

Alanbrooke] ever fully realized that the greatest British feat of operational maneuver, not only for the war but of the twentieth century, had not been the work of Monty [the 8th and later the 2nd Army] or Alex [the 8th Army in Italy] but of Slim. . . . It [the Indian Army] had remade itself by 1944 and 1945, perhaps in some ways aided by the quasi autonomy that allowed Auchinleck, Savory, Slim, and many others to get on with the business of forging a battleworthy weapon, with few interventions from above. . . . The war in Burma was the war the Indian Army had, and it got on with preparing to win it, accepting whatever new structures or doctrines were necessary. It seems safe to predict that Slim's campaigns will be deemed examples of the military art far longer than Monty's victories.[42]

The 33rd Corps

For clarity's sake, the following narrative will cover the movement and battles of the 33rd Corps, under the command of Lt. Gen. Sir Montague Stopford, in the north in and around Mandalay, and then will switch to the advance and battles of the 4th Corps in the south in and around Meiktlia. The 33rd Corps HQ held a formal meeting on the 20 December and laid out the new plan. The formations now attached were the 2nd British, 19th Indian, and 20th Indian divisions, the 254 Armoured Brigade, and the 268th Brigade. They were tasked

> to capture YE-U and SHWEBO, To capture MONYWA,
> To capture MANDALAY and to advance south of the Corps
> axis . . . 19 Ind Div to capture SHWEBO. . . . 19 Div will go
> across the Irrawaddy after the capture of SHWEBO and will
> probably be directed on MAYMYO thence to operate from the
> east of Mandalay. [This would be partially true.]. . . 2 Div will
> operate south from YE-U—SHWEBO area on Mandalay. 20 Div
> will operate against MANDALAY from the south-west.[43]

The 19th Indian Division was ordered to deploy on the northern side of the Shwebo Plain, then advance south, cross the Irrawaddy, and create two bridgeheads at Thabeikkyin and Kyaukmyaung in mid-January. After accomplishing this, the 19th was to be prepared to advance on Mandalay from the north in mid-February.[44] The division's march across the Shwebo Plain was quicker than expected, although the Japanese forces on the plain had a different perspective. Elements of the IJA 31st Division composed the formation on the Shwebo Plain. According to the Japanese records:

> Fierce fighting took place beginning 26 December along the entire Shwebo Plain advance line from Kanbalu to Yeu. About the 7th of January, a strong enemy force approached the main positions in the Shwebo area and another enemy group stood ready to encircle the right flank of the Division. Anticipating an all-out attack by two divisions within a matter of days, the 31st Division commander was faced with deciding whether to stand at Shwebo and probably incur heavy losses or to withdraw to the stronger defensive positions beyond the Irrawaddy River. On 8 January, key points of the Division's positions were subjected to heavy mortar fire and air bombings. On that same day, Colonel Tetsujiro Tanaka, a 15th Army staff officer, arrived from Maymyo with orders to halt defensive operations at Shwebo and prepare for immediate withdrawal to the Irrawaddy. Emphasis was placed on defending the bridgehead at Sagaing in order that the enemy should not capitalize on the shift and seize that vital point. The retreat of the 31st Division was started at once.[45]

As the 33rd Corps moved across the plain, they deployed patrols forward to cut off the various roads and capture or destroy any Japanese units in the area.[46] The 19th Division's units and formations followed the ritual of all-round defense and protection patrols on the perimeter. The first major clashes occurred when the 98th Brigade surrounded the village of Leiktu in early January 1945. At times, elements of the IJA 31st Division put up stiffer resistance. The units of the 19th were able to clear the Japanese out of their positions. It became apparent that the 31st was trying to hold up the 19th, so as to allow other elements of the IJA time to withdraw across the Irrawaddy River, to fight another day, and to allow more time for the IJA on the eastern side of the river to prepare for the coming crossing. Each evening the battalion and brigade set up box formations to offset any Japanese counterattacks. The Japanese rearguards were pushed out and the advance continued.[47]

The 2nd British, 20th Indian, and 19th Indian divisions had closed in on the town of Shwebo. The Japanese rearguards that were caught in the various pincers were easily destroyed. The 19th Indian Division now turned due east toward the Irrawaddy River. The 62nd Brigade pushed hard, as did the 98th Brigade. On 17 January 1945, the 33rd Corps ordered the 19th Division bridgeheads to be established across the Irrawaddy River. The Corps specifically stated, "19 Ind Div (a) Will est two br heads each not in excess of one inf bde gp EAST of the IRRAWADDY in the areas THABEIKKYIN SR 73 [the 98th Brigade] and KYAUKMYAUNG SR 60 [the 64th Brigade]. These will be strongly dug in in anticipation of enemy counter attacks."[48] The 62nd Brigade had established a divisional base at Onbauk to support the bridgeheads.[49] By late January 1945, the 19th Indian Division had established bridgeheads on the eastern bank of the Irrawaddy River north of Mandalay.[50] The Japanese launched a counterattack by crossing the river and landing a significant number of troops on the Irrawaddy's western side at Kabwet to the north of the bridgeheads.[51] This was easily destroyed by a flying column from the 98th Brigade. Fighting in and around the two bridgeheads continued unabated. As one Indian officer noted:

> The battle went on all one long night and inside the bridgehead the fire fell heavily from low-trajectory, quick firing Japanese guns, since the contending forces were at such close quarters with each other . . . towards dawn the fire slackened. It seemed that the Jap had shot his bolt and failed to hurl us into the river. . . . Throughout the next day Mitchell bombers skillfully attacked his forward positions and obvious strong-point earthworks, though in spite of this the fighting continued on for some days.[52]

Within the 98th Brigade bridgehead, the fighting was as intense. At different times, various companies from the battalions were detached to escort wounded or provide support to other defensive positions within the bridgeheads. During this period, the 98th Brigade sent out fighting patrols to destroy Japanese counterattacks forming up outside the bridgeheads. The 98th Brigade was holding the line, but the divisional commander, Maj. Gen. Pete Rees, felt their performance left room for improvement.[53] He sent a message to all units of the division, pointing out some of the minor mistakes that had been made over the past two months. He recommended that units "go on learning from the mistakes and be conscious of them, profit from them and teach all new lessons to new members of the division."[54]

Due to the 20th Indian and 2nd British divisions having established bridgeheads to the south of Mandalay (see below for more detail), Japanese pressure against the 19th Indian Division's bridgeheads had begun to weaken by early February. On 2 February, the 33rd Corps issued an order for the final envelopment and capture of Mandalay and the destruction of the Japanese forces in the area. It specifically stated:

> To isolate MANDALAY by coordinated advances by 19 Ind
> Div from the NORTH, by 2 DIV from the WEST and by the
> 20 Ind Div from SW and SOUTH. As 19 Ind Div is furthest
> from Mandalay and is likely to meet the strongest opposition it is
> desirable that operations of 2 and 20 Divs should develop as early
> as possible with a view to threatening the enemy's communications
> on the EAST bank of the IRRAWADDY and thereby compelling
> him to relax his pressure in front of the 19 Ind Div.[55]

The Japanese 15th Division was now preparing the city of Mandalay for defense. As Japanese sources noted:

> The construction of the defenses had, however, been slower than
> had been anticipated. In the Monglong Hills, north of Madaya,
> and at Kyaukmyaung on the 15th Division front, except for some
> simple field positions, defenses were still in the planning stage.
> The construction and repair of roads and waterworks had just been
> started. Military discipline and morale had, however, improved
> vastly under the new commanders and the units faced the future
> with full confidence in their ability to hold the Irrawaddy line and
> drive the enemy back.[56]

The author John Masters, then GSO 1 of the 19th Indian Division, gives a very interesting and illuminating description of both the advance of the 19th Indian Division and the drive and professionalism of the divisional commander, Maj. Gen. Pete Rees, in his book *The Road Past Mandalay*. John Masters described a conversation with a staff officer from the 33rd Corps, where the staff officer stated, "Your general's a superb soldier, but we are having difficulty finding out what he's doing. And he doesn't always pay strict attention to the orders that the Corps Commander would wish for. General Pete sometimes thinks the 19 Division must win the war singlehanded."[57] He wrote about General Rees: "I became very fond of Pete, for his military aggressiveness was combined with a rare personal gentleness and unfailing good manners."[58] It was during this period that once again the Indian Army showed its ability to innovate, as General Rees created an ad hoc infantry/armored/artillery column to advance quickly to the northern outskirts of Mandalay. The force was named, with a hint of British humor, the Stiletto Force. This force was to protect the flank of the main attack into the city.

The force, now fully mobilized, pushed hard toward Mandalay and was able to brush aside any Japanese opposition. As one of the commanders noted, "I was sure the Japanese were right off balance and in considerable disarray."[59] This was partially true, as elements of the Japanese 15th Division started to reinforce sections of Mandalay Hill and Fort Dufferin. Elements of the IJA 18th Division from the 33rd Army were detached to the 15th Army to help defend in and around Mandalay.[60] The 64th Brigade had shifted toward the east to cut the Maymyo and Mandalay Road and the 62nd Brigade was ordered to seize Maymyo itself. John Masters noted that the Japanese were still full of fight, as units and formations from the 19th Indian Division closed in on Mandalay from the west, north, and east. He stated, "Pete and I spent an unpleasant hour under [the] western slope [of Mandalay Hill] on two successive days. Every movement, particularly of vehicles, drew prompt and accurate fire from 105s and 155s [Japanese artillery pieces]."[61]

We will look at some of the tactical actions of the 98th Brigade inside the city of Mandalay, chiefly the fighting for Mandalay Hill and Fort Dufferin. (I would recommend a battlefield visit to the present-day Mandalay city to cover this fighting. Much of the area has not changed dramatically from how it was during the fighting in 1945.) This description will give some idea of the heavy fighting within an urban environment, something that is often lost when people think of the Burma Campaign. The 98th Indian Brigade began to move out toward Mandalay on 23 February. The three battalions of the 98th Indian Brigade—the 4/4th Gurkhas, 2nd Royal Berkshire (partially depleted due to the battle for the Kabwet bridgehead), and 8/12th Frontier Force Regiment—leapfrogged one another in the advance toward Mandalay. The 8/12th FFR reached Madaya, fifteen miles north of Mandalay, on 7 March, and the northern outskirts of Mandalay itself two days later.[62] As various units from both the Stiletto Force and 98th Brigade marched south, all reported the sighting of the dominating feature of Mandalay Hill. As John Masters noted: "we could make no further advance until we took Mandalay Hill."[63]

The 1/15th Punjabis, as part of Stiletto Force, pushed into sight of the Hill and occupied part of a hill to the northwest of Mandalay Hill. Reports were coming in that the Japanese were clearly reoccupying and strengthening their positions on the hill, and various discussions ensued about who would attack the Hill. In the end, after much debate, a decision was given that the 4/4th Gurkhas would attack the Hill. Their commanding officer, Lieutenant Colonel McKay, made an impassioned plea for his battalion to seize Mandalay Hill; Lieutenant Colonel McKay knew the hill well, as he had served in Mandalay in the 1930s.[64] A company commander in the Royal Berkshires stated: "The Gurkhas were quite the stoutest-hearted soldiers with whom one could wish to serve. . . . They were the right men for the job."[65] The 4/4th Gurkhas and two companies of the 2nd Royal Berkshire regiments were given orders to seize Mandalay Hill and the base area lined with Japanese defenses. (There are regimental plaques to both regiments on the hill to this day, honoring the dead and wounded. There is also a memorial to the dead Japanese.) The attack went in on the evening of 8/9 March. By dawn on the 9 March, the Gurkhas and Berks had secured the northern reaches of the Hill. The Japanese would carry out countless local counterattacks in an effort to dislodge the Gurkhas and the Berks. The advance continued and after much heavy hand-to-hand fighting, including the use of drums of petrol ignited by Very lights, the Hill was declared cleared by 12 March, although the Japanese still held on to the southern reaches of the hill among the small pagodas.[66] John Masters described the "clearance operations" as "a gruesome campaign of extermination began, among the temples of one of the most sacred places of the Buddhist faith. . . . Our infantry fought into tunnels behind a hail of grenades, and licking sheets of fire from the flamethrowers . . . under the stench of burning bodies . . . the battalions fought their way down the ridge to the southern foot—to face the moat and thirty-foot-think walls of Fort Dufferin."[67]

Simultaneously, the 8/12th FFR, 98th Brigade, was ordered to seize Fort Dufferin. The 8/12th FFR was ordered to attack Fort Dufferin from the north.[68] The first attack was ordered on 10 March to coincide with the attack on Mandalay Hill. The original orders sounded more like orders for a Napoleonic siege operation, stating that "medium guns over open sites blast four holes in wall on west side of gate. This to be followed by artillery concentrations with smoke to allow troops to approach the bridge . . . to get through to the breaches. One company to pass through first company to secure a box inside the fort."[69] If the breach and box were firmly held, the two remaining companies were to join the rest of the battalion. At 1315 hours on 10 March, the breaches had been formed. D Company, with C Company on its left, attacked across the bridge at 1345 hours. D Company was able to get onto the bridge, but was pinned down by the Japanese fire. Supporting artillery and tank fire dueled with the Japanese defenders. C Company also became pinned by the Japanese fire, and an order was called to fall back at 1600 hours. A smokescreen was laid, and the two companies withdrew.[70] Airpower was heavily used through this period. Bombers dropped thousand-pound bombs with delay fuses.[71]

On 11 March, C Company was sent to clear the southern area of Mandalay Hill; as noted previously, the 4/4th Gurkhas had already cleared most of the remaining area. As C Company moved, it was hit by Japanese fire from the fort and forced to retire. On 12 March, a second attack against the southern area was launched, this time with armor support, and the area was cleared by early afternoon. During the time that C Company was operating, various other patrols were sent out to monitor Japanese movement along the fort. On 15 March, orders were received that a third attack, this time at night, was to be launched against the northwest area of the fort, with the support of the 64th Brigade.[72]

A series of detailed reconnaissance patrols was carried out;[73] B Company was first to cross the moat, in sixteen assault boats with five flamethrowers, followed by A Company. The initial attack was to be silent, but would have the support of artillery when needed. At 0050 hours on 17 March, B Company had crossed; the Japanese took notice as the company moved toward the breaches,[74] and, as Major Williams noted, "all hell broke loose."[75] Supporting artillery was called for, but B Company could not force its way into the breaches. At 0340 hours, the company was ordered to withdraw and was able to extricate itself, with artillery support, by 0630 hours. The company had suffered nine wounded, including Maj. D. D. Slattery, the commander.[76]

The 8/12th FFR were held in reserve for a few days and then joined the rest of the 98th Indian Brigade in an attempt to destroy the retreating Japanese troops from Mandalay and link up with the 2nd British and

20th Indian divisions to the south.[77] The battle for the fort continued; by the 19 March, there were more than twenty breaches in the walls, due to the heavy fire from artillery and air attacks. On 20 March, five Anglo-Burmese came out of the fort to report that the Japanese had withdrawn from their positions and were heading south. In the end, the 8/12th FFR was not present for the final flag raising of the Union Jack with General Rees at the destroyed Government House.[78]

During this period, the rest of 98th Brigade and units from the Stiletto Force fought street by street in the western part of the city.[79] The 19th Indian Division had performed well during its previous four months of active service. It had marched across the Shwebo Plain and carried out successful patrols and outflanking movements against the Japanese rearguards. It formed boxes during the evening without being ordered to do so. When tasked with a dangerous operation, the seizure of Mandalay, it carried out orders to the best of its ability under the circumstances. The divisional commander, Major General Rees, sent a message to many of his battalion and brigade commanders, commending them for their professionalism. Lieutenant Colonel Sheik from the 8/12th FFR received one: "kindly express to the FFR my admiration of their gallantry today [17 March] and my regret at their casualties. . . . I have seldom seen such a gallant attack and only wish it could have been favored with better luck."[80] In the end, some elements of the Japanese 15th Division were able to extricate themselves to fight another day; however, the momentum was clearly with the XIV Army as Operation Extended Capital was reaching its stated aim: the destruction of the Japanese Burma Area Army.

Let's now shift the narrative to the battles to the south and southwest of Mandalay. The advance of the veteran 20th Indian Division, under the command of Maj. Gen. D. D. Gracey, was also rapid since the Japanese had left only rearguard units on the Shwebo Plain. The 20th operated at the southern end of the Shwebo Plain, while the 19th moved down from the north and the 2nd British Division and 268th Indian Brigade operated in the center. Orders for the 20th Indian Division were to advance to Monywa "with all possible speed" on the Chindwin and seize it, and then deploy south in the Myinmu area along the Irrawaddy River.[81]

While units of the 20th Indian Division crossed the Chindwin on 3 December 1944, units from the 100th Brigade were detached to rebuild the road for supplies, which was a constant headache for the commanders. On 31 December, the 100th Brigade crossed the Chindwin[82] and continued to advance. The continuing innovation with the XIV Army was on display. The 14/13th Frontier Force Rifles continued to adapt their successful fighting practices and organization, Sher Forces, to the open plains of Burma.[83] Sher Forces aimed to have units operating farther afield that would disrupt the lines of communications of any retreating Japanese force. There were still other orthodox fighting patrols of larger strength than the Sher Forces sent out on the flanks of the battalion.[84]

The battalion was moving rapidly and gave specific instructions for marching under such circumstances. After one hour and forty minutes, the battalion was directed to rest for twenty minutes. The men were to form themselves into small boxes, with some men on the outside of the perimeter to keep watch. As the battalion moved forward, Sher Forces were sent forward and companies deployed on the flanks when terrain permitted.[85] When the battalion came into enemy contact, a company was immediately sent around the flanks of the village to cut off any escape routes, while the rest of the battalion infiltrated from multiple directions.[86] Each evening, the battalion set up box formations for protection and[87] received air drops to keep them well supplied.[88] In mid-January, the 20th Indian Division was given orders to "(a) . . . est one inf bde gp in the area of the confluence of the MU and IRRAWADDY RIVERS with the object of leading the enemy to believe that a crossing in force is to take place at MYINMU . . . (b) . . . plan to cross the IRRAWADDY WEST of MYINMU with the object of capturing KYAUKSE LF 62 and ISOLATING MANDALAY from the south."[89] The 20th Indian Division was to make the crossing in early February and advance to Kyaukse and block any Japanese troops retreating from Mandalay in the north and link up with troops from the 4th Corps coming north from Meiktila.[90]

As the 14/13th and the rest of the 20th Indian Division approached Myinmu, reports came in that Japanese rearguards were attempting to pull back and cross the Irrawaddy River to the south. As the division moved south to Myinmu, it carried out extensive patrolling to locate and destroy any Japanese forces, arriving at its destination on 2 February. Orders were given for the crossing of the Irrawaddy River on the 2 February. Intelligence predicted that there would be strong counterattacks against the bridgeheads.[91] There were reports that there were elements of both the IJA 31st and 33rd divisions in the area. The 14/13th FFRifles and the 100th Brigade immediately set up patrol bases in the area to locate any Japanese on the northern bank of the Irrawaddy River. A major Japanese attack was launched against A Company, 14/13th FFRifles, a few days after its arrival. A Company withdrew and, receiving support from C Company, by evening had been reestablished in its old positions. On 7 February, the battalion was pulled back and given instructions to prepare for the crossing of the Irrawaddy River.[92]

The 32nd Brigade had crossed on 13 February and seized a bridgehead at Kyigon. Within the first day, the Japanese made a series of counterattacks against the bridgehead. Fighting ensued and there were delays in the crossings on the 14 February. While the 32nd spent the first few days consolidating their bridgehead, the reserve brigade, the 80th, cleared Japanese rear parties on the western bank of the river.[93] The 100th Indian Brigade was to form the "main" bridgehead for the division at Myinmu, and units moved forward on the night of 12/13 February.[94] The fighting in this bridgehead for the coming week, especially for the 14/13th FFRifles, was described by the division commander, Major General Gracey, as the fiercest fighting of the whole campaign.'[95] The 14/13th was to be the second unit to cross and was to pass through the bridgehead established by the 2nd Border Regiment and occupy the village of Lingadipa, and then spread out to the south near Kanlan Ywathit and establish a front of thirty-five hundred yards. The battalion began to cross at 0430,[96] with C Company in front. The men were given two days' rations and ordered to carry enough ammunition for the same period. By 0900, all companies had crossed the river, except mules and other transport, which were not scheduled to arrive until the following day. The landing was unopposed and all went according to plan for the first day, with the villages of Yekadipa and Lingadipa cleared of enemy troops with flanking attacks and heavy patrolling.[97] During the first evening, B and C companies were formed into a box south of Lingadipa.[98] A Company dug in in the village of Yekadipa, while D and HQ companies held a position on the riverbank.[99]

On 14 February, B and C companies moved south toward Aunzeya and a ridge at Kanlan Ywathit. C Company took Aunzeya without incident, and on 15 February B Company seized Kanlan Ywathit.[100] In the meantime, however, units of the Japanese 2nd and 33rd divisions, specifically the 1st/3rd Battalions, 16th Regiment, supported by tanks and artillery, had been moving toward the bridgeheads of the 20th Indian Division, forcing the battalion to spend the next four days fighting defensive actions to protect their positions.[101]

On 16 February, the battalion's patrols reported an increase in enemy activity to the south, including a large Japanese force forming up south of B Company. B and C companies were ordered to have all patrols fall back and dig in well at Kanlan Ywathit, while A Company was sent south to support the other two companies at Kanlan Ywathit. The patrols and companies were fired upon as they withdrew to Kanlan Ywathit, and by 2300 hours on 16 February, the Japanese were launching attacks against the positions of B and C companies, who were aware of the likelihood of attack due to reports of patrols in the area. The Japanese twice managed to penetrate the perimeters of the box formations,[102] but all those who succeeded in getting inside were killed by the Indian troops.[103] After these two heavy attacks, ammunition shortages became critical for both B and C companies. By 0300 hours on 17 February, the larger Japanese forces had surrounded the boxes. Both A Company and battalion HQ were also under attack by the Japanese, and by 0330 hours, both companies had been forced to withdraw to the 9/14th Punjab Regiment's lines.[104] The Japanese, surprised by the withdrawal, did not follow up the force too closely. The 33rd Corps artillery opened fire on the former B and C company locations, hitting the Japanese, with two hundred guns, and at 0615 the battalion sent forward patrols to the old positions and came upon empty trenches from which the Japanese had withdrawn. A Company was sent forward to the village south of the ridge and reported "no enemy seen."[105]

The battalion moved to the south of the ridge, dug in, and carried out extensive patrolling in the surrounding area. On the night of 17/18 February, a series of Japanese patrols attempted to penetrate the companies' positions but was repulsed. This was followed by a more intensive attack against B Company's positions on the night of 18/19 February. After two attacks, the Japanese had penetrated at a few points but were killed upon reaching the inside of the box. Casualties forced B Company to pull back after artillery fired upon its position, but within minutes of the barrage, the company had moved back in again. Elements of the 7th Light Cavalry and the 4/10th Gurkha Rifles fought and supported the 14/13th Frontier Force Rifles. This new ad hoc battlegroup pushed on to the village of Talingon. The Japanese then attacked the ad hoc battlegroup for five days and nights. The village would change hands multiple times. The FFRifles and Gurkhas, with close air support, punished the Japanese for their efforts.[106] An officer from the 7th Light Cavalry recorded his thoughts on the fighting in and around the village. He stated: "As we bumped across paddy fields in two up formation, neither ourselves nor the Japs realized what a slaughter-house Talingon was going to prove for them, or what hard nerve-wracking days and nights it could give us. . . . We were attacked by Banzai yelling Japs and this combined with the unforgettable stench of rotting carcasses inside their positions, made a very grim night of it."[107]

The commanders assessed that more than five hundred Japanese had been killed, including two battalion commanders.[108] The 14/13th FFRifles had accounted for another four hundred dead Japanese over the previous two weeks, but it too had suffered. Forty-six men had been killed and more than one hundred wounded.[109]

By 21 February, the 80th Brigade had crossed into the Myinmu bridge-head; on 28 February, the two bridgeheads were connected by active patrolling. The divisional artillery had moved over by 5 March. The brigades began to push west and east to expand their bridgeheads and link up the 2nd British Division to the east and the 4th Corps to the south. Intelligence had reported that more than thirteen Japanese battalions had been involved in the counterattacks, drawn from four different divisions, the 31st, 33rd, 53rd, and 2nd.[110] By the beginning of March, the 20th Indian Division was involved in the fighting to link up with the 4th Corps to the south, the destruction of the Japanese south of Mandalay, and the advance down the Irrawaddy River.[111]

The division had adapted rapidly to the conditions of the central Burma plain. When advancing, it combined the tactics of both open and jungle warfare styles. It kept up its reputation as an expert patrolling formation with the location and destruction of Japanese rearguards. When in defense of the bridgeheads, patrols provided information of any imminent attack, and deployment was in all-round defense formations. These ensured destruction of the Japanese attacks against their bridgeheads. The 20th Indian Division had once again been able to maintain the initiative and destroy the IJA when the time came. Its veteran status in 1945 was well maintained.

The British 2nd Division, another veteran formation, under the command of Maj. Gen. C. G. G. Nicholson, from the fighting of 1944, was the last formation in the 33rd Corps that crossed the Irrawaddy River. As noted above, the 2nd Division moved down the central path of the Shwebo Plain and was involved in the fighting in and around the town of Shwebo with the 19th Indian Division. As was noted on 20 December 1944, the "2 Div will advance with all possible speed on the main axis east to Shwebo."[112] As with the rest of the 33rd Corps, the 2nd Division closed in on the Irrawaddy River. The orders from 2 February stated that the 2nd

Division was to cross north of the 20th Indian Division and establish one bridgehead to the west of Sagaing, with two brigades, and clear the area of the enemy.[113]

Due to the lack of assault boats and rafts, the crossing of the 2nd Division would have to wait until the 20th Indian Division had established its two bridgeheads. On 24 February, the 5th Brigade crossed the Irrawaddy River, with the 4th and 6th brigades ready to cross. Major artillery and smokescreens were laid on. Of the two crossings, one was successful, and by the morning of 25 February, a two-battalion bridgehead had been established. Tanks, infantry, and artillery were shipped over into the bridgehead over the following days. Japanese opposition was light, especially compared with the 19th and 20th division bridgeheads. Japanese sources noted: "The 31st Division had completed 60 to 70 per cent of the positions covering the Sagaing approaches and had established a fairly strong field defense complex. Construction of infantry positions in all other 31st Division areas was about 30 per cent completed while heavy gun positions were approximately 50 per cent completed."[114] On 27 February, the 6th Brigade crossed, and the 4th Brigade followed. The bridgehead was rapidly expanded, and the brigades pushed out to link up with the 20th Indian Division. By 5 March the 2nd Division was concentrated in the bridgeheads and the link up with the 100th Indian Brigade of the 20th Indian Division had occurred. The division was ready to push on to Ava and close the southern approaches to Mandalay.[115]

Within thirty-six hours of the 20th Indian Division's crossing of the Irrawaddy River, the 7th Indian Division and the 4th Corps had also crossed further south at Nyaungu on the night of 13/14 February 1944.[116] The Japanese High Command was still not aware that a major landing was taking place at Nyaungu; General Kimura still believed that this attack was a feint and that the main landings were happening to the north in the 33rd Corps area. The decisive phase of Operation Extended Capital was coming to a culmination point. Now let's shift the narrative to the southern area of operations for the 4th Corps.

IV Corps

As previously noted, the 4th Corps, under the command of Lt. Gen. F. W. Messervy, had shifted its focus, after receiving orders from General Slim and XIV Army HQ. The 7th Indian Division, another veteran formation under the command of Maj. Gen. G. C. Evans, had been moved on 29 December 1944 by motor transport from the Kohima region to Tamu. From Tamu, the march progressed due south to Kalemyo and then onto Kan. On 19 January 1945, the 4th Corps commander, Evans, issued an appreciation of the mission. He was clear what the main mission of the 4th Corps was:

> My object is to get a sufficiently strong force to MEIKTILA
> IN TIME to be able to cut off all Jap forces retiring from the
> MANDALAY area and in conjunction with 33 Corps to destroy
> them. . . . 7 Div with 4 inf Bdes at their disposal, and if necessary,
> a Tank Regtl group and a Medium Bty in sp can seize PAUK first
> and then establish a bridgehead over the IRRWADDY without
> undue delay. Every effort must be made by rapid envelopment
> tactics to destroy and disintegrate enemy rearguards before the river
> is reached. . . . Once across the IRRAWADDY I must deploy a
> hard-hitting force, strong in tanks and arty, against MEIKTILA
> while continuing to engage the enemy in the YENANGYAUNG
> area and preventing them from interfering with the crossing of the
> Corps or threatening the Corps administrative airhead.[117]

At Kan, the 7th Indian was divided up into different battlegroups. The 89th Indian Brigade was sent out on the flank of the division to protect the advance from any Japanese forces in the area on the march toward Pauk. There was a minor skirmish in Pauk, but then the brigade and the 1/11th Sikh moved on toward the Irrawaddy River.[118] As the brigade marched south, depending totally on mules for its transport, it sent out constant patrols on the flanks and forward of the unit. Each night, the brigade created box formations and sent out patrols on the edges to counter any Japanese movements.[119] As units of the 7th Indian Division closed in on the Irrawaddy River shore from the west, plans were drawn up for the crossing. A major deception plan, Cloak, had been created to lure the Japanese into thinking that the major corps crossing would occur to the south at Yenangyaung and not at Nyaungu. The 28th East African Brigade was sent south opposite Chauk to entice the Japanese that movement was still going south. The Japanese fell for the ruse. They also started to realize that there was a major buildup now south of the 33rd Corps. They had minimal understanding that the full force of the 4th Corps, the 7th Indian Division, the 17th Indian Division, parts of the 5th Indian Division, and the 255 Armoured Brigade were about to launch a major threat to their rear.[120]

The 33rd Brigade was in the lead to seize the bridgehead at Nyaungu. On the evening of 13 February, the first units started to cross the Irrawaddy River; within a day, there would be three battalions across the river.[121] (The landing sites can still be clearly identified today.) As with previous parts of the narrative, let's focus on the actions of one battalion, the 1/11th Sikh, as part of the 89th Indian Brigade, to gain a more detailed picture of the operation. The 1/11th Sikhs was to land south of the main landing site, Nyaungu, near Pagan. This was to be a subsidiary crossing to tie down more Japanese troops in the area.[122] While the battalion was stationed on the west bank, it carried out patrols to find and eliminate any retreating Japanese forces in the area.

On 12 February, the battalion had sent over a series of patrols to the eastern bank of the river to report on Japanese movement. The initial information indicated that the town of Pagan was unoccupied, but on the night of the crossing, 13/14 February, reports came in that Japanese troops were moving toward the landing areas and Pagan. The first boats to cross were fired upon, creating confusion. Then a boat was seen crossing over from the eastern side of the river with a white flag, approaching the positions of the 1/11th Sikh. It proved to contain Indian National Army (INA) troops who wished to surrender.[123] A second landing party was sent across[124] and received the surrender of the remaining INA troops in Pagan.[125] By the morning of 14 February, the whole battalion had crossed. Positions were immediately dug for the day, and patrols were sent to push out to the east to make contact with the rest of the 89th Brigade and the division. Contact was established the following day, 15 February.[126] The 89th Brigade held the western side of the bridgehead, while the 33rd held the east and southeast sides. All units of the division received orders on 16 February to start expanding the bridgeheads to allow for the remainder of the 4th Corps to arrive, assemble, and pass through.

The 1/11th Sikh was ordered to move south toward Chauk on 17 February 1945. B Company was pushed forward down the main road on 18 February. The battalion was in charge of a large area of land, and what followed clearly illustrates some of the problems that arose when fighting in open terrain with orders to cover a large area. Forward patrols engaged the Japanese, who were moving north. B Company was reinforced with tanks and battalion mortars in order to press an attack on a large concentration

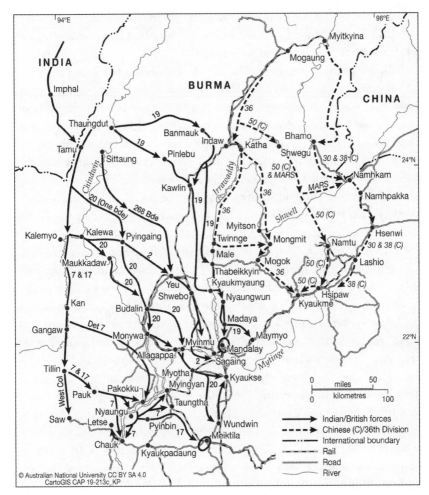

Operation Capital and Extended Capital

of Japanese forming up. The battalion HQ and CO moved forward and occupied a pagoda, and B Company moved forward to attack the retreating Japanese.[127] In doing so, the battalion failed to sweep the area around the road for enemy positions, allowing a large force of Japanese to attack the battalion HQ in the pagoda.[128] HQ did not have company troops for protection, and in short order was fighting for its life, until a troop of tanks came and provided support, enabling the HQ to extricate itself.[129] B Company also returned and destroyed the attacking Japanese force.[130] The outcome was ultimately successful, but luck was a major element of the outcome—that the battalion had been able to overcome the Japanese so quickly, and that neither B Company nor battalion HQ had been overwhelmed by the bypassed Japanese forces.

Following this engagement, the 1/11th withdrew a few miles back and set up company-sized box formations covering the routes to the north. Patrols were sent far and wide to locate and destroy any remaining Japanese forces. The lucky escape of 18 February brought home the point of continued, vigilant patrolling.[131] D Company was attacked heavily on the night of 19 February at Tetma, but the Japanese failed to destroy its position. The front remained quiet for the next few days.[132] On 21 February, other elements of the 89th Indian Brigade, the 2nd King's Own Scottish Borderers (KOSBs), and the 4/8th Gurkhas moved south to help the 1/11th Sikh hold the western side of the bridgeheads. At this point, elements of the 17th Indian Division had entered the bridgehead and were patrolling. (We will come back to this point.) The Japanese failed to identify the 17th Indian Division, under the mistaken impression that it was still in India.[133]

On 23 February, another attack came in against D Company, and again the Japanese were repulsed. The next major attack did not happen until 11 March, again in the Tetma area. Patrols reported that the Japanese were preparing for attacks against Tetma. Two Sikh patrols attacked the Japanese, thinking they were moving against only a forward ambush party. They succeeded in dispersing the Japanese force, which proved to have over one hundred troops stationed in the position. Not realizing the numbers they were up against, the patrols suffered heavily,[134] but still forced the Japanese to withdraw.[135] A Company relieved D Company at Tetma on 13 March and was attacked on the evening of 15 March. Once again, the Japanese were defeated with heavy losses. The 1/11th Sikh was ordered into reserve on 22 March. It returned to the front on 27 March and participated in the destruction of the Japanese caught on the Irrawaddy Plain.

While the 7th Indian Division and the formations and units under its command created the bridgehead and secured the lines of communications, their main effort was still to support the efforts of the 17th Indian Division and the 255th Armoured Brigade and its push toward Meiktila, to which we will now turn our attention.

Battle for Meiktila

The 17th Indian Division, under the command of Maj. Gen. "Punch" Cowan,[136] was stationed in Imphal at the end of January 1945. The various units of the division carried out training as lorry- and air-transport battalions.[137] On 5 February, the 17th was ordered south toward Nyaungu on the Irrawaddy River. It received the following order: "To seize MEIKTLIA-THAZI area in sufficient strength and in time to cut off all the JAP forces retiring to the SOUTH from the MANDALAY area and in conjunction with 33 Corps to destroy them."[138] It reached its destination on 17 February and was given two hours' notice to move across the Irrawaddy River into the 7th Indian Division bridgehead. The divisional plan was to strike out south of the bridgehead and seize Pyinbin, and then move northeast and seize Taungtha with the 48th Brigade. Meanwhile, the 63rd Infantry and 255th Armoured brigades were to move south of Taungtha and seize Mahlaing. The airstrip at Thabutkon was to be seized by the 63rd and 48th brigades so that the 99th Indian Brigade could be flown in. The 48th Brigade was to move south to Thabutkon and prepare for attack on Meiktila. At that point, the division would be within eight miles of Meiktila, having covered a distance of about eighty-five miles from the bridgehead.

The Japanese were not in strength in the area; however, intelligence was reporting that the Japanese would push forces into the region as they recognized the major threat to their communications and rear. Units from the 15th and 53rd Japanese divisions had been identified as possible reserves for a battle in the Meiktila region, as they withdrew from the Mandalay region. As stated by the Japanese sources: "Around Meiktila, which the 53d Division has been assigned to fortify, positions were still in the reconnaissance stage."[139] There were also reports that elements of the 18th and 56th from northern Burma may be shifted to the central front.[140]

As with previous sections, let's turn the narrative to unit-level engagements. The reform and the professional standards of the XIV Army had clearly been embedded and learned across the various formations, as will be noted by the actions below. For some of the units and commanders, this campaign truly was "Payback" for the losses and defeat of 1942. The 4/12th Frontier Force Regiment,[141] as part of the 48th Indian Brigade, crossed the Irrawaddy River on 18 February. The 17th Indian Division and 255th Armoured Brigade were sharing a small bridgehead with the 7th Indian Division, and the resulting overcrowding provoked the 17th to send small patrols out to the south to Pyinbin crossroads so that the rest of the division could move forward.[142] The 4/12th FFR, with the rest of the 48th Indian Brigade, was able to seize Pyinbin without opposition on 21 February 1945 and began sending out patrols to find and eliminate Japanese positions to the south and east of Pyinbin. On 23 February, the battalion moved toward Taungtha, and seized it the following day. On 26 February the battalion arrived at Mahlaing, reoccupying the same area it had held during the campaign of 1942.[143] Throughout the period between crossing the Irrawaddy River and arriving in Mahlaing, the battalion and brigade had built "box formations" during the evening and sent numerous patrols forward, both to reconnoiter and to engage the enemy. The opening up of the terrain dictated larger boxes, but these were still established with an all-round defense formation. The battalion by this point was being supplied completely by air, as the Japanese had closed the road behind the division at Taungtha.

On 28 February, the 48th Indian Brigade moved south to attack Meiktila, with the 63rd Indian Brigade moving on foot on its right to seize the southern approaches. The 255th Armoured Brigade, with two attached infantry battalions, was sent to the left of the 48th Indian Brigade in a flank attack to seize the airfield to the east of Meiktila and attack the town from the east.[144] The 4/12th FFR moved south as the 1/7th Gurkhas led the brigade attack along the road into Meiktila. As the battalion moved south, it harbored and sent out patrols to locate any Japanese positions. On the evening of 1 March, D Company was sent forward into Meiktila as a fighting patrol, and seized the twin pagodas at point 298334 by 2200 hours. Early the next morning, on 2 March, A and B companies moved into the town with orders to seize the railway line,[145] supported by two squadrons of the Royal Deccan Horse. Six hours of fighting through various bunkers with the tanks providing support cleared the railway area. D Company followed behind and, supported by a troop of the 5th Probyn's Horse, cleared the remaining Japanese positions along the railway line.[146] By 5 March, the town had been cleared of Japanese troops, and the 4/12th FFR[147] was immediately sent to clear the airstrip at the east entrance of the town. Over the course of the next five days, the battalion sent out patrols from its box formations to locate and eliminate any Japanese positions in the area to the south and east of the town.[148] The 5 March marked the closing of the "hammer and anvil" for the XIV Army. All the formations within the 4th Corps and the 33rd Corps had reached their initial objectives. Now they set out to systematically destroy the Burma Area Army, which was caught between Meiktila in the south and Mandalay in the north.[149]

It was in early March that the Burma Area Army realized the danger to their defensive plans for Central Burma, noting in unit documents: "The battle around Meiktila, which had been considered a minor operation was now becoming very important because of the strategic location of Meiktila. The Area Army commander was convinced of the inadvisability of leaving the command of such an important and complicated battle situation to the 15th Army commander."[150]

While the 4th Corps was massing from Pagan to Meiktila, the XIV Army continued to use deception. The new operational term was Conclave. The main intent of this part of the deception phase was that "the enemy is aware of the presence of tps of 4 Corps in the MEIKTILA area. He does not know, however, that the whole Corps is concentrating there, nor does he know in which direction our next move from MEIKTILA will be made. To conceal from the JAPS for as long as possible the fact that a force of the size of a corps is concentrating at MEIKTILA."[151]

The 17th Indian Divisional GOC, Major General Cowan, decided on a bold policy for the defense of Meiktila, while maintaining Conclave. His land communications lines had been cut, and supplies arrived both by air drop and air landings. To deal with the potential for a Japanese counteroffensive against his division, Cowan adopted an offensively oriented plan to defend Meiktila.[152] He set out to destroy the Japanese units as they assembled for attacks, proving once again his adaptability to a new situation.[153]

Cowan set up six major harbors around the town, from which mobile strike formations of combined tank/infantry units (columns)[154] were to seek out and destroy the Japanese forces building up nearby. Each harbor had a company-sized unit supported by medium machine guns (Vickers) (MMGs) and mortars as protection forces when the mobile unit moved out. Static defenses[155] were created around the Meiktila airstrip east of the town and inside the town itself.[156]

A series of major mobile attacks in the region was carried out. One example of the success of this tactic—which also demonstrates the professionalism of both the infantry and the tank units involved—was an attack carried out by the 4/12th FFR and the 5th Probyn's Horse on 10–11 March. The battalion, with B Company in the advance guard, was sent out with two squadrons of Probyn's to the northwest to clear any Japanese roadblocks on the road to Mahlaing.[157] The infantry advance guard was transported on the tanks. Six miles outside Meiktila, they encountered a sizeable Japanese force. Fighting ensued, and continued throughout the day, with each side unable to dislodge the other. The decision was made to harbor for the night near the defended area, and B Company sent out patrols to locate any holes in the Japanese defense.[158] Early on the morning of 11 March, D Company was brought forward and made an encircling movement, successfully infiltrating some of the Japanese positions, rather than attempting to make a frontal attack. The attack was met by heavy artillery fire and was called off.[159] Lieutenant Colonel Smeeton of the 5th Probyn's Horse decided to attack the positions without infantry support, and a group of tanks swung from the left flank and engaged the bunkers at point blank range. One tank was disabled, but most of the Japanese guns were destroyed. The two companies and Probyn's Horse withdrew toward Meiktila. The battalion had suffered nine killed and forty-seven wounded during the two days' fighting, while the Japanese had suffered more than two hundred killed.[160] The battalion continued to carry out constant patrols, attached to various tank formations and other units, for the remainder of the month, and was successful in ambushing and destroying Japanese locations.

The 7/10th Baluch was part of the 63rd Indian Brigade.[161] The battalion had been successful in deploying ambush parties ahead of the main advance toward Meiktila during late February. On 28 February, the battalion had moved across by foot to set up roadblocks on the Kyuakpadaung-Meiktila road, establishing defensive boxes on both sides of the road and sending out patrols to the surrounding area to locate and clear Japanese positions. From 1–3 March, D Company held the roadblock as the rest of the battalion made sweeps, in cooperation with A Squadron of 5th Probyn's Horse, around the road southwest of Meiktila. Over the course of the next few days, they killed approximately 150 Japanese,[162] and themselves lost ten killed and forty-nine wounded.[163] Each night the companies created boxes and prepared for a Japanese counterattack. The companies sent many foot patrols out to contact the enemy.[164]

The battalion was engaged in normal foot patrolling for the first few weeks of March in the area to the west of Meiktila. There were three patrol bases set up, at Oknebok, Letpankagaw, and Mezalibin.[165] Both reconnaissance and fighting patrols were launched in the area to locate and disrupt any Japanese movements.[166] As Japanese troops amassed north along the Pindale Road, the battalion was shifted to the area north of Meiktila. On 11 March it carried out its second major combined tank/infantry "column" attack.[167] C and D companies were ordered to destroy any Japanese five miles up the road. D Company moved north riding on the tanks and was shot at within minutes. C Company moved north to support the attack, coming in on the right flank. After a few hours of fighting, the Japanese were forced to pull back, having lost fifty killed, compared to only one killed and four wounded for the 7/10th Baluch. For the next week, the battalion set up patrol bases and operated alongside tanks in various sweep operations as well as carrying out more local foot patrols in the area north of Meiktila.[168] As with earlier operations, the battalion built up and reinforced its box formations each day and carried out daily patrols.[169]

The 7/10th participated in several tank/infantry sweeps during the last week of March. The most successful was carried out over the course of two days, 27–28 March, when the battalion had been moved northwest to deal with the last Japanese defenders near Mindawagan Lake.[170] The battalion attacked a Japanese position in and around Hill 850. C Company, supported by tanks, was sent in to seize the position. The rest of the battalion moved up to consolidate the hill before a Japanese counterattack could be launched, digging in on the position. The Japanese, having lost over a hundred killed, failed to attack. The 7/10th Baluch, by contrast, lost four killed and seventeen wounded.[171] The Japanese began to fall back from Meiktila in the north as a road link was established with the 5th Indian Division.

The 17th Indian Division were successful in operating as lorry-transported infantry in the approach to Meiktila. Units set up boxes each evening, with constant patrols sent out to locate and destroy any enemy troops in the area.[172] Neither had been overrun or surprised during the advance. The 4/12th FFR moved into and successfully fought in a built-up area of Meiktila, and the 7/10th Baluch effectively established roadblocks and set up ambushes on foot in the southwestern region of Meiktila. Both battalions adopted infiltration tactics when Japanese defenses proved too strong to attack frontally, adapting effectively to the changing situations of the battlefield during the approach to and defense of Meiktila. Mounted patrols and attacks with tank support were successfully carried out. They had learned the lessons of the campaign of 1944 when dealing with strong Japanese positions: infiltrate and, if possible, have heavy supporting weapons such as tanks available. General Leese, GOC ALFSEA, in a letter to General Alanbrooke, noted this apparent transformation of the XIV Army. He stated, "Frank Messervy and 'Punch' Cowan have handled the operation with their usual dash, and we have made a clean break in three days to the satellite MEIKTILA airfields. It is a very fine performance, especially since the troops have not been accustomed to this type of open warfare."[173]

As with all units of the 17th Indian Division, the 1st Sikh Light Infantry

(SLI)[174] had spent the month of January and part of February in Imphal. It was a war-raised regiment, and the 1st Battalion would represent the first "blooding" for the regiment. It would prove its worth at Meiktila. The chief elements of training for the battalion included emplaning, deplaning, loading jeeps, company attacks, patrolling, and harboring.[175] The 99th Brigade had been earmarked for an "airlanding" operation. On 28 February and 1 March, the battalion, along with the rest of the 99th Indian Brigade, flew from Palel to the Thabutkon airstrip. A company (COY) commander, Major Maling from the 1st SLI, reported:

> the scene on the strip was full of action—Dakotas and Commando
> planes roaring in with accompanying dust clouds; a divisional air
> drop of supplies in progress a few hundred yards away with up
> to thirty supply planes circling for the drop; AA gunners British
> and American stripped to the waist and digging feverishly and
> continual flow of MT; infantry and equipment moving from the
> strip to the Battalion harbours, made a stirring picture.[176]

On the afternoon of 1 March, the 1st SLI was ordered to proceed toward Meiktila to protect the divisional HQ, but these orders were changed on the approach to Meiktila. A company was posted to the 48th Indian Brigade to establish a roadblock to the northeast of the town. D Company set up a box that was to become known as Able Box just north of the town center, and the rest of the battalion was posted to the northern side of the town.[177] As the battalion moved around and set up defenses, it carried out numerous patrols in and around the positions, which had been established in all-round defensive lines.[178] The first major test for the battalion came on 3 March. A Company, stationed on the roadblock to the northeast of the town, had protected the roadblock from a Japanese night attack on 2/3 March. That morning, a squadron of tanks from the 5th Probyn's Horse arrived to support its positions. Orders were received to proceed further north to destroy a Japanese roadblock, with the men of A Company carried on the tanks. As the tanks began to move forward, they came under fire from west of the road. The SLI dismounted and followed closely behind the tanks. The position was cleared using tank/infantry cooperation. The Japanese lost four artillery pieces in the action, and after it was over the SLI and Probyn's were pulled back to the original roadblock.[179]

On 4 March, the battalion was withdrawn to Meiktila. A and C companies were placed in Area B at Kyigon, while B Company was placed at Charlie Box, and D Company at Able Box. Unlike the 4/12th FFR and the 7/10th Baluch, the 1st Sikh Light Infantry was part of the static defense scheme;[180] they were to prepare their positions in each box and dig and set up defenses. Then a series of patrols, both for fighting and for reconnaissance,[181] was to push out toward the north and northwest to disrupt any Japanese attempts at a counterattack.[182] Most of the battalion's patrolling and fighting activities were concentrated along the main northern road from Meiktila toward Pindale. The Japanese were applying heavy pressure along this road, and many of the battalion's attacks were against superior numbers. Because of this, orders were to hit the Japanese positions and withdraw, not become committed in a fight. The fighting was not always one way, as the IJA regrouped. As Major Maling noted in his diary after a difficult skirmish on 10 March, "this reverse was a great blow to the Battalion and was more of a shock, as up to then we had matters very much our own way. It also marked the beginning of a week of unpleasant small engagements on the Pindale road during which we suffered heavily. . . . From the 11th of March our patrols were under constant observation and accurate shelling from enemy 105 guns."[183]

On 14 March, A Company relieved D Company at Able Box. Soon after this transfer, the Japanese attacked the box, and were repelled. On 15 March, D Company was sent, with a company of the 1/3rd Gurkhas, to dislodge a group of Japanese stationed to the north of Able Box. After a day of heavy fighting, the Japanese pulled back. On 17 March, all units of the 1st Sikh Light Infantry[184] (except for A Company, which was given the task of continuing to hold Able Box and to patrol up the Pindale Road) were ordered to the airstrip to the east of the town to combat the Japanese attacks in that area.[185]

The fighting in and around the Meiktila airstrip was fierce.[186] The 1st Sikh Light Infantry, ordered to clear the area to the north of the airstrip, encountered a considerably larger force of Japanese in the area on 18 March. The attempt to clear the area was successful in some villages, but overall the Japanese were too strongly dug in, and orders were received to pull back. B Company, having suffered extensive casualties, had to be amalgamated with D Company. On 19 March, the battalion was released from the 99th Indian Brigade and sent out to the east of the airstrip along the Meiktila-Thazi-Mandalay railway line, to ambush and engage the Japanese in hit-and-run attacks. The battalion operated in this role for the next week; while battles raged to the south, southeast, north, and northeast of Meiktila, the 1st Sikh Light Infantry destroyed countless Japanese reinforcements trying to reach the fighting. The battalion had become very adept at employing hit-and-run tactics, and the fighting patrols successfully surprised Japanese patrols, both lorry-bound and on foot. By the end of the month, the battalion had been re-attached to the 99th Indian Brigade and was engaged in destroying the remnants of the Japanese forces to the south and southeast of Meiktila.[187]

As noted previously, the intense defensive fighting in and around Meiktila marked the first engagements for the 1st Sikh Light Infantry, and it suffered numerous casualties in action. In spite of its lack of battle experience, the battalion effectively carried out patrols and defended its respective boxes during the first weeks of March.[188] It did encounter difficulties when tasked with clearing heavily fortified positions to the north of the airstrip, but no more so than other units. When asked to carry out hit-and-run raids along the railway line, the battalion performed extremely well, creating small patrol bases to attack the incoming Japanese. Troops were never caught out and destroyed, even against larger Japanese forces, and withdrew when required to do so. The 1st Sikh Light Infantry received praise from Major General Cowan[189] and Field Marshal Auchinleck[190] for their performance,[191] and officers serving with other units of the 17th Indian Division and the 4th Corps also commended their abilities.[192]

As already noted, the 5th Probyn's Horse[193] was used in support of the infantry during the advance on and defense of Meiktila and enjoyed success in destroying Japanese positions.[194] During the Meiktila operations, the regiment built or returned to previous boxes at night and set up all-round defense positions. As with the 7th Light Cavalry in the 33rd bridgeheads, the tanks were arrayed in the perimeter to give covering fire for the whole box.[195] During the fighting in and around Meiktila, the regiment was often divided up and squadrons were detached to various infantry formations, although there were occasions when the regiment fought as a whole unit. One example of a mobile column was the attack on the Mahlaing Road with 4/12th FFR on 11/12 March 1945.[196] The organization of such an attack is as follows: the column was divided into four groups. The "advance guard mounted troops" group consisted of three troops of the 16th Light Cavalry (armored cars) and one troop of Probyn's.[197] The "advance guard" had one squadron of Probyn's with one company of 4/12th FFR. The "main body" column consisted of HQ, HQ 4/12th FFR, a field ambulance, and one company of the 9/13th FFR rifles. The "rear guard" comprised one troop of Probyn's, one company of the 4/12th FFR, and one section of the 21st Mountain Battery.[198] An interesting anecdote from this attack was the apparent lack of concern on the part of Lieutenant Colonel Smeeton for the Japanese antitank gunfire. In the column's daring dash, more than ten Japanese guns were destroyed. However, an antitank round did hit—and pierce—the side of Smeeton's turret but did not explode.

Another example of the hit-and-run tactics employed by the mobile columns was the attack north of Meiktila on 14 March, by A and C squadrons. They were ordered to make a wide sweep of the region east, north, and west of the Myindawgan and Meiktila lakes, and to engage and destroy any Japanese located in these regions. The column moved out up the Mandalay Road at 0930 hours; after traveling for two hours and resupplying with fuel, it turned northwest toward the Pindale Road. The squadrons moved forward by having one squadron holding a position, while another came through and passed forward. West of the Pindale Road, near Leindaw, the column came into contact with Japanese artillery positions.[199] The attack was ordered ahead as heavy artillery fire came in on the tanks, wounding Lieutenant Colonel Smeeton.[200] An air strike was ordered, silencing the guns. The tanks moved on toward the village of Leindaw, engaging more artillery targets, and called in artillery fire on various located Japanese positions. By the end of the day, the column had returned to Meiktila with one damaged tank and four wounded. The Japanese had lost over forty killed, and six guns (known, more probable) were destroyed.[201]

Over the remainder of March, the regiment was sent on several more column attacks. A and C squadrons operated mostly in the northern area north of Meiktila, spending every day on hit-and-run and supporting attacks. Only on 25–26 March did the two squadrons have two days for rest and tank maintenance. B Squadron operated to the east of Meiktila, supporting the efforts of the 99th Indian Brigade to hold the airstrip. After the 99th was pulled back, it continued to provide support to the 9th Indian Brigade, also in the area. On 28–29 March, the regiment was assigned to operate as one unit and sent north to link up with troops moving south from Mandalay.[202]

During the previous six weeks, the regiment had performed very well in the role of infantry support and in the hit-and-run columns. If the unit found itself outside Meiktila overnight, it adopted a box formation with supporting infantry and held the perimeter. The regiment successfully defended all boxes and was never forced into a withdrawal during the fighting. It had learned the important basics of infantry/tank cooperation and adapted this knowledge to the open terrain of Burma.[203] The regiment had destroyed more than one hundred Japanese artillery pieces during the fighting, and had annihilated many Japanese in their forming-up positions before launching attacks against the town of Meiktila. General Leese sent a letter to the brigade commander, Brigadier Pert, stating, "I have heard so much of the splendid fighting of your tanks during the last four weeks. They have played a decisive part in this battle."[204] Lieutenant General Messervy followed this up with a letter to Pert on 7 April 1945. He stated, "you and your two regiments of the IAC (Indian Armoured Corps), Probyns and Deccan, have had the chance at last of showing the world what the IAC can do. You and they have seized that opportunity in splendid and traditional style."[205]

By the end of March, units from the 5th Indian Division, under the command of Maj. Gen. E. C. R. Mansergh,[206] were making their way into the Meiktila fighting. The 9th Brigade was flown into the airstrips in and around Meiktila. An account from the 17th Dogra Machine Gun Battalion highlights the desperate fighting in the last days of March. A COY was attached to the 9th Brigade and was flown into and took up position outside of Meiktila. The following account was recorded by the battalion commander, Lieutenant Colonel Bristow:

> On the night of the 24–25 March 1945 the MG section commanded by No. 7462 Hav. Wakil Singh . . . on the Meiktila perimeter. After heavy shelling the enemy attacked his position with three tanks and infantry at 2000 hours. Waiting until the attackers were close he opened accurate fire which drove the infantry to ground, and made the tanks close down. Later the tanks attacked alone supported by the fire of the infantry. Opening fire with his M9 grenade discharger he damaged one tank. That again stopped the attack, and eventually the damaged tank was towed away. Two hours later the remaining two tanks attacked. One MG pit received a direct hit, which put the gun out of action and wounded all the crew. One tank penetrated and overran the section position, and as by then all M9 grenades had been fired the section had no anti-tank weapon. The Havildar and his men attacked the tanks with hand grenades and drove them back, while the remaining MG

continued to pin the enemy infantry to the ground. The enemy finally withdrew at 0400 after a struggle that lasted eight hours. At daylight 21 Jap bodies were counted in front of the section position.[207]

The performance of all Indian Army and British Army units in the fighting around Meiktila can best be summarized in a telling statement by the enemy. Lieutenant General Hanaya of the Japanese 33rd Division noted that "since 29th February allied tanks thrusted deep into our positions everyday. . . . In this fighting the co-operation among allied infantry, artillery, and tanks was made admirably."[208]

Destruction and Conquest

The 7th Indian Division and the 33rd Corps had not been idle during this period. The 7th Indian had pushed out from the bridgehead and was tasked to follow the 17th Indian Division and reopen the road to Meiktila, so supplies could come overland. The 7th Indian Division began operations on the 6th, when the 89th Brigade pushed south toward Chauk. Their mission was to pull Japanese force in their direction. The 114th Brigade would operate toward the important town of Kyaukpadaung. The 33rd Brigade was pushed toward Taungtha and Myingyan in the east. These brigade attacks were opening the overland route into Meiktila.

By 15 March, various units had been pushing toward their objectives; however, the Japanese in and around these sectors were becoming better organized. The force was a "hodge podge" of forces that had been engaged in the north, but were able to withdraw as well as some formations from southern Burma. The IJA 33rd Army had taken charge of the area, and had moved in many units and formations in an attempt to break up the efforts of the 4th Corps. Japanese reserves, the 18th, 53rd, and 49th divisions, were coming to the area.[209] General Kimura understood he needed to reopen access to Meiktila if he wished to withdraw his forces from the north. As stated by the Japanese command, "the battle at Meiktila would decide the fate of the Japanese forces in Burma."[210] General Honda received a report from his Chief of Operations Staff, which was very gloomy. It was clear that attrition had set in; many units and formations were down to 33 percent effective strength, and much of the artillery had been captured or destroyed by the XIV Army. The British XIV Army had advantages, mobile armored columns, and control of the air. General Honda earmarked the main counteroffensive to seize the airfields.[211] The good news for the 7th and 17th Indian divisions was that the 5th Indian Division had arrived into the bridgehead. Two brigades from the 5th Indian Division, the 161st and the 123rd, were pushed forward to support the 33rd and 114th brigades. The 9th had already been flown into Meiktila.[212]

The XIV Army had intercepted much of the Japanese radio traffic and understood a major Japanese counteroffensive was in the making. The intelligence stated that the main effort would be through Chauk and along the Irrawaddy River in an attempt to destroy the bridgeheads and cause major disruption to the XIV Army's offensive capability. The 114th Indian Brigade was pulled from the Meiktila road battles to the western side of the Irrawaddy to support the 28th East African Brigade and protect the western flank of the XIV Army. The 89th and 28th East Africa (EA) and 114th brigades on the eastern and western sides of the Irrawaddy River waited for the Japanese counterattacks. By 17 March, the attacks came in heavily on both sides of the river. Fighting would continue for six more days, and the three brigades were able to block the Japanese counterattacks. At the same time, the 5th Indian Division had continued its advance through Myingyan and Taungtha in an effort to reach the 17th Division and the 255th Armoured Brigade at Meiktila.[213]

Between 27 and 30 March, the 17th Indian Division made contact with the 5th Indian Division from the Taungtha-Mahlaing road, and with the 20th Indian Division to the northeast. Having established communication, the three divisions turned their attention to destroying remnants of the Japanese forces north of Meiktila. Air support had been a major enhancer to this success. March was the high-water mark in terms of close air support from the 221st Group and partial support from the 224th Group. The squadrons flew more than twenty-one thousand hours, 4360 close air-support sorties, 2085 sorties against Japanese lines of communications, and another twenty-three hundred sorties to support transport aircraft.[214]

The Japanese were rapidly pulling back from their defeats in the Mandalay-Meiktila regions, and Slim realized that an all-out race for Rangoon was in the offing. The Japanese command understood that they had failed in the defensive plans for central Burma. It had also become clear to the Burma Area Army command that the 15th Army was a shadow of its former self, and needed to extricate as quickly as possible. The 33rd Army was given the task of trying to stop the XIV Army from advancing down the Rangoon road. It set up defensive positions to the south.[215] The final phase of the destruction of the IJA Burma Area Army was now possible. Slim and the XIV Army knew that they had to capture the port before the monsoon broke, in order to avoid the problems of getting sufficient supplies forward by air during the rains. He issued orders for the 5th and 17th Indian divisions to make a dash down the main Mandalay-Rangoon road and seize Rangoon,[216] followed by the 19th Indian Division, which was to follow in support and try to keep the road open. The 7th and 20th Indian divisions were sent down both banks of the Irrawaddy River to search out any Japanese trying to escape. The 2nd British Division[217] was pulled back, due to a lack of adequate supplies for all formations stationed in central Burma.[218] To carry out this final phase of Extended Capital, much reorganization and planning needed to occur. This will be the story of the next chapter.

4

The Race to Rangoon

The final drive to Rangoon once again highlighted the high level of professionalism that the XIV Army had achieved by 1945. As the various formations of the XIV Army engaged and destroyed the IJA 15th and 33rd armies in and around the Irrawaddy River region, planning for the final thrusts commenced. As with the previous planning for Capital/Extended Capital, the XIV Army command group reorganized and revised its initial planning for the advance on Rangoon. The overall aim was still the same as in December 1944: destroy the Japanese Burma Area Army and seize Rangoon as quickly as possible, and before the onset of the monsoon. On 18 March, General Slim issued his first guidance on the final drive to Rangoon. As he stated:

> Messervy's 4 Corps, with the 5th and 17th Divisions and 255 Tank Brigade, would strike at the Japanese about Pyawbwe and prepare for the thrust south. Stopford's 33 Corps, with the 2nd British and 20th Divisions, would clear the area Mandalay-Maymyo-Wundwin-Mahlaing-Myinggyan, freeing all its roads and railways for our use. The 7th Indian Division, already on the Irrawaddy River, would then replace the 2nd British and the corps would position itself for the advance south. The 19th Division would, as the 2nd and the 20th moved west, take over the security of the area from Mandalay to Meiktila. In phase 3, 4 Corps would push down the railway axis and take Rangoon. 33 Corps, moving on both banks of the Irrawaddy, would capture Chauk and cut off Yenangyuang by a flanking movement on Magwe . . . then Prome and finally Rangoon, if possible before 4 Corps could

reach it. . . . At start of Phase 3, the 19th Indian Division would come under direct Fourteenth Army control and would be used to protect the left flanks and communications of 4 Corps.[1]

One fundamental issue for the XIV Army was logistics to maintain the formations in the field. While a railway had been built up in the region, it would not be fully operational until the end of April. Supplies of petrol and ammunition were making their way down from Imphal, but there was going to be an issue of keeping up the logistical chain as the army moved south. Air supply already operating at the furthest limits and capacity was once again called on for even more. The RAF transport pilots were now operating at 196 hours a month and the USAAF were at 204 hours a month. The American transports would remain in support of the XIV Army until Rangoon had fallen.

The 221 Group was far exceeding normal operating levels in an effort to maintain close air support for the XIV Army. SEAC organized a committee on 28 March 1945 to discuss how best to maximize air supply as the XIV Army moved south. It was agreed that the transport could achieve even more hours and better streamline the effort. A decision was made to supply the 4th Corps drive south of Toungoo with air supply, while all operations north of Toungoo were to be supplied by rail and road. The 33rd Corps drive would be supported by transport aircraft for one division, while the rest of the corps would rely upon rail, road, and inland water transport.[2] Water transport had been built up since the crossing of the Chindwin. Planning would achieve the movement of five hundred tons a day to the Irrawaddy River and then 370 tons down the Irrawaddy River to supply the 33rd Corps.[3] While the supply system was being pushed to its highest limits, Slim understood that he would still need to take more risks in his final drive. He and his staff decided that the British 2nd Division, after carrying out clearing operations in the southwestward area of Myingyan, would be flown out to India. The formation would then be held in reserve for future amphibious operations.[4]

While the planning for the XIV Army's advance continued, SEAC and ALFSEA also discussed the need for resurrecting and revising Op Dracula, an amphibious landing at Rangoon. The XIV Army had also requested this, as both they and SEAC recognized that although the two corps, the 33rd and the 4th, had the capability to reach Rangoon, they would need reinforcements almost immediately to deal with any threats to the lines of communications to the north. Ultimately, the planners decided that an amphibious landing would need to occur no later than the first week of May, due to the monsoon. While there were various divisions in reserve, including the 23rd Indian and the 81st West African, the decision was made that the 26th Indian from the Arakan serving under the 15th Corps would be used for the amphibious landings, which would also be supported by an airborne operation. The British Chiefs of Staff approved the landings,[5] recognizing that the overland advance, particularly by the 4th Corps to seize the airfields in and around Toungoo by the end of April, would be fundamental to Dracula. Air support for the landings would be flown from Toungoo as well as from Ramree Island in the Arakan.

Overland Advance: 4th Corps

On 1 April 1945, the Japanese Burma Area Army was in full retreat following its failure to destroy the XIV Army bridgeheads and boxes throughout the Meiktila and Mandalay regions. British intelligence on the state of the Burma Area Army by this stage was very accurate; the 4th Corps Operations Instruction, No. 139, 5 April 1945, illustrates this. It reported that "the JAPS have just suffered a resounding defeat. . . . Since 1 Jan 1945 they have lost some 18,000 men . . . and about 255 guns. . . . In consequence, there is at present only one JAP Div in Burma which approaches full strength."[6]

Within the XIV Army, logistics depots for both air supply and river communications were being built up. The various corps HQs were moving forward and setting up command posts as the advance to the south was being organized.[7] Both the 33rd and 4th Corps received their clear and simple orders from the XIV Army in early April. As the 4th Corps operational order stated on 5 April:

33 Corps on completion of the task of destroying all organized enemy resistance in the area MANDALAY-KYAUKSE-MYITTHA-WUNDWIN-MYINGYAN is operating to (i) capture SEKIPYU; CHAUK; MAGWE (ii) Advance SOUTH subsequently astride R.IRRAWADDY . . . [the 4th Corps] 3. To secure TOUNGOO with all possible speed as a preliminary to further operations Southwards . . . 4. The operation is to be phased as follows:- (ao PHASE A 17 Div will capture PYAWBWE area.

Target date 7 Apr. (b) PHASE B 5 Div (less 9 Airborne Bde GP) will pass through 17 Div and secure an airhead at PYINMANA, (target date 15 Apr.) 17 Div will move forward as close as possible behind 5 Div to PYINMANA and will take over its protection and further development. (c) PHASE C 5 Div will surround and secure TOUNGOO, with the assistance of an airborne build up of 9 Bde GP from MEIKTILA. Target date for capture of TOUNGOO 25 Apr. 5. Speed is all important and risks must be accepted to obtain it. Every day is precious.[8]

The 5th and 17th Indian divisions were fully mechanized and had armor support.[9] The 17th Indian Division and elements of 255th Armoured Brigade pushed out toward Pyawbwe by the end of March. The 17th Indian Divisional GOC, Major General Cowan, decided to envelop the town from all sides. Cowan's planning was as follows: the 48th Indian Brigade was to attack the town from the north along the main road; the 99th Indian Brigade was to attack from the northeast; the 63rd Indian Brigade was to attack from the west. Meanwhile, elements of the 255th Armoured Brigade, under the command of Brigadier Pert, were to swing around to the west of the town and cut off the Rangoon road and attack from the south. This attack group was named Claudcol, and included two squadrons of the 5th Probyn's Horse, two squadrons of the 16th Light Cavalry, the 7/10th Baluch, the 6/7th Rajputs, the D Company 4/4th Bombay Grenadiers, and the 59/18th Royal Artillery (self-propelled). By 6 April, Yindaw was taken. The 63rd Brigade would provide support to Claudcol while all formations moved on toward their objective, Pyawbwe. The Japanese put up a heroic resistance, but were hampered by various units from the 17th Indian Division moving against them from multiple angles; the IJA 18th Division records noted that it was savagely attacked.[10] Probyn's Horse described the advance to the south of Pyawbwe:

After the bund areas had been cleared up to the raid, it was seen that the remaining enemy had retreated into scrub enclosed by a small bund north of the Pyawbwe road. No. 3 troop advanced to give fire support. No. 1 troop crossed the main road to clear the enemy from West to East, took some time, and the squadron then rallied in the area of the cross-roads while mines and a road block were lifted. Any Japs who had escaped retreated straight through

the village and on southwards, but over 150 dead were counted on
the ground.[11]

It was at this juncture that the 4th Corps missed an important opportunity. On 7 April, as the various columns closed in on the Japanese positions
south of Pyawbwe, they came close to destroying the 33rd Army HQ.
After a fierce fight, the British armoured columns turned north to engage
the 18th Division. Orders were given for the 33rd Army as a whole to break
contact or break out of various encirclements and withdraw further south
from the 8/9th of April.[12]

Claudcol surprised Japanese forces south of the town at Ywadan on 9
April and killed more than two hundred men. Claudcol, after destroying
many of the Japanese in the area, turned north toward Pyawbwe. Probyn's
commander, Lieutenant Colonel Smeeton, noted:

> We were sitting down again at our interrupted meal when we
> heard the distinctive whine of Japanese tanks coming south from
> Pyawbwe. . . . We ran to the line of tanks nearest the road and
> climbed into their backs as the crews scrambled for their places.
> Bahadur Singh jumped up with me, and seeing the gunner's place
> still empty, took it himself. He was the best game shot in the
> regiment. . . . As it [the Japanese tank] came opposite us I leant
> forward and touched Bahadur Singh's shoulder. A dagger of flames
> shot from the barrel of his gun, the enemy tank glowed redly, and
> immediately with a great belch of flame blew up.[13]

The last remaining Japanese tanks in Burma were caught in a vicious
crossfire, and many were destroyed that evening. Claudcol had inadver-
tently smashed into the retreating Japanese 33rd Army, which had been
ordered on 9 April to withdraw from Pyawbwe. On the morning of 10
April, Claudcol turned north toward Pyawbwe. As noted above, after the
war, it became clear that the Japanese 33rd Army HQ had been in Ywadan
and was able to escape as Claudcol moved north, while the IJA 18th Division was crushed.[14]

On 10 April, the rest of the 17th Indian Division and 255th Armoured
Brigade moved in from all sides to destroy the remnants of the Japanese
18th Division now caught inside Pyawbwe. The 5th Indian Division followed up behind the 17th, clearing out any small pockets of resistance.

Heavy fighting ensued on the 10th and the 11th, and more than two thousand Japanese were killed in the town.[15] The tally of losses was notably lopsided as Probyn's Horse, by contrast, lost one officer and two Indian soldiers.[16] Slim described the fighting thus: "by dawn on the 11th, the whole of Pyawbwe was in our hands. Such defenders as survived had made off south and east in the darkness, many of them only to be hunted down by our mobile columns. . . . The skill which Messervy and Cowan had handled the battle was matched by the dash and resource of their troops."[17]

The 5th Indian Division, minus the 9th Brigade, moved through and around the battle at Pyawbwe to follow up the advance to Toungoo. Once again, the units and formations continued to follow previous experience and adapted to the new requirements of the battlefield, such as the 2/1st Punjab, 123rd Indian Brigade, which had operated north of Meiktila in a combined armored and infantry force. This battalion had been successful in opening the road to Meiktila and destroying Japanese counterattacks in the earlier battles around Meiktila.[18] As the battalion moved forward, it continued to carry out foot and mechanized patrols, and to establish a box formation each evening. Japanese opposition was dislodged using encircling and infiltration methods. On 11 April, the battalion was re-formed into "Applecol,"[19] along with tanks from the 255th Armoured Brigade, and tasked with protecting the eastern flank of the 17th Indian Division's drive against Pyawbwe. For the next three days the column was involved in clearing the area of Japanese troops to the south of Pyawbwe near Yamethin.[20] Due to the need for speed and bypassing pockets, the 123rd Brigade passed through Yamethin on 11 April. However, more than three hundred Japanese moved back in and reoccupied the town. A decision was made, due to the threat to the lines of communications, that the 123rd Brigade would need to retake the town. The brigade started to fight into the northern section of the town on 12 April, and the 2/1st Punjabis were ordered to clear out the southern section of the town on 13 April. After a series of heavy firefights, the battalion slowly cleared the town toward the southeast. Due to a minefield, the attack was held up. Divisional-level artillery support was called in. The 5th Division pounded the Japanese positions. An airstrike was put in during the early hours of 14 April and the battalion followed up with another attack. The use of artillery and infiltration tactics cleared out the enemy by noon on 14 April.[21]

The fighting in both Pyawbwe and Yamethin had delayed the schedule. The 9th Brigade was moved to support the rest of the 5th Division. The

19th Indian Division was also released to push south and add more protection to the flank of the 4th Corps advance. The pressure was on to get
forward as quickly as possible. The 161st and 123rd brigades, 5th Division,
pushed hard toward Toungoo, with support from the 255th Armoured
Brigade. The Japanese 33rd Army was attempting to create blocks on the
advance. On 19 April, the northern sections of Pyinmana had been seized
by the 161st Brigade. The 2/1st Punjab and the rest of 123rd Brigade proceeded south with great speed. The Japanese 33rd Army had almost been
captured once again, but had been able to break contact and retreat south.[22]

The 5th Indian Division's progress was catching up with the original schedule. On 22 April, the airfield at Toungoo was seized three days
ahead of the original schedule. The 2/1st Punjab set up boxes and patrolled
around the airfield, frustrating Japanese attempts to disrupt traffic at the
airfield. The Japanese troops in the area were becoming increasingly disorganized, and patrols were turning into mopping-up operations against
minimal opposition. As the 17th Indian Division and 19th Indian Division proceeded, the 5th Indian Division continued to focus on destroying
any retreating Japanese troops in the area.[23] The Japanese 28th, 15th, and
33rd armies were now at a very low ebb, and many units were on the
verge of complete destruction. Meanwhile, the Burma Area Army was
in the dangerous position of being in Rangoon as the British XIV Army
closed in from the north. The Burma Area Army HQ would be moved
to Moulmein on the east side of the Sittang River by 27 April.[24] The 5th
Division took the town of Pyu three miles to the south, and by 25 April the
area around Toungoo had been secured. The 17th Division now moved
forward to strike toward Pegu, while the 19th Division fell in with the 5th
and prepared for any Japanese counterattacks. The two divisions carried
out foot patrols in the jungle areas on both sides of the road and inflicted
heavy casualties on the retreating enemy troops.

On 26 April, the 4th Corps HQ moved into Toungoo, where two
airfields needed to be repaired as quickly as possible. By 30 April, there
were three RAF and USAAF wings operating on the airfields in support
of the drive to Rangoon as well in support of Op Dracula. On 28 April,
17th Division moved through the 5th and advanced to Pegu; the 19th was
now in charge of the defense of Toungoo. The 17th Indian Division was
organized into three brigade groups at this stage; each group would have
a strong armored component. The advance guard was the HQ 255th Armoured Brigade, 9th Royal Horse, 7th Light Cavalry, 16th Light Cavalry,

18th RA (S.P.), 6/7th Rajputs on tanks, 1/3rd Gurkhas in trucks, and an Indian Engineer detachment.[25] Japanese opposition was getting weaker as the 17th and 255th advanced. The issue was logistics, chiefly petrol for the vehicles. As an officer from the 7th Light Cavalry noted on 26 April:

> At Milestone 114 we had to halt as petrol was exhausted and B echelon was not in sight. The fifty-two Shermans of the Deccan thundered past us here, and behind them came our petrol trucks which nearly thundered past us as well in their eagerness to get somewhere at any cost. We managed to stop them and refuel. . . . The Japs were really on the run now; the difficulty was to catch them. . . . The 17th Division with its armour was hardly delayed.[26]

Slim also noted, "the troops of 4 Corps were already on reduced rations, having given up food for petrol and ammunition, but the knowledge that they were only forty-seven miles from Rangoon . . . spurred them on."[27]

The flank of the 17th Division needed protection. The 4th Corps became aware of elements of the Japanese 33rd Army operating to the east of the Sittang River and was moving south toward Pegu. The 9th Brigade, 5th Indian Division, was flown into airfields in the Shwegyin-Waw area to destroy any Japanese counterattacks. Elements of the 19th Division also were used to destroy the Japanese forces to the east of Toungoo, as the Rangoon road came under Japanese artillery fire. After a series of fighting patrols, the flank was protected by early May.[28]

It was during the advance that an interesting episode occurred. On 25 April Smeecol, from the 5th Probyn's, captured three Indian National Army (INA)[29] officers. The officers informed Probyn's Horse that the INA divisional commander, Col. Aziz Ahmed Khan, wished to surrender his division. Over three thousand INA soldiers and officers surrendered on 26 April, and the POWs were taken over by the 5th Indian Division. Probyn's then proceeded forward to support the 63rd Brigade of the 17th Indian Division.[30]

General Slim and the XIV Army HQ still recognized that there were Japanese forces to the west and to the east. By 27 April, with the withdrawal of the Burma Area Army HQ, the 15th and 33rd armies were ordered to withdraw to the east across the Sittang River.[31] Pegu was a key junction point for a possible Japanese defense. Intelligence had come in from British POWs who were rescued outside of Pegu that Rangoon was free of Japanese forces. On 29 April, the final plans for the attack into Pegu were set. The initial attacks to the north of the town were unsuccessful. It was recognized later that the Japanese forces in Pegu were trying to keep it clear, as Japanese forces from Rangoon were trying to cut through Pegu to the east and across the Sittang River.[32] On 30 April a new plan was created to clear Pegu as quickly as possible. The orders were clear:

> 1. One battalion [the 4/12th FFR] of the 48 Ind Inf Bde was to cross the Pegu River, . . . advance South down the West bank and capture Pegu railway station. 2. 63 Ind Inf. Bde with one sqn Royal Deccan Horse was to capture the high ground attacked on the previous day, and exploit on down the main road as far as the road bridge over the river in the centre of town. 3. 255 Ind Tk Bde less 116 RAC . . . were to move South east from the road at M.S. 53.5 across country to attack Kammannat, other villages to the South, and then attack North East and meet up with 62 Ind. Inf. Bde. on the road bridge.[33]

The 99th Brigade would operate to the east and destroy any Japanese trying to escape to the east.[34]

The Japanese defense and the terrain in the area stymied some of the attacks. By 1 May,[35] the eastern side of Pegu had been cleared of Japanese. By 2 May, the rest of the units were able to seize their assigned objectives. It was during this period that the monsoon finally broke; rain had started on 1 May, and became torrential on 2 May. The Pegu River was flooding, stalling the drive to Rangoon. The airfields at Toungoo were also starting to flood, and from this point the weather compelled RAF and USAAF planes to fly back to Meiktila.

The units and formations of the 4th Corps during this period successfully adapted to the changing battlefield conditions, combining the tactics of open and jungle warfare when patrolling and in preparing defensive measures. When required, troops encircled and infiltrated Japanese positions by foot and mechanized means.

The 4th Corps, as well as the XIV Army as a whole, was by this time an outstanding military force. They had overcome major logistical issues and continued the advance toward Pegu. They had adapted to as many different challenges as the enemy, terrain, and weather threw up. The original timings for the advance to Pegu fell behind schedule, only for the 4th Corps to push even harder and arrive into Toungoo and Pegu ahead of schedule. Before we end the narrative of the taking of Rangoon, we will switch and discuss the efforts of the 33rd Corps along the Irrawaddy River basin.

The Irrawaddy River Advance

As stated above, the final advance to Rangoon was to be carried out on two prongs: (1) the 4th Corps on the road and railway network from Meiktila to Pywabwe to Pegu; (2) the 33rd Corps advanced along the Irrawaddy River basin. The XIV Army once again showed its flexibility in two ways: the 7th Indian Division was "chopped" from the 4th Corps and placed alongside the 20th Indian Division, and the organization of the 7th Division shifted from a heavily motorized force to one that would rely heavily upon animal transport once again, as the 20th Indian Division remained heavily mechanized. The 7th Indian Division, with the 268th Indian Brigade in support, marched in early April to seize Seikpyu and Chauk. The Japanese forces in the area attempted to hold in various towns. The progress was slow due to the Japanese rearguards, who were putting up a stiff fight. By 12 April, the 7th Division and the 268th Indian Brigade were finally in a position to envelop and attack Mt. Popa, Seikpyu, and Chauk. The 20th Indian Division had been on the move on the left flank of the 7th. By 12 April, the 20th had reached Natmauk, more than sixty miles in three days. The 32nd Brigade was then earmarked to push south toward Magwe with speed.[36]

With the loss of Pyawbwe, along the 4th Corps axis of advance, senior Japanese commanders in the Burma Area Army feared for the 28th Army, which was operating in the Arakan. General Kimura would not allow orders for the 28th Army to withdraw. Some others on the Burma Area Army staff did not agree, and slowly started to withdraw the 28th Army. Orders were received by the Japanese forces in the Irrawaddy River basin to hold at all costs, to allow for the 28th Army to extricate itself and withdraw to the east. The 7th Indian Division at the same time moved its formations into action to destroy the Japanese in and around Chauk. As the 7th Division closed in, chaos reigned as reports came in that Japanese forces were withdrawing, while units came up against determined resistance. After a series of actions, the Japanese defenders started to withdraw by 18

April. General Evans, GOC, 7th Division, ordered the 114th Brigade to push south to Salin. At the same time, the Japanese defenders on Mt. Popa were finally cleared out by elements of the 268th Brigade. The leadings elements of the 20th Indian Division had reached the northern outskirts of Magwe. The Japanese efforts to hold the area were collapsing, as the 33rd Corps was pushing hard to clear the enemy in the south. The Japanese were forced to withdraw further south in an attempt to find crossing points that were not under pressure from the 33rd Corps.[37]

By 25 April, all the first objectives of the 33rd Corps had been reached. New orders were issued for the Corps by Lieutenant General Stopford. The orders for 33rd were clear: "33 Corps will (a) seize PROME earliest possible. (b) destroy enemy forces attempting to escape EAST. (c) adv with all speed on RANGOON with max force possible."[38] This advance would entail the clearances of major Japanese defenses, as the 28th Army was still attempting to extricate itself from the west to the east.

As the 89th and 114th brigades, 7th Indian Division, recrossed the Irrawaddy River on 25 April and proceeded south, the terrain through which they were traveling changed, from flat and open to hilly and jungle-covered. They were to destroy any Japanese forces that were attempting to withdraw from the Arakan to the east. This meant that the division was to be resupplied by air, and that each brigade operated almost independently of the other. Each battalion organized its own airdrops. The march south on the western side of the river was characterized by constant skirmishing and patrolling.

The 4/8th Gurkhas were involved in a significant engagement at Taungdaw as part of the 89th Indian Brigade, which was tasked with seizing the important valleys west of the Irrawaddy River.[39] The 1/11th Sikhs were able to seize and deny access to the Japanese in the Shandatgyi valley.[40] The fighting for the Sikhs foretold what was to come. As noted, "a counter-attack, with the fanaticism of despair behind it, now fell on the Sikhs, and they were hard put to hold on to their positions."[41] The 4/8th Gurkhas moved through the 1/11th Sikhs, and pushed twelve miles west to Taungdaw valley, to hold it on 11 May.[42] B Company placed itself on the floor of the valley close to the western edge where the track crossed the Mu Chaung by a ford, with C Company on the ridge above, and A and D companies with battalion HQ several miles to the east. B Company's position was not optimal,[43] but there was not much to be done, as the Japanese were moving in to destroy the positions from the north—the Japanese, "whose only chance of survival—since surrender was still unthinkable—was to break the ring."[44] Both Gurkha companies began to dig in, in preparation for the confrontation with the Japanese, who within a few hours had arrived and begun to probe B Company's positions. The Japanese began to move with purpose during the evening of 11 May, when C Company patrols spotted forty Japanese soldiers moving toward B Company. A mortar barrage dispersed the Japanese temporarily, but more enemy troops were spotted as they moved into position in the early hours of 12 May. A second attack was broken up by mortar fire called in by C Company.[45] The two companies in Taungdaw were attacked for three days without respite and continued to hold out.[46] The Japanese managed to penetrate between the two forward companies, and the remaining two companies stationed to the east on 13 May.[47]

On 13 May, A and D companies were ordered to make flanking moves from the south and north, respectively, and link up with the companies in Taungdaw. Both companies made slow progress due to the numbers of Japanese in the area, and settled down to dig in for the evening without having achieved their objective. A Company could not break through, but succeeded in drawing off many of the Japanese, enabling D Company to make a move from the north. They linked up with A Company on 15 May and pushed through to the rest of the battalion.[48] General Evans stated: "although surrounded and cut off for three days and two nights, they held and smashed every attack."[49]

The 4/8th Gurkhas and the rest of the 7th Indian Division had retrained thoroughly in Kohima, learning the basics of jungle warfare once again. When faced with the open plains of central Burma, the 7th Indian Division adapted to those conditions, and then reverted to jungle warfare as the formation proceeded south. The defensive layout and encircling movement of the battalion at Taungdaw denied a large portion of the 54th Japanese Division access to the Irrawaddy River and the possibility of escape to the east. For the period from 25 February to 21 May, the battalion accounted for 508 Japanese killed (counted), an estimated additional three hundred probably killed, and many more wounded. The battalion itself lost one British and one Gurkha officer and thirty-two other ranks killed, as well as more than one hundred wounded. Unquestionably, the battalion and the 7th Indian Division as a whole had proven themselves when confronted with the changing conditions of the campaign of 1945.[50]

The 20th Indian Division had continued its southerly advance as well.

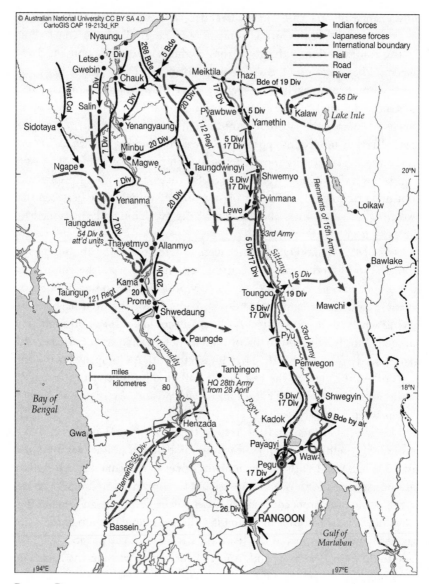

Race to Rangoon, 1945

The 20th Indian Division had seized the town of Allanmyo on 28 April. Fighting in Allanmyo was fierce at times. The 14/13th FFRifles noted: "the enemy were putting up fierce resistance and by 3pm hand to hand fighting was taking place in the village."[51] By 3 May, units from the division had entered Prome from the north and the east. Strangely, there was no fighting, as the INA had occupied the town.[52] The brigades leap-frogged one another as they pushed south of Prome toward Shwedaung and Paungde. An armored column pushed as far south as Tharrawaddy by 17 May, sixty miles north of Rangoon.[53] On 6 May, Lieutenant General Stopford held a meeting to discuss the future operations in the Irrawaddy River basin. The 33rd Corps was now to defend their occupied areas, and wait for the fighting units from the 28th Army as they attempted to break out to the east. Throughout the rest of May and part of June, both the 7th and the 20th Indian divisions fought bands of Japanese forces retreating from the Arakan in an attempt to reach the Sittang River in the east.[54] Mountbatten reported, "they were beaten back with heavy losses."[55]

Fall of Rangoon: Op Dracula

As noted previously, the planning for a revised amphibious landing to seize Rangoon was heavily debated in mid-March and SEAC, ALFSEA, and the XIV Army agreed that there was a need to launch Op Dracula, no later than early May. After many discussions and planning meetings, on 17 April, the green light was given for Dracula. Interestingly, only divisional-, corps-, and army-level commanders within the XIV Army were made aware of the operation. The 26th Indian Division, commanded by Maj. Gen. H. M. Chambers, from the 15th Indian Corps in the Arakan, was earmarked as the main formation to carry out the landing. An airborne battalion would be dropped at Elephant Point to deal with any Japanese defenses at the mouth of the Rangoon River.[56] Mountbatten specifically stated "to carry out an amphibious and airborne operation with the object of the early capture of Rangoon should this not have been previously achieved by the Fourteenth Army from the north."[57] The 26th Indian Division's order on 22 April was a little more detailed. It stated, "26th Indian Division, with naval and air support, will assault land in the Rangoon River and capture the general area Syriam-Kyauktan with a view to establishing a firm base there from which subsequent operations can be conducted against Rangoon."[58]

The 26th Indian Division was an experienced unit, having been fighting in the Arakan region since 1944. It had recently carried out an amphibious landing on Ramree Island in March. The landing was set for 2 May, and naval preparations were well underway. The Royal Navy had organized eight convoys to sail to support the landing and the rest of the XIV Army—a massive effort. They planned for the landing of over forty-one thousand men, twenty-six hundred vehicles, and just under twenty thousand tons of supplies in the first twenty-four days of the first landing.[59] The naval force drew heavily from the Eastern Fleet. The carrier force sailed on 23 April from Ceylon to meet the amphibious task force, assembling off Ramree Island. The invasion task force had six convoys, the slowest sailing on 27 April, while the main convoy left on 30 April. The carrier task force had four escort carriers and supporting destroyers; the Royal Navy, 3rd Battle Squadron, with two battleships, two escort carriers, four cruisers, and six destroyers, sailed to the Andaman Islands to intercept any Japanese naval attacks against the amphibious task force. A Royal Navy destroyer task force operated south of Rangoon and intercepted Japanese merchant shipping carrying Japanese troops to Moulmein from Rangoon. The RAFs 224 Group would provide further air cover, as well as elements of the 221 Group, which would operate from Toungoo, recently seized by the 4th Corps. The USAAF provided twelve B-24 and B-25 squadrons and two Dakota squadrons to provide air lift for the airborne battalion that was to drop on Elephant Point.[60] Close to forty squadrons were in support.[61]

On 1 May, the RN, RAF, USAAF, and USN attacked enemy positions at the mouth of the Rangoon River. Royal Navy minesweepers moved and cleared out the entrance to the Rangoon River. A Gurkha airborne battalion dropped at Elephant Point and cleared out any of the remaining Japanese defenders.[62] On 1 May, RAF aircraft spotted signs on the top of buildings in Rangoon, stating, "JAPS GONE." Intelligence had been coming in that the Japanese were withdrawing from Rangoon and attempting to escape Pegu to the east. The fighting in Pegu had confirmed the likelihood of the Japanese withdrawal from the city.[63] By 0215 on 2 May, the first landing craft entered the Rangoon River estuary, as the monsoon was breaking. Two battalions from the 36th Brigade landed on the west bank of the river by 0700, while the 71st Brigade landed on the eastern bank by 0800. Reports came in immediately from patrols that the Japanese had withdrawn from both sides of the river. The buildup of the brigades accelerated, and reconnaissance units were pushed as far forward as possible to ascertain the whereabouts of the Japanese. As more intelligence came in to confirm that Rangoon was an open city, the two brigades were reembarked on landing craft and pushed farther up the river to get to Rangoon ASAP.[64]

By 4 PM on 3 May, the first troops landed at the Rangoon docks. The various battalions spread throughout the city. By 5 May the Rangoon airfield had been seized and the northern suburbs cleared. One of the battalions, the 2/13th FFRifles, stated that they had expected to fight the Japanese to the last man in Rangoon. However, upon arrival, they were able to easily round up mostly INA, who had been left behind by the Japanese. The battalion noted many patrols trying to find any large groups of Japanese soldiers, to no avail.[65] The 26th Division HQ was set up in the Government House on 5 May. The 71st Brigade moved north to meet the 4th Corps outside Pegu. A formal link-up between the 26th and 17th Indian divisions occurred on 6 May. Within fourteen days of arriving on the Rangoon docks, the port was open to receive the convoys that were sailing to supply the XIV Army. With the meeting of the 26th and 17th divisions, the 15th Corps ceased to exist as the XIV Army took command of the forces in Rangoon. Slim best summarized the feeling within the XIV Army when he wrote: "We were back!"[66]

General Slim now issued orders for the 4th and 33rd Corps to deal with the Japanese who were clearly trapped west of the Sittang River. He stated that the XIV Army was

> to intercept and destroy as many as possible of the enemy as
> they attempted to reach the east bank of the Sittang. To prevent
> the Japanese concentrating and reorganizing in the Moulmein
> area. . . . 4 Corps to destroy all enemy attempting to cross the
> Pegu Yomas west to east. . . . 33 Corps to destroy all the enemy
> in the Irrawaddy Valley . . . to effect a junction between the 20th
> Division [with the 26th Division] south of Prome.[67]

Some of these operations have been referred to as "mopping-up" operations, as if the level of violence was much less. To many of the soldiers, NCOs, VCOs, and officers, it was just as violent.

The actions of 1/11th Sikhs at Kabaing, on 21 May 1945, highlighted these sorts of operations and that the Japanese were still very much a force to be reckoned with. The battalion had been ordered to the area, as intelligence was coming in that elements of the Japanese 28th Army were on the march east to the Sittang. As the battalion arrived, intelligence stated that there were more than one hundred Japanese in the village. The 1/11th Sikhs decided to attack the village from the southwest, after occupying the hills in the area. They would be resupplied by air. A COY laid on fire from the northwest in an attempt to cover the advance of D COY across a rice field. As the Japanese defenders became aware of the threat to their southwest, they were caught in the open by a very accurate mortar barrage. D COY closed in with bayonets and cleared the village, killing more than seventy Japanese soldiers, though some were able to escape. The 1/11th Sikhs lost three KIA and eleven WIA. By nightfall, the battalion had been resupplied by air. Wounded were evacuated on 22 May by air, after an airstrip had been cleared from the jungle.[68]

Two officers offered their thoughts regarding "mopping-up" operations for their battalions in their memoirs. These operations in May and June were a foretaste of the major "breakout" battles of July. (Please see the following chapter for a description of the breakout battles.) Maj. John Hill from the 2nd Royal Berks, 19th Indian Division, stated, "we learnt in the course of the next two months that mopping up is not the easy form of campaigning that the name implies—against the Japanese anyway. . . . We were in for more fire and movement operations, a number of close quarter battles."[69] An officer from the 4/8th Gurkhas, 7th Indian Division, Maj. Denis Sheil-Small, wrote, "The Japanese fought to the last gasp wherever we found them; they died singly, in fives, in tens and in hundreds with a fanaticism that was awe-inspiring."[70]

Conclusion

The XIV Army at the end of the advance and taking of Rangoon was a professional force that was prepared to deal with any contingency that arose. It has been contended that the victories of 1945 were due in significant part to the Imperial Japanese Army's difficulties in providing supplies and reinforcements to Burma. This situation certainly helped the XIV Army by limiting the numbers that the Japanese could send into battle. Whether Japanese supply problems created any advantage for the XIV

Army is a more questionable assertion, considering that both British and Indian formations were also suffering from serious supply shortages. Many of the units fighting in Mandalay, in Meiktila, and on the subsequent advance to Rangoon were on half-rations to cope with the small quantities of supplies that were getting through to them. Only reopening the port of Rangoon ensured that the XIV Army was properly supplied—which partially explains the impetus for the race to Rangoon.

As had happened in the fighting of 1944, provision of supplies and air support had some impact on the outcome of battles, but these were secondary to the vastly improved tactics and training deployed by British and Indian troops in the jungles and open terrain of central Burma. As Field Marshal Slim noted, "[air power] could not stop movement on the ground; it could only impede and delay it." He also proposed that a large box formation could hold out against a Japanese attack almost indefinitely, as long as it had unlimited access to resupply by air. He went on, however, to say that "troops thus cut off even if fed and maintained, eventually lose heart, and air supply is so easily interrupted. . . . An adequate relieving force [is required]."[71] The relieving forces would, of course, need to be adequately trained and able to adapt to conditions on the battlefield.

The campaigns of 1945 clearly demonstrated that the XIV Army was capable of adapting to the changing conditions of the terrain. When troops were pulled out of the line in the autumn of 1944 and jungle tactics further evaluated, the senior commanders also recognized that future fighting would eventually involve a very different terrain: the open central plains of Burma. They could easily have been caught on the back foot emerging from the jungles of the Indo-Burma region, but by foreseeing the potential problems, they were able to adapt quickly and successfully to the change in terrain. The Japanese High Command in the Burma Area Army did not realize that the jungle-oriented XIV Army would also be able to operate in the open at a high level of efficiency, incorporating tanks and artillery into its operations. Indian, East African, and British units carried out an aggressive defense when required and pressed forward otherwise, seeking out and destroying Japanese concentrations. The XIV Army did not fall back on a linear style of defense, but continued to use boxes and mobile patrols to claim no-man's land and keep the Japanese alert. The XIV Army had achieved a new level of professionalism; it was a fully modern, properly trained army, capable of dealing with almost any tactical situation with which it might be presented, by land, sea, or air. As Slim noted, "my Indian divisions after 1943 were amongst the best in the world. They would go anywhere, do anything, go on doing it, and do it on very little."[72]

The personnel reforms of Indianization and recruitment allowed the army to continue along the path to this high level of professionalism. As of 1945, there were Indian officers serving as commanding officers of battalions, as well as in senior positions in the brigade-, divisional-, and corps-level staffs. New recruits were provided with a high standard of basic and specialized training before they were deployed to units in the field. British battalions were suffering from a lack of reinforcements and began in March/April 1945 to rely upon the Indian Army to provide replacement infantry battalions. This would not have been possible without the foresight of the senior officers who advocated the broadening of recruitment of both officers and men. Far from the conflict and controversy that opponents of Indianization had predicted, relations among officers were cordial and professional. Indian and British officers performed well throughout the campaign in both junior and senior positions. Those who had been skeptical of the abilities of Indian officers to serve with and in command of British officers and to lead men in battle had been definitively proven wrong.[73]

Indian troops mingle with troops from the 81st West African Division in 1944.

British and West African troops in the Arakan, 1945.

Polish officer and a soldier from the 81st West African Division, Arakan, 1945.

Lieutenant J. K. Rduch (or J. K. R. Duch) of the 5th Battalion, Gold Coast
Regiment (5 West African Infantry Brigade, 81st West African Division), giving
fire orders to a mortar crew of the 102nd Mortar Battery during the Third Arakan
Campaign, January 1945. He was originally from Krakow and was seconded from
the Polish Armed Forces to the RWAFF for the duration of his service.

Troops of the 11th East African Division on the road to Kalewa, Burma, during the Chindwin River crossing.

A Consolidated Liberator B Mark VI of No. 356 Squadron RAF releases thousand-pound bombs over the target during a daylight raid on the Japanese Army Headquarters at Kyaukse near Mandalay, Burma, February 1945.

Air Vice Marshal S. F Vincent, Air Officer Commander-in-Chief of No. 221 Group RAF (*center*), watches Hawker Hurricanes take off from Sadaung, Burma, on a strafing operation during the advance on Mandalay, with Lt. Gen. Sir William Slim, Commander of the XIV Army (*right*), and Group Cap. D. O. Finlay, Commanding Officer of No. 906 Wing RAF (*left*) in March 1945.

An aerial view of Fort Dufferin at Mandalay under an Allied aerial attack, March 1945.

Troops of the Indian 19th Division in action against Japanese positions on Mandalay Hill overlooking the city, March 1945.

A 5.5-inch gun of 19th Indian Division in action against the walls of Fort Dufferin, Mandalay, 9–10 March 1945.

Sherman tanks of Probyn's Horse (5th King Edward VII's Own Lancers), 255th Armoured Brigade, advancing on the road between Myaungyu on the Irrawaddy bridgehead and Meiktila, March 1945.

The crew of Douglas Dakota Mark III, of No. 238 Squadron RAF (*left to right*),
Flying Officer J. Creech (navigator), Flight Lieutenant T. J. Bayliss (pilot), and
Leading Aircraftman I. Fiddes (nursing orderly), in a bomb crater by their damaged
aircraft after it was shelled by the Japanese before take-off at Meiktila, Burma.

On the road to Rangoon: Major General D. T. Cowan (center, wearing glasses),
GOC, 17th Indian Division, at a staff conference.

Men of the 6/7 Rajputs mop up Japanese resistance in Pyawbwe north of Rangoon,
April 1945.

Landing craft carrying troops of the 26th Indian Division proceed up the Rangoon River, May 1945.

Indian troops of the 20th Division search for Japanese at the badly damaged railway station in Prome, 3 May 1945.

Gen. Sir Claude Auchinleck, Commander-in-Chief India, inspecting troops from the 7th Indian Division, 1 August 1945.

Admiral Mountbatten reading the Instrument of Surrender in Singapore, 12 September 1945, to the Japanese representatives.

Japanese prisoners of war working to repair the taxiing strip at Saigon airfield, Vietnam, December 1945.

5

The Final Battles

6 May 1945, 1630 hours: The 1/7th Gurkha Rifles, 48th Brigade, 17th Indian Infantry Division—"Punch" Cowan's "Black Cats"—squelching toward Rangoon through the sodden terrain created by an early monsoon met the 1st Lincolns of 26 Indian Infantry Division moving north from Rangoon, reoccupied on 3 May, the Japanese having pulled out several days previously. It was an (almost) theatrical close to the most brilliant campaign conducted by any British general during the Second World War.[1] The 1/7th Gurkhas had fired the opening shot of the Burma campaign in January 1942. The 17th Indian Division had been nearly destroyed at the Sittang River in February 1942. That was the point where Cowan became its commander.

Fighting through the retreat, rebuilding, playing a key role at Imphal and at Meiktila, and then leading the drive down the Rangoon road, with five of its battalions from 1942 still with it, Cowan's splendid division almost had the satisfaction of leading the XIV Army back into Rangoon. But as it slogged toward its rendezvous with the 26th Division, Cowan's Gurkhas up to their chests in monsoon floodwaters, the last crisis of the campaign broke—SEAC's land forces commander, Gen. Sir Oliver Leese, Bt., sacked Bill Slim.

It is one of the most remarkable episodes of Britain's war. Far more dramatic than Churchill's well-known descent on Cairo in the wake of Rommel's pummeling of the 8th Army in the summer of 1942, which led ultimately to Auchinleck's replacement by the team of Montgomery and Alexander, it remained virtually unknown—or, at least, unmentioned—for decades. Slim drafted a chapter for his memoir, *Defeat into Victory*, published in 1956—but then decided not to use it.[2] No echo of the event appeared in the final volume of Churchill's memoirs, *Triumph and Tragedy*, published in 1953. Field Marshal Lord Alanbrooke made his wartime diaries available to Sir Arthur Bryant, who used them as the basis for a two-volume study of Churchill and the British Chiefs of Staff during the war. Published shortly after *Defeat into Victory*, the second volume, *Triumph in the West*, says absolutely nothing about the command crisis in Burma in May 1945.[3] Finally the five-volume official history, *The War against Japan*, in its concluding volume (published in 1969, shortly before Slim's death) gave the episode a single sentence (to which is attached a totally misleading footnote).[4] Despite what almost amounts to a conspiracy of silence, what happened is now reasonably clear—even if still somewhat hard to understand.

The explosion of May 1945 has its origins in the reorganization of the SEAC command structure in the autumn of 1944. Mountbatten's original SEAC land forces commander was Gen. Sir George Giffard. His command, the 11th Army Group, was Slim's immediate superior during the crucial period of the Indian Army's reshaping and the battles of 1944—the "Admin Box" fight and Imphal-Kohima—which both revealed a new Indian Army and shattered a large part of the Japanese Burma Area Army. Slim worked very smoothly with Giffard (who, although a British Army regular, had spent much of his career working in an imperial setting, in this case Africa). In *Defeat into Victory* he would pay a clearly heartfelt tribute to Giffard, with particular emphasis on his character. After praising his qualities as a soldier, Slim added this: "*The* quality that showed through him was integrity, and that was the quality which, as much as any other, we wanted in our Army Commander."[5] This statement is usually taken not only as a tribute to Giffard but as a not very oblique condemnation of Lt. Gen. Noel Irwin, who had been Slim's superior in 1942–1943 and who had tried to scapegoat him for his own failures during the woebegone first Arakan campaign. But, in the light of what happened in May 1945, it may have referred to Oliver Leese as well.

The characteristics that commended Giffard to Slim, and that made for their smooth and effective teamwork in 1944, were also exactly what made his fraught relationship with—and eventual removal by—the supreme allied commander, South East Asia, Acting Vice Admiral Lord Louis Mountbatten all but inevitable. And it was this development that marked the beginning of the powder train that exploded as Rangoon fell.

Mountbatten was controversial during his lifetime and remains so.[6] He owed his swift rise to Churchill. When he became the supreme allied commander in South East Asia, he had just turned forty-three and was only a substantive captain in the Royal Navy. He was, however, a great grandson of Queen Victoria and had been a dashing destroyer captain (an image not entirely accurate but buttressed by the very successful propaganda film *In Which We Serve*, made by Noel Coward, who hero-worshipped Mountbatten and played the leading role, a destroyer captain based on Mountbatten). By the time the film premiered in 1942, Churchill had made Mountbatten chief of Combined Operations, with the acting rank of vice admiral and a seat on the Chiefs of Staff Committee. The chairman of the committee, the acerbic Gen. Sir Alan Brooke, had a very low opinion of Mountbatten as the exasperated entries in his diaries show, and, again, controversy followed in his wake. Combined Operations under his leadership played a major role in "Jubilee," the Dieppe fiasco in August 1942. Nonetheless, Churchill a year later, in August 1943, made him Southeast Asia Command's "supremo" during the Anglo-American summit at Quebec. (Alan Brooke thought no one became a supreme commander with less aptitude for the job.) But Churchill's decision was based on a shrewd political assessment. Anglo-American tensions in Southeast Asia were at their peak in 1943 over American suspicions that the British were not serious about reopening an overland route to China by reconquering north Burma.[7] Mountbatten, young, vigorous, and charming, already known to, and liked by, Roosevelt, would be a reassuring choice. (The same need to placate the Americans over Burma would lead Churchill to embrace the controversial Orde Wingate and his unproven "Long Range Penetration" tactics at the same time). Churchill scored a major political success at Quebec, removing Burma as a major source of Anglo-American friction. Brooke, who told his diary that Mountbatten would need a first-class chief of staff to "pull him through," gave him one in Lt. Gen. Sir Henry Pownall, a highly competent and vastly experienced staff officer. Nonetheless, a clash was almost certainly unavoidable between the competent but utterly uncharismatic Giffard (vastly senior to "Dickie") and Mountbatten, whom many beside Brooke regarded as an overpromoted lightweight whose rise owed more to royal connections, publicity seeking, and Churchill's patronage than to command talent. The friction set in almost immediately. Pownall, as his diaries show, was sympathetic to Giffard but saw clearly that he was not even making an effort to "play." When Mountbatten moved SEAC headquarters from Delhi to the more tranquil atmosphere of Kandy in Ceylon (Sri Lanka), Giffard simply refused to move the 11th Army Group headquarters so far from the Burmese battlefront. He had a point but distance from the supreme commander clearly had great attractions for Giffard. The breaking point came in mid-May 1944 when Pownall (who liked Giffard personally) was given the unpleasant task of telling him that he was to be replaced. The change did not in fact take place until November and when it did Giffard was replaced with someone who would be a better fit for Mountbatten but a disastrously bad fit for the theater's key commander: Slim. Brooke sent east Lt. Gen. Sir Oliver Leese, Bt.

The root of the problem that then swiftly developed lies in the fact that no military institution has an unlimited supply of top-class command talent, and the heart of Britain's war effort was the war against Germany. Alan Brooke lamented in his diary the lack of strong candidates for general officer appointments. Brooke's priority was his army's performance in the German war and he concentrated its talent there. Leese's initial rise was due to Monty, Brooke's protégé. Leese had been Monty's student at the Staff College and Monty would always regard him as "1st class," bringing him from divisional command at home to take over a corps in the 8th Army. When Monty left the 8th Army to become the allied land forces commander for Overlord, Leese succeeded him. Brooke at that point began to express reservations about his performance. By August 1944, he was telling his diary that "my doubts about the value of Oliver Leese are being confirmed. He was certainly not anything outstanding as a commander."[8] Despite this, Brooke chose Leese to succeed Giffard. Why? Leese was creating problems within the Anglo-American command structure in Italy. He could not work with the commander of the American 5th Army, Gen. Mark Clarke, and had forced a major change in the plan devised by Field Marshal Sir Harold Alexander, the allied army commander in Italy, for an offensive against the Gothic line, the last German defensive position in northern Italy. Leese insisted the entire 8th Army be switched to the eastern side of the Italian peninsula, across the intervening Apennine Mountains, so that he could have a separate sphere of operations, free from Clarke and the Americans. This posed major logistic problems, delayed Alexander's offensive, and probably contributed to its frustration. Moving Leese to SEAC would solve a problem in Italy (Brooke noted in his diary that Leese's departure "was greeted with considerable joy" in the Italian theater).[9] Fixing a problem in Italy, however, would create a far larger one in SEAC. Many years later, reviewing his wartime diaries, Brooke added a series of notes that amounted to second thoughts on a number of issues. The entry of 26 May 1944 records his meeting with Lt. Gen. Sir Henry Pownall, Mountbatten's chief of staff, who told him "that Dickie wants to get rid of George Giffard." The Chief of the Imperial General Staff added: "I am very sorry for it." Writing in the 1950s, Brooke added this: "Dickie Mountbatten made a fatal mistake in getting rid of Giffard, who would have done him admirably, and better than Oliver Leese."[10]

In November 1944, the 11th Army Group was replaced by Allied Land Forces, South East Asia, and Lt. Gen. Sir Oliver Leese, Bt., became Slim's immediate superior. Leese, an Etonian and Grenadier Guardsman (and a baronet), wrong-footed himself with Slim (grammar school and Indian Army) immediately.[11] Alexander, who had worked with Slim and taken his measure during the retreat in 1942 from Burma when he had been the theater commander with Slim commanding Burcorps under him, advised Leese not to take his 8th Army staff with him—good advice Leese ignored, bringing with him a number of staff officers headed by his tactless chief of staff, Maj. Gen. G. P. Walsh. The 11th Army Group had been built on the framework of the Indian Army's Eastern Army and so, in addition to Giffard's good relations with Slim, there was a strong presence of the Indian Army. Then 11th Army Group morphed into Allied Land Forces, South East Asia. Slim (who had known Leese when they both were instructors at Camberley) noted in his memoir that many of the XIV Army's old friends vanished from ALFSEA and that Leese and his 8th Army staff had a lot of "desert sand" in their shoes and made it clear that the 8th Army was the standard to be aimed at—"rather inclined to thrust Eighth Army down our throats." Not only did Slim and his army miss Giffard—"we saw him go away with grief"—but "we also thought that the Fourteenth Army was now something."[12] To Leese, thoroughly imbued with the 8th Army mystique Monty had carefully crafted, this was *lese majeste*. He complained to Brooke that the XIV Army did not understand modern weaponry and told his wife that for Slim to think of himself and his army as being in the same category as Monty and the 8th was the mark of someone who was "almost a megalomaniac."[13] There was something else as well, noted by another Gurkha Rifles officer: Leese "in common with many British Service Generals disliked the Indian Army."[14] This was an old institutional rivalry, dating back to the late eighteenth century when Royal officers, arriving in India with their units, found an army larger than the regular British army, officered by men of lesser social status whose commissions came from a company of merchants.

Slim and Leese were thus set on a collision course from the outset and this was aggravated by Slim's command style and by his relationship with Mountbatten. The first wartime operation Slim, then a brigadier, conducted in November 1940 at Gallabat on the frontier between the Sudan and Italian-occupied Ethiopia was a failure. Slim believed that failure was the result of his decision to choose the more prudent, rather than the bolder, course.[15] He never had to learn a lesson twice. The rest of his wartime career was marked by a preference for the bolder and riskier but far more promising course of action. It was also marked by a determination to make his own plans and carry them out. Leese and ALFSEA soon felt the impact of Slim's command style: "I always went on the principle that my plans, as long as they carried out the general directions I received from above and did not require more resources than I had under my control, were my business and did not require anybody's approval or sanction," Slim wrote years later.[16] The recipient of that letter, Brig. Michael Roberts, later told Slim's official biographer, Ronald Lewin, that "Mountbatten got a bad bargain when he swapped Giffard for Leese. Bill was quite frankly insubordinate in his dealings with Leese, but he was an expert in knowing when he could be insubordinate—and for 'could' you could substitute 'should.'"[17] Slim himself admitted as much in *Defeat into Victory*. Recording a directive from ALFSEA on 27 February 1945 to take Mandalay and then secure Rangoon before the monsoon, Slim mildly remarked that he had already, in December 1944, given this order to the XIV Army's corps commanders and therefore no changes in his plans were necessary. Slim effectively cut ALFSEA out of the loop—Leese was informed, not consulted. Of course Slim could only do this because Mountbatten allowed him to.

Mountbatten was chosen for SEAC because Churchill expected that Burma would be reconquered as a by-product of the maritime and amphibious strategy he wanted implemented in the theater. At no time was the prime minister ever interested in the XIV Army's campaign. The strange American obsession with China would be satisfied, he hoped, by Wingate's bold design for clearing north Burma. SEAC would meanwhile retake Singapore—always Churchill's prime objective in the theater. The problem with the prime minister's idea was, however, that in the circumstances actually facing SEAC, it was unworkable. In 1943 (and 1944 and early 1945) the British simply did not have the resources for it, nor would they until after the European war ended, and, even then, they would need American help to implement it. The Americans, whose resources, particularly in air transport, were crucial to the XIV Army's campaign, would support it because it promised to open their road to China. They had zero interest in seeing the Union Jack rehoisted in Singapore. Therefore SEAC's actual campaign (as opposed to ceaseless hopeful planning exercises) became the XIV Army's. Even his sharpest critics agreed that Mountbatten was very good at spotting talented subordinates whose success would redound to his credit. Slim and his army were delivering victories even if not the victories for which Churchill yearned. Moreover, as Mountbatten's relations with Giffard soured, a direct connection with Slim was inevitable. In the Admin Box battle and even more during the protracted Imphal struggle, Mountbatten was crucial to Slim, leading the fight to extract from the Americans (and other theaters) the Dakotas that were the key to the XIV Army's great victory—Mountbatten personally knew Churchill (and FDR) as well as the members of the Combined Chiefs of Staff and could operate at a level Slim could not. He saw that Slim got and kept the Dakotas XIV Army needed.[18] By the time Leese arrived, the Slim-Mountbatten axis was well established. During the Sea or Bust (SOB) phase of the campaign in 1945—by which time it was clear that the XIV Army was going to deliver SEAC a stunning victory—Mountbatten played a key role in beating off the last challenge to Slim's lifeline, when the Americans threatened to remove their Dakotas—Rangoon after all was not *their* objective. Churchill was mobilized to browbeat George Marshall on behalf of "Mountbatten's campaign." The Dakotas stayed. The XIV Army rolled on.

SOB linked up with Dracula on 6 May. Slim had moved the XIV Army headquarters from Imphal to Meiktila, where he was marooned on that day by monsoon rains that closed airstrips. The following day the airfields reopened and Slim planned to leave for Rangoon. However, he was told Leese planned a visit and waited for his arrival. After pro forma congratulations Leese "abruptly said he had decided to make a change in [the XIV Army's] command." Slim was shocked. Leese then quickly added that Slim would remain in Burma but not with the XIV Army. That headquarters, now gilded with victory, would relocate to Delhi and, under the command of Lt. Gen. Sir Philip Christison, Bt. (who had commanded 15th

Corps in the Arakan), plan the return to Malaya, Operation Zipper. Slim would take over a new XII Army scheduled to be quickly reduced to corps size—which would mop up and handle occupation duties. Slim turned this down flat. Since, he said, he had lost Leese's confidence, he intended, as soon as he handed over to Christison, whom he asked Leese to send to Meiktila quickly, to return to India and retire. Nonplussed, Leese urged him to take time to decide, perhaps taking a few days' leave to visit his wife (who was at the hill station of Shillong in Assam). Slim simply reiterated that Christison should arrive quickly to avoid any hiatus in command. On this note the meeting ended.[19] What had happened?

On 3 May, Leese had met Mountbatten at Kandy. The supreme commander was suffering from amoebic dysentery, one of the treatments for which he pronounced "particularly revolting and uncomfortable." Leese had come to discuss command in Burma. Mountbatten already had some doubts about Leese apparently. There had been a clash that left him pronouncing Leese "a vain, stupid, dangerous man" and a "bully."[20] If this was his assessment of Leese, it makes what followed even more remarkable. Leese told Mountbatten that Slim was tired. Moreover, Zipper would be an amphibious operation and Slim was "not proficient" in amphibious operations. Christison was, as shown by his handling of the landings on Akyab Island in the final weeks of the Arakan campaign. If this was Leese's case, it was not only weak but virtually nonexistent. Doubtless Slim was tired—so were most senior commanders in the XIV Army at this point—but there is no shred of evidence that he ever gave any sign of being too tired to carry on. As for Combined Operations experience, Akyab was an absolutely ludicrous case to cite. The Japanese had evacuated the island. The pilot of an army light observation plane, flying over the island, could see no sign of a Japanese presence but could see crowds of civilians waving to him. He landed and "took" Akyab. The amphibious assault force, already embarked, landed as a training exercise. Mountbatten had been chief of Combined Operations. How could he not have spotted the utter fraudulence of this claim?[21] However, for whatever reason, he allowed Leese to approach Slim about a change of command, albeit with very strict guidelines. Lt. Gen. Sir Frederick ("Boy") Browning, who had replaced Pownall as Mountbatten's chief of staff, was present at the interview. On 24 May he sent Alan Brooke a letter describing it: "The Supreme Commander informed Oliver that he could not countenance any change which might carry the slightest indication that Slim was being removed from his command. He informed Oliver he should handle the matter extremely carefully, that he had the highest opinion of and confidence in Slim, and he would not consider anything that might affect Slim's future."[22] This (if accurate) should have warned Leese off. It didn't.

The next phase of the story fully justifies the comment of Mountbatten's official biographer: this episode "still inspires a degree of incredulity in the reader."[23] Leese's meeting with Mountbatten was observed by Browning; for the next chapter we have to rely on the unpublished memoirs of Christison.[24] Leese flew to Akyab, where he met Christison and briefed him on the meeting at Kandy, a briefing totally at variance with what Browning told Alan Brooke had taken place. Leese, according to Christison, said that Mountbatten felt Slim was tired and should be relieved. Leese also told Christison that he had asked Mountbatten, as the supreme commander, to handle Slim's removal but Mountbatten had told him that, as Slim's immediate superior, it was his job. Then, telling Christison that he was to take over the XIV Army, Leese flew off to Meiktila. After his meeting with Slim, he sent a message to Brooke explaining what he had done and returned to his own headquarters, apparently feeling that everything was settled and that Slim had accepted the situation. This was a disastrously bad misreading of the situation.

Slim himself said nothing immediately to his staff, leaving on the de-layed visit to Rangoon, where he spent 8 May in conferences with com-manders there. When he returned to Meiktila on 9 May, he told key members of the XIV Army staff in confidence before leaving for a brief visit to his wife in Shillong. At this point the XIV Army pushback began. Slim's staff was, in his words, "restless," a very mild term for what began to happen. When Slim returned on 12 May, he told his corps commanders and sent Leese a message saying he would return to India and another to army headquarters in Delhi saying he wished to retire. He also asked Leese where Christison was. Slim behaved impeccably, telling his distraught staff that their loyalty belonged to the XIV Army and cautioning them not to indulge in any "quixotic nonsense." But if Slim was absolutely correct, the XIV Army was not. His chief of staff, Brig. "Tubby" Lethbridge, threat-ened to lead the XIV staff on a sit-down strike, risking his own court martial, to force the whole episode into the open. A corps commander and two division commanders threatened to resign. As the word spread, the anger and revulsion grew. A colonel on Slim's staff raged, "Oliver 'Twist' and Mountbatten must be out of their minds," adding, "I never trusted that affected, silk-handkerchief-waving guardsman." John Masters, a Gurkha Rifles officer then serving as the senior staff officer to the 19th Indian Infantry Division, later observed that the XIV Army had become an extension of Slim's personality. Slim did not have to put up an open fight—the army he had created did it for him.[25]

There is a very revealing account of an encounter between Slim and one of his staff planners, Col. Denis O'Connor, during these fraught days. O'Connor told Slim how sorry he was that the XIV Army was losing him. Slim put his hand on O'Connor's shoulder and said, as O'Connor remembered it for Slim's official biographer, "Don't worry, my boy. This happened to me once before and I bloody well took the job off the chap that sacked me. I'll bloody well do it again." Lewin downplayed this as "temporary animosity" but there is no reason not to think it reflected exactly what Slim thought at that moment. The man who had defied a medical verdict that he was done with soldiering after his Gallipoli wounds, who had beaten Irwin's attempt to make him the scapegoat for his own failings, and who against every obstacle imaginable led the XIV Army to victory was highly unlikely to tamely accept rustication at the hands of a distinctly second-level player like Oliver Leese. All he had to do was stay calm, ratchet up the pressure by repeatedly asking where Christison was, calmly ask for retirement, and let the reaction of his army speak for him.

At this point, a week into the drama, the SEAC hierarchy went into panic reverse. Leese sent Walsh back to Meiktila on 17 May to try to persuade Slim to accept command of the 12th Army. Slim calmly pointed out that the XII Army was in fact to amount to barely more than a corps command and reiterated that he planned to "go quietly." He then pointedly asked when Christison would arrive. Privately he characterized Walsh's visit as an attempt to park him in Burma "until [they] find [a] better man."[26] It was Leese's last throw because by now the XIV Army's manifest and near-mutinous fury was powerfully reinforced by a thunderbolt from London. Gen. Sir Claude Auchinleck, commander-in-chief, India, professional head of the Indian Army, was in London for consultations. He took the matter up with Alan Brooke, who of course already had Leese's message about his visit to Meiktila on 7 May. Mountbatten, who had much more sharply attuned political instincts than Leese, had begun to feel queasy telling Brooke, in an exculpatory letter written after all was over, that he had become "very worried when he saw what was happening, and was intending to take the matter up with Leese."[27] It was too late.

The CIGS—who did not rate either Leese or Mountbatten highly—knew perfectly well who had led the XIV Army to victory. He fired off two broadsides on 18 May. To Leese: "I wish to make it quite plain that I consider the manner in which you have attempted to carry out changes in highest appointments under your command has been most unsatisfactory and highly irregular." He then reminded Leese that recommendations for senior command changes should have come from Mountbatten and "no definite action could even then be taken without my approval." Mountbatten was told any change of command proposals ought to have come from him and was then given this backhander: "I have expressed my surprise and displeasure [to Leese] that he should have discussed the matter with Slim at all. I have also made it clear that I have every confidence in Slim whose record has been outstandingly successful, and that unless very strong arguments can be adduced I have no repeat no intention of agreeing to his supersession by Christison." The famous Alan Brooke temper, honed in clashes with Churchill, settled the issue. Mountbatten went into full back pedal, writing two letters to Brooke claiming that Leese had exceeded his instructions (he could hardly deny he had allowed Leese to go to Meiktila), adding a long list of complaints against Leese and asking Brooke what he ought to do. The answer, on 19 June, was brutally clear, as was the scorn: "You ask for my advice. I can only tell you what action I should take if I were in your place. I should feel that there was no alternative but to replace Oliver Leese at the earliest possible moment."[28] Long before this exchange, Slim's total victory was clear. His repeated vain demands for Christison's appearance were followed by an ultimatum: he would hand over to Stopford of the 33rd Corps and leave for India. This produced on 23 May a message from Leese: Slim was to stay with the XIV Army and Stopford would take over the XII Army (which in fact was the 33rd Corps retitled). The whole business was, Leese explained, a misunderstanding. On the next day Slim flew to Calcutta, saw Leese, and went on to Kandy, where Mountbatten—not yet in receipt of Brooke's thunderbolt—asked him if he was willing to continue to serve under Leese. Slim indicated he was—doubtless with his tongue firmly in his cheek—but added that the XIV Army had no confidence in Leese.

Leese then suggested that Slim be given home leave (he had not been in Britain for seven years). He and his wife flew home together with Gen. Sir Richard Gale, the commander of Britain's Airborne Corps. Gale had been assessing the possibilities for airborne operations in SEAC. Slim, who knew Gale, showed him the draft of his official dispatch covering the XIV Army's great campaign. Gale found the story very impressive and said so. "Yes," Slim replied, "you wouldn't think they'd sack a chap for doing that."[29]

Christison's face was (partially) saved by being named the acting XIV Army commander in Slim's absence. Slim's home leave was marked by civic receptions, promotion to full general, a visit to Chequers, and then a meeting with Brooke, who told him that he would be succeeding Leese at ALFSEA. Mountbatten conveyed Leese's dismissal to him, in a letter that also informed him his successor would be Gen. Sir William Slim.

On 10 July, Brooke interviewed Leese on his return. His diary entry for the day shows some sympathy for Leese. Why is made clear in a note written some years later: "at the bottom of my heart I had a feeling, and still have a feeling, that, although he may have been at fault, he had a raw deal at the hand of Mountbatten."[30]

What was Brooke hinting at? Was Mountbatten not merely convalescent but complicit in the attempt to sidetrack Slim? There is no definitive answer to this but suspicions existed at the time and linger on. Mountbatten could be devious and was both avid for renown and very protective of his own, largely self-created reputation.[31] Slim had delivered all of SEAC's victories. In May 1945 the early nuclear conclusion of the Japanese war was unforeseen. The next step for SEAC after Rangoon was Zipper, the invasion of Malaya and reconquest of Singapore—and Slim was set to lead the XIV Army in what would be the victorious culmination of SEAC's mission. In his version of what had transpired at Kandy, given to Christison almost immediately afterward, Leese mentioned rumors that the supreme commander was jealous of Slim—before switching to Slim's alleged fatigue and lack of amphibious proficiency. Leese would maintain for the rest of his life that he, not Mountbatten, was responsible—a view with which Mountbatten's official biographer concurred. But suspicion remained. Brooke clearly thought there was more to it (as did Brooke's biographer, David Fraser), and Brig. Michael Roberts, a close friend of Slim's, later told Ronald Lewin, Slim's biographer, that toward the end of his life Slim had come to believe that Mountbatten was behind Leese's action.[32] Leese was a Guardsman and the Guards were known for unswerving loyalty to the chain of command, which Leese certainly demonstrated toward Mountbatten. On his deathbed Slim said to Mountbatten, who was paying a farewell visit, "We did it together, old man."[33] Acknowledgment—or reminder?

The last word possible at this point may be given to Maj. Gen. Julian Thompson in his study of the Burma campaign:

> It is hard to determine what part Mountbatten's jealousy of Slim played in the attempted sacking of the great general by the lesser men placed in authority over him. The account in Mountbatten's official biography is evasive and reflects little credit on Mountbatten's loyalty to Slim who had won all his battles for him.
>
> Neither does it say much for Mountbatten's integrity as a commander. Leese on the other hand, for all his faults, was straight, and readers must judge for themselves where the ultimate blame lies.[34]

A case perhaps where the Scottish verdict "not proven" seems appropriate.

As high drama played out in the command stratosphere, the business of wrapping up the Burma campaign continued. The fall of Rangoon led to a major reshuffle of the structure of ALFSEA—some of it planned, some not. The next big operation in SEAC was Zipper, the return to Malaya. After a great deal of the to-ing and fro-ing inseparable from planning any SEAC operation, with multiple references to London and Washington, the date was set for late August. Headquarters, XIV Army, moved to Delhi to begin planning. Christison, who became SEAC's equivalent of a substitute teacher, became acting commander of the XIV Army during Slim's absence in England (he would then become acting commander of ALFSEA when Leese left in July, being replaced at the XIV Army by Lt. Gen. Sir Miles Dempsey, another Monty favorite but one far more clever than Leese). In Burma Stopford, his 33rd Corps having morphed into the XII Army, conducted the final stages of the campaign. Stopford had Messervy's 4th Corps (although Messervy left on leave and was replaced by the talented Lt. Gen. Francis Tuker, a Gurkha Rifles officer who had commanded the 4th Indian Infantry Division with great distinction in the Desert, Tunisia, and Italy). All the relabeling had not however changed the reality on the ground: the war in Burma was the Indian Army's war.

Stopford's order of battle was five Indian divisions (5th, 7th, 17th, 19th, and 20th) plus two independent brigades (the 255th Indian Tank Brigade and the tireless 268th Indian Infantry Brigade) plus the 82nd West African Division and the 22nd East African Brigade. A single British brigade (the 6th Brigade of the 2nd British Division) remained. Moreover, the British component of the Indian divisions, declining steadily since 1943, was now evaporating like spring snow under a scheme designed by the War Office in London, Python.

From the time that France left the war and British mobilization went into overdrive, the War Office, the Ministry of Labour and National Service, and the War Cabinet knew that a long war would produce a manpower crisis for the army. The manpower demands of the RAF, the Navy, the war industry, agriculture, the necessary minimum civilian economy, and the huge government machine that supervised and coordinated it all meant that the size of the army would be much smaller than in 1914–1918. In the course of the war Britain raised eleven armored divisions (four of which were disbanded during the conflict), thirty-five infantry divisions (ten being disbanded subsequently), and two airborne divisions.[35] Once the number of units committed to action began to climb, in and after 1943, the issue of replacements became critical (hence the disbandment of some units to provide reinforcements to others). There were only so many young men of the right physical category available to the army out of a population of some forty-five million (the smallest demographic base of any of the major combatant powers). By 1943 the bottom of the barrel was in sight. This had two consequences: a "comb out" of men from other units to furnish infantry replacements (70 percent of the army's combat casualties were in infantry rifle companies), and a prioritization of theaters. By 1944 the top priority was Montgomery's British units (even so the War Office could not cover the 21st Army Group's casualties fully after July and more disbandments—"cannibalization"—ensued). The 8th Army in Italy was suffering from a shortage of replacements and the poor quality of many of the rather reluctant infantrymen combed out from the rear. In India Command and SEAC the problem was at its worst—and insoluble. By autumn 1944, British infantry battalions there averaged about 18 percent below strength, the replacement pool was almost empty, and the most rigorous comb out of the rear-area units could do no more than put a Band-Aid on a deep wound. The prediction was that by November British infantry units in the XIV Army would be eleven thousand men short.

Then, in September 1944, the War Office announced a major change in the plan known as Python, which governed the length of service for British personnel in India and SEAC. Hitherto set at five years, it would drop to three years and eight months.

The change in Python was driven by the growing concern in both the War Office and the War Cabinet about the state of mind of British troops serving in the East and the conditions in which they served. The focus on the European war meant that whatever happened in Burma was an afterthought in the British press, while the conditions experienced in India and Burma were Spartan behind the lines, grim at the front. Home leave was virtually impossible and prolonged family separations put a heavy strain on morale. It was clear in London by the autumn of 1944 both that the European war was entering its final stages and that the Japanese war was likely to last at least a year beyond its end—and possibly longer. Those British personnel with years of eastern exile already served could clearly not be asked to serve on without adverse reactions both at home and in the ranks. Hence the revision of Python. From that point on, however, every British soldier in the XIV Army had a calendar in his head with a date circled—the day he became eligible for return home. Touring his army, Slim noticed that British soldiers, instead of reciting their regimental affiliations, would tell him their time served in the East (and thus how long until their Python eligibility). In the course of the XIV Army's campaign in 1945, both of his British divisions were returned to India—their logistic demands were too heavy and the inability to keep their units up to strength meant that their combat effectiveness was eroding. Slim noted that in his Indian divisions, the attenuating strength of their remaining British battalions put a heavier burden on the Indian battalions, who noticed and resented the fact. As a result British battalions were being steadily swapped out for Indian battalions, whose casualties could easily be replaced and which comprised professional soldiers, not the tired, "browned off" conscripts of a citizen army.[36]

There matters stood when Germany surrendered. Zipper was next. The 34th Corps, commanded by Lt. Gen. Ouvry Roberts (who had led the XIV Army's 23rd Indian Infantry Division through the Imphal battle), was planning it. Both British divisions, the 2nd and the 36th, were scheduled to participate, despite bleeding men due to Python, when London suddenly pulled the rug out from under SEAC's planners (not for the first time). Churchill's great wartime coalition dissolved shortly after VE Day and Churchill formed a "caretaker" Conservative government pending the general election set for 5 July. Zipper was now set for 9 September. On 6 June, Mountbatten was told by the secretary of state for war, Sir James Grigg, that he would announce in Parliament on 8 June that eligibility for Python would drop immediately to three years and four months. All Python-eligible troops would be sent home as fast as transport could be made available, *without having to await their replacements.* This was driven obviously by the impending general election and aimed both at the service vote in SEAC (which in the event went to Labour) and at the voters at home with family members serving there.[37] No thought was given to the fate of Zipper. The result there was simple—its British component vanished. The 36th Division (only two brigades strong to begin with) would no longer be functional for combat. Neither would the 2nd Division, which now would lose ten thousand men to Python by September. The return to Singapore, so long sought by Churchill, would be the work of the Indian Army and of XIV Army in particular.[38] Four of Slim's divisions were its backbone. The last act in Burma was also a XIV Army affair, even if the headquarters in charge was now labeled the XII Army.

The XIV Army's drive on Rangoon had splintered what was left of the Burma Area Army into two groups. The remnants of the 15th and 33rd armies had been driven by the 4th Corps's blitz down the Mandalay-Rangoon corridor eastward in the Shan and Karen Hills, where, harassed by Force 136, which supplied and directed guerrillas, they were slowly withdrawing toward Thailand. Neither was in any shape to resume serious offensive operations. Maj. Gen. Pete Rees's 19th Indian Division, responsible for safeguarding the long supply line from Meiktila to Rangoon, was probing into the hills to ensure that the Japanese continued to withdraw. The speedy rehabilitation of the port of Rangoon—by the end of May it could handle the maintenance requirements for the XII Army and its share of administrative support for Zipper—made the Mandalay-Rangoon road less important. It also, finally, relieved the burden on the Dakota squadrons that, despite the monsoon, had continued to be vital links in Slim's supply chain. The workload of the RAF Dakota squadrons had actually increased since the American squadrons, in accordance with Marshall's stipulation in March, had begun to redeploy from SEAC to China the moment Rangoon fell.

The precarious supply situation may have eased but there remained one last battle for Slim's army, because one Japanese army, Lt. Gen. Sakurai

Shozo's 28th, remained in Burma. This army had defended the Arakan and had begun in March, as Slim's 33rd Corps drove down the Irrawaddy valley, to withdraw through the passes in the coastal mountains, the Arakan Yomas. Sakurai's intention was to link up with the rest of the Burma Area Army in the hope of blocking the XIV Army's drive on Rangoon. However, the XIV Army simply moved too fast. When Rangoon fell, most of the 28th Army was still west of the Irrawaddy. Cut off from resupply and reinforcement, with two great rivers in full monsoon spate, not to mention the XIV Army being between it and safety, the 28th Army nonetheless planned—surrender being unthinkable—to cut its way through to rejoin the 15th and 33rd armies in the hills east of the Sittang. Sakurai's headquarters had already crossed the Irrawaddy and taken refuge in the Pegu Yomas, a range of hills between the Irrawaddy valley and that of the Sittang. A number of rear-area units were gathered there, as were bits of the Rangoon garrison (including some naval units now functioning as infantry). The Pegu Yomas were very sparsely inhabited, so foraging for food yielded little. Sakurai could not remain there long but with many of his fighting units, including most of his 54th Division, still west of the Irrawaddy he had to wait until they caught up with him before tackling the 4th Corps cordon in front of him in the Sittang valley. To do so, Lt. Gen. Miyazaki Shigesaburo's 54th Division had to get past the 7th Indian Division and the 20th Indian Division lining the east bank of the Irrawaddy. At a very high price in casualties he did so, joining Sakurai in the Pegu Yomas by the end of May. Sakurai now had about thirty thousand men, many of them, however, from administrative and rear-area units. The commander of the Burma Area Army, Lt. Gen. Kimura Hyotaro, secure in Moulmein, at first entertained the fantasy that the 28th Army could hold out in the Pegu Yomas until early 1946. Reality quickly asserted itself and Sakurai was ordered in mid-June to break out, cross the Sittang, and link up with the remnants of the Burma Area Army—a decision Sakurai had already taken.

The decision was, of course, the embrace of a suicidal course of action. The 28th Army was not really a coherent fighting force. Many of its troops were from administrative formations; even its combat units were fragmented. All were hungry, many were sick (and there were virtually no medical units left). They had no artillery, no air support, and only rare and intermittent radio contact with Kimura and therefore little chance of coordinating with other Japanese forces. The monsoon was at its height; when they emerged from the Pegu Yomas they would have to traverse the flood plain of the Sittang, a monsoon-created swamp. Waiting for them were three of the best divisions in the British Empire's best field army: Rees's 19th Indian, Cowan's 17th Indian, and Evans's 7th Indian. Air support was abundant (whenever the monsoon permitted) and since the 4th Corps controlled the hard-surfaced road so was armored firepower. Every division had its full complement of artillery and there was no shortage of ammunition. To add one final touch to the 28th Army's handicaps, the 4th Corps had an intelligence windfall. On 2 July 1945, a patrol from 17th Indian's 1/7th Gurkha Rifles clashed with a Japanese patrol on the eastern edge of the Pegu Yomas. They killed nineteen Japanese, and found a soaked briefcase whose contents, when examined by intelligence officers, proved to be Sakurai's 14 June operation order to all his units laying out in complete detail how each of the four groups into which he had divided his force would move out of the Yomas and cross the flood plain and then the river. Now the 4th Corps knew everything but the date—and the capture of a Japanese liaison officer on 18 July supplied that.[39]

On 19 July, the 28th Army, carrying some two thousand wounded with them (those who could not be moved were given a hand grenade with which to commit suicide), came out of the Pegu Yomas onto as perfect a killing ground as any planner could imagine. Tuker did not have to put many of his infantry at risk. The official historians decided against describing in detail what happened.

The swampy flood plain claimed many; British and Indian gunners many more. In daylight hours the RAF bombed and strafed anything that moved. For those who reached the riverbank, the monsoon-swollen Sittang may have proved deadliest of all. A thousand yards across, flowing at twelve knots, it claimed hundreds of Sakurai's tired, sick, and hunger-weakened troops. One British post alone counted six hundred bodies floating by. Of the four hundred Naval Guard Forces (from the naval shore establishments in Rangoon) who made it to the banks of the Sittang, only three survived. The center of the Japanese effort was the sector held by the 17th Indian Infantry Division. A few miles downstream the 17th had been nearly destroyed thirty-seven months before (1/7th Gurkhas had lost better than half their strength). Slim had spoken of the campaign of 1944–1945 as payback. On the banks of the Sittang the 17th Indian had its own personal moment of retribution.

Less than half of the 28th Army made it across the river.[40]

By early August, apart from stragglers, no formed body of the Imperial

Japanese Army remained in Burma. Slim was about to take over ALFSEA. Lt. Gen. Ouvry Roberts was preparing to lead Zipper, all of whose divisional units had served under Slim, in the return to Malaya. The Indian Army had won its last great campaign under the British flag. Then two flashes "brighter than a thousand suns" changed war and the shape of the world forever.

Appendix 1: The Official Historian's File

Maj Gen. Stanley Woodburn Kirby, who headed the team that produced the five-volume series *The War against Japan* in the Cabinet Office official histories series covering Britain's role in World War II, faced some very thorny issues. The first volume had to cover the fall of Singapore, at a time when most of the senior participants were still alive. The constraints imposed by this led Kirby to write his own book on the subject, which was published posthumously. In the third volume of the official series, Kirby and his team produced a devastatingly candid appraisal of Orde Wingate's Chindit operations, which led Wingate's fervent defenders to present the Cabinet Office with a petition demanding a rewrite. Finally, Kirby had to deal with Oliver Leese's attempted coup against Bill Slim. About that the official history says: "Leese . . . told [Slim] in private that he proposed to place Christison in command of 14th Army and that he (Slim) would remain in command in Burma." To this is appended the following footnote: "Slim was not however prepared to accept Burma Command and the proposal was later dropped on orders from Mountbatten."[41] While the restraint in handling a command crisis rooted in a personality clash is perhaps understandable in an official history, Kirby was clearly not satisfied with this anodyne treatment. He wrote a full narrative of it: *The Full Story of the Attempt to Remove General Sir William Slim (Commander 14th Army) from His Post Immediately after the End of His Victorious Campaign to Clear Burma and the Recapture of Rangoon.* He appended to his narrative copies of his correspondence on the subject with Auchinleck, Mountbatten, Leese, Christison, Walsh (Leese's chief of staff), Browning (Mountbatten's chief of staff), and Air Marshal W. A. Coryton, who commanded the RAF in Burma at the time. There are also copies of cable traffic between Mountbatten and Brooke as well as a copy of the chapter on the episode that Slim wrote for—but did not use in—his memoir. This comprehensive collection—the best that, at this point, we are likely to have on the subject—is at the Liddel

Hart Center for Military Archives at King's College, London. Kirby stipu-
lated that it should not be opened until 1975, when the thirty-year closure
on World War II records expired and then only if Mountbatten, Slim, and
Leese were dead. The last of that trio to die was Leese, who died in 1983.
The file was therefore not available to Slim's official biographer, Ronald
Lewin, who nonetheless ferreted out most of the story, while pulling his
punches a bit where Mountbatten was concerned, as noted in the text. The
contents of Kirby's summation of the incident have been incorporated in
the text (the file appears never to have been used before by writers on the
subject). But several points deserve reiteration:

The commander-in-chief, India, Gen. Sir Claude Auchinleck, the professional head of the Indian Army, was neither consulted nor informed
before the most distinguished of the Indian Army's serving generals was
removed from command. He found out about it from Brooke (he was in
London at the time) and promptly told Brooke it would be disastrous for
Indian Army morale.

Both Coryton and, much more pointedly, Browning put their finger
on Leese's jealousy of Slim—"swollen head" and "extreme jealousy" were
Browning's terms—as being the root of the affair.

On 6 May, after meeting Leese at Kandy and telling him he could raise,
very carefully, with Slim taking a period of leave, Mountbatten wrote a
letter to Brooke expressing his dissatisfaction with Leese's conduct of affairs and his relations with other services and the Americans. He also told
Brooke that he had told Leese: "if he thought victory entitled him to be
insubordinate he would find himself in trouble." (He had previously sent
Browning to Leese's Calcutta headquarters with the same message.) Yet
he had told Leese only a few days previously that he should approach Slim
about leaving the 14th Army "on a friendly basis and handle it extremely
carefully." The doubts expressed in the text about Mountbatten's role are
underscored by Kirby's unpublished narrative. Either the supreme commander was totally muddled or he had a two-track strategy: If Leese could
quietly slide Slim aside, well and good. If, however, there was trouble,
Leese was expendable.

6

The XIV Army's Last Campaigns

The final campaigns of the 14th Army were some of the most controversial in the history of the Indian Army. From 1945 until the eve of independence in South Asia in 1947, the 14th Army and the Indian Army were involved in occupation responsibilities throughout the former Imperial Japanese Empire. In the immediate aftermath of the Second World War, the Indian Army found itself carrying out occupation duties not just in British colonies such as Burma, British Borneo, Hong Kong, Singapore, and Malaya, but also in Siam (Thailand), the colonies of French Indo-China (FIC), the Netherlands East Indies (NEI, later Indonesia), and Japan. Some of these occupation duties were fairly peaceful, such as in Burma, British Borneo, Hong Kong, Malaya, Singapore, Siam, and Japan.[1] The Indian Army's involvement in FIC and the NEI was to prove one of its most controversial and final violent assignments.[2] In both places, Indian Army divisions found themselves, as one officer would later state, in the position of "piggy in the middle."[3] The divisional and corps commanders had to navigate a minefield of political issues, involving emancipation of Allied prisoners of war and civilians, disarming more than three hundred thousand Imperial Japanese soldiers, and eventually fighting counterinsurgency campaigns against nationalist guerrillas who perceived them as instruments of the returning French and Dutch colonial administrations.[4] For some battalions, the campaigns during this period involved fighting almost as bitter as anything they had encountered against the Japanese in Burma.[5] This chapter will first focus on the "quieter" reoccupation operations and then shift to the difficult occupation duties in FIC and the NEI, as many viewed these duties as a continuance of operations from Burma and the occupation of Japan as a larger Allied effort.

Strategic Context

When His Majesty's Government (HMG) in London agreed to expand the area of responsibility for South East Asia Command (SEAC) with regard to occupation duties in July 1945 at Potsdam, Germany, this put SEAC in the position of relying upon the largely volunteer Indian Army to carry out the mission.[6] The difficult operations were further hampered by a poorly defined strategy; mission statements appeared to change over the course of the occupation, and indicate considerable gaps in understanding between SEAC, His Majesty's Government, and India Command on what the Indian Army's remit and goals should be. Attempting to define, and articulate, why the Indian Army should be involved in occupation duties in non-British colonies and as a result find itself fighting a counterinsurgency campaign against nationalists that had nothing to do with India or the British Empire presented a number of problems for both the viceroy, Lord Wavell, and the commander-in-chief India (c-in-c I), Gen. Sir Claude Auchinleck.

While the Indian Army's involvement was being discussed and debated in New Delhi, the Indian Army itself quietly got on with carrying out its difficult duties with competence and dispatch. They were commended on all sides for their professionalism.[7] To supply but one example from this period, consider the performance of the 23rd Indian Division in the NEI by assessing awards listings for gallantry and leadership: the Distinguished Service Order, Military Cross, and Military Medal. Nine DSOs were given to commanders during the Burma Campaign, three in the NEI. Seventy MCs were given out in Burma; twenty-three were given out in the NEI. Last but not least, one hundred Military Medals were awarded in Burma, and another thirty-eight in the NEI. Then consider that the 23rd served just over one year in the NEI, compared to just under three years in Burma against the Japanese.[8] One need only refer to the various war diaries and divisional and regimental histories to see that, for the men, VCOs, and officers, these campaigns were a strange continuation of the Second World War—and one that some authors felt should not have occurred.[9]

As noted above, Lord Louis Mountbatten, commander of SEAC, arrived in Potsdam, Germany, on 24 July 1945, to meet with the Combined Chiefs of Staff. There he was informed that SEAC would be taking over responsibility for more of South East Asia—chiefly Borneo, Java, and Indo-China, all of which had previously been under the control of South West Pacific Area, or General MacArthur's command. At first, Mountbatten did not feel that this would be too large a task for SEAC to take on. SEAC had already been planning Operation Zipper, the amphibious attack and campaign for Malaya and Singapore.

It was during the meetings in Potsdam that Mountbatten was advised of the planning for the atomic bomb drop on Japan. He was sworn to secrecy but told to prepare for the possibility of an early Japanese capitulation. Mountbatten duly informed SEAC HQ in Kandy, Ceylon, without revealing information about the atomic bomb, to prepare for potentially imminent capitulation, and to begin planning to manage the enlarged area of responsibility that SEAC had inherited. SEAC HQ responded to this information with concern, fearing that Operation Zipper would not go forward if an early capitulation occurred. Military and political leaders in SEAC and London considered the invasion and re-occupation of Malaya and Singapore of particular psychological importance, necessary to wipe clean the humiliation of the Malayan and Singapore capitulations in 1942.[10]

Mountbatten immediately set out to prepare SEAC, chiefly formations from the XII and XIV armies, to seize strategic areas from the Japanese in Burma and then prioritize specific areas expected to be handed over to SEAC control. On 13 August SEAC established priority areas as follows: Malaya, Saigon, Bangkok, Batavia (NEI), Surabaya (NEI), and Hong Kong. With this plan in place, SEAC was able to move quickly, and naval forces were able to begin carrying out Operation Zipper in short order.[11]

The increased level of responsibility caused consternation for some senior British officers, including Gen. Sir William Slim, commander of Allied Land Forces South East Asia (ALFSEA). As he wrote: "The area of South East Asia Land Forces had suddenly expanded to include Malaya, Singapore, Siam [Thailand], [NEI], Hong Kong, Borneo and the Andaman Islands. . . . In two of them, Indo-China [FIC] and [NEI], nationalist movements armed from Japanese forces had already seized power in the vacuum left by the sudden surrender."[12]

Another major issue for Generals Slim and Auchinleck, back at India Command, was that Operation Python,[13] the repatriation scheme for British personnel, was also in full force. Many conscripted British officers, NCOs, and soldiers were being released from service due to pressure on the British government to end conscription with the war's end. With the expanded area of operations for SEAC and the need to reoccupy many areas, SEAC needed formations that were going to provide the capacity required for occupation duties. The political reality of Operation Python meant that this duty fell to the professional Indian Army.[14] General

Auchinleck stressed to Mountbatten[15] that it was not a forgone conclusion
that all the Indian Army troops that were needed could come from India
Command. SEAC had asked for the 7th Indian Division to deploy to Siam,
the 20th Indian Division to deploy to Indo-China, and the 23rd and 25th
Indian divisions to deploy to Malaya, and then the 23rd moved to the NEI,
with the 5th Indian Division following on.[16] Auchinleck specifically cited
the need for troops for internal security duties in India, which would be
necessary later in the year and into 1946 as communal tensions increased.[17]
It was clear that the political situation in India was extremely delicate;
Mountbatten understood this and was quick to respond to Auchinleck
that he saw the need to be cautious. Even so, neither they nor HMG were
prepared for what would be required of the Indian Army in the NEI and
FIC.[18]

Even as planning went ahead, formations were earmarked and assigned; as shipping began to move, inter-Allied relations deteriorated. The
American general Douglas MacArthur announced that he wished for all
commanders to stop movement and for no landings to take place in the
Japanese Empire until the formal surrender in Tokyo Bay had taken place.
At this point, this ceremony was planned for 28 August. MacArthur's rea-
soning was that Japan had not yet signed any surrender treaty, and that
unilateral action by theater commanders could prejudice the surrender
process, and ultimately lead to the Japanese commander of forces in South
East Asia, Field Marshal Terauchi, refusing to obey surrender orders from
SEAC.[19] It was well known that communications between Tokyo and field
commanders were erratic at best during this time,[20] and while some of
MacArthur's points may have been valid,[21] Mountbatten and SEAC were
outraged. They complained bitterly to the Combined Chiefs, pointing
out that some of their forces were already six days out from Rangoon
and preparing to land in Malaya. The British Chiefs of Staff agreed with
Mountbatten, but HMG in London disregarded these concerns and told
Mountbatten and SEAC to halt the invasion of Malaya and follow Mac-
Arthur's instructions. To add insult to injury, not all Allied forces did
the same. The Russians ignored MacArthur and continued to destroy the
Japanese Army in Manchuria; even worse, the American general Albert
Wedemeyer,[22] serving with the Chinese Nationalist forces, did the same.[23]
This delay contributed significantly to the subsequent issues that arose in
the occupations of both the NEI and FIC; British/Indian forces lost time
and traction in dealing with both Japanese and nationalist groups, the latter

of having successfully filled the political vacuum that had been created with the Japanese surrender.[24]

The British/Indian Army mission for occupation duties continued to evolve over the next several months. Issues remain unresolved to this day regarding the intent of senior commanders and what actually occurred especially in FIC and the NEI. Overall, the commanders had three specific aims in entering into each area: rescue Allied Prisoners of War (POWs), disarm the Japanese military, and maintain law and order to ensure internal security.[25] The ability of commanders to carry out these orders was compromised by the delay imposed by General MacArthur and the ensuing internal political maelstrom. The plight of the POWs was an excellent example of this; as Slim noted: "Our men and those of our Allies were daily dying in their foul camps; thousands were at the limit of weakness and exhaustion."[26]

SEAC's campaigns in all the occupied areas began almost simultaneously; however, while the NEI campaign lasted through most of 1946, the FIC campaign was over for all intents and purposes by the end of February 1946 and the operations in Siam and Japan differed in timings but were generally peaceful. This chapter will first focus on some of these peaceful operations, as well as the more difficult and violent operations in FIC and the NEI, and end with the occupation duties in Japan. The Indian Army provided the 268th Infantry Brigade, from the recent Burma campaign, for the occupation forces in Japan, which was commanded by Maj. Gen. D. T. Cowan, former GOC, 17th Indian Division.

23rd and the 25th Indian Divisions Return to Malaya

The planning for the invasion of Malaya, Operation Zipper, had been laid in May 1945 and the initial plans called for an amphibious invasion in mid-August. The planning shifted to a peaceful landing as intelligence came out from Malaya that the Japanese would not oppose the landings.[27] As noted above, the date for the landings was delayed by General MacArthur. The political reoccupation of Malaya had been established since 1943 by the Malayan Planning Unit. There would be a military administration for an initial period of time in Malaya.[28] The 34th Corps was given command of the operation; the 25th Indian Division was given the responsibility of the landings south of Port Swettenham, while the 23rd Indian Division was given orders for landings northwest of Port Dickson.

The first units and formations from both divisions began to land at their respective beaches on 9 September.[29]

The landings did not go quite to plan in either area; the actual landings suffered due to poor reconnaissance and tide timings. Various vehicles were lost as they dropped into the ocean too far from the shore or were caught by the muddy tides and the actual landing zones had difficult road networks and large ditches. As noted in an official report, "conditions on the beaches were chaotic, vehicles drowned in scores as there were no decent exits from the beaches, and the roads became choked with ditched tanks which tore up the road services."[30] The issues for the 23rd Indian Division were in a similar vein. The IJA only had twenty thousand troops in northern Malaya; however, many commanders recognized that, had the Japanese opposed the landings, there would have been significant casualties. The 23rd divisional history noted, "it did occur to some to wonder what would have happened had this been an operation of war with the Japs massing from the north against the 25th Division."[31]

By the 10 September, the chaos of the beaches had been settled and the various units from both the 23rd and the 25th divisions began to move inland and toward Kuala Lumpur. By the 12 September, elements of the 25th Division had reached Kuala Lumpur, as reports had been coming in that rioting had occurred. The ceremonial entry of the British into Kuala Lumpur, the capital of Malaya, occurred on the 13 September. Lt. Gen. T. Ishiguro, commander of the 29th Army, surrendered all the Japanese forces on the Malayan peninsula to the commander of the 34th Corps, Lt. Gen. O. L. Roberts.[32] For the coming days, thousands of Japanese troops formally surrendered to British and Indian troops as various towns were re-occupied. The 7/16th Punjab described one scene, where the Japanese 94th Infantry Division and Japanese Naval forces were going to surrender to the 25th Indian Division. The battalion diary noted that "the march past took an hour and the state of the ground after 10,000 men had passed can well be imagined. . . . They started with a General Salute, when a thousand or more swords flashed from their scabbards. After this every man on the parade was searched. Then each officer in turn laid his sword reverently at the feet of the G.O.C."[33] By the middle of October, the Japanese forces in Malaya had formally and ceremonially surrendered without any issue.[34]

As the Japanese cooperated, General Slim disbanded the 34th Corps. The reoccupation of Malaya had been very smooth, but the power vacuum left in other sectors of SEAC were starting to flare up. The 14th Army HQ in Singapore met on 28 September, and the 23rd was earmarked to shift to the NEI to deal with the rising tensions. By early October, the first elements of the 23rd Indian Division were shifting to Java.[35] See below for a detailed description of the 23rd Indian Division's experience in NEI.

5th Indian Division Returns to Singapore

As the 23rd Indian Division and 25th Indian Division moved toward the Malay peninsula, the 15th Corps and the 5th Indian Division were to proceed to Singapore as part of a massive Royal Navy flotilla. On 4 September, Lt. Gen. S. Itagaki, 7th Area Army commander, met Lieutenant General Christison on HMS *Sussex* and surrendered the Japanese forces in Singapore and the Malayan province, Johore.[36] The Japanese delegation also handed over the maps of the mines in the sea opposite Malaya and Singapore. On 5 September, the first elements of the 5th Indian Division landed and began to accept the surrender of the Japanese forces on the island, estimated at more than seventy thousand men. By 8 September, the whole island had been reoccupied, just in time for the 15th Corps HQ to land on 9 September.[37]

On 12 September one of the main events of the war in Southeast Asia occurred: The Japanese formally surrendered all their forces in Southeast Asia to Lord Mountbatten and the Allied representatives at the Municipal Buildings of Singapore.[38] As Lord Mountbatten stated:

I have come here to receive the formal surrender of all the Japanese forces within South-East Asia Command [noting that the area of responsibility had greatly expanded]. . . . In addition to our Naval, Military and Air Forces which we have present in Singapore today, a large fleet is anchored off Port Swettenham and Port Dickson, and a large force started disembarking from them at daylight on the 9th of September. . . . This invasion would have taken place on the 9th of September whether the Japanese had resisted or not. I wish to make this plain; the surrender today is no negotiated surrender. The Japanese are submitting to superior force, now massed here.[39]

Eleven copies of the surrender were signed. The delegations left the building and Mountbatten read an Order of the Day. Mountbatten stated:

I wish to warn, too, of the situation you find when you proceed to liberate other territories in this command. In the new territories you will be occupying, the Japanese have not been beaten in battle. You may well find, therefore, that these Japanese who have not been beaten may still fanatically believe in the supreme superiority of their race. They may try to behave arrogantly. You will have my support in taking the firmest measures against any Japanese obstinacy, impudence, or non-cooperation.[40]

A Union Jack that had been concealed in the infamous Changi Jail was hoisted, and the national anthems of the Allies were played.[41]

Mountbatten had made it clear to all Allied forces in Southeast Asia: "There will be no fraternizing whatever between Japanese and Allied forces. In dealing with Japanese your behavior will be guarded and coldly polite. . . . Any Japanese who came to receive orders or report should be kept at arm's length."[42] (This order would not be carried out by the 20th Indian Division in FIC, which is discussed below.) Singapore became SEAC HQ, with all subsequent operations in the area directed from there.

By 15 September, the 161st Brigade of the 5th Indian Division had crossed over to Johore, moving to meet up with elements of the 25th Indian Division. Allied prisoners of war had been rescued and treated for illness and injury, and thousands were evacuated from Singapore by the end of September. The GSO I of the 5th Indian Division, Lt. Col. J. F. Carroll, noted, "the bearing and morale of our prisoners of war was a sight I shall never forget; it has made one proud of one's fellow man. They were magnificent, despite the appalling times they had been through and endured."[43]

By mid-October, the 5th Indian Division and the 25th Indian Division had shifted boundaries and had formally linked up on the Malayan peninsula. By the end of October, the 5th Indian Division had processed more than one hundred thousand Japanese prisoners;[44] shortly after, they were ordered to the NEI to support the efforts of the 23rd Indian Division in maintaining law and order in Java, which is discussed below.

7th Indian Division Ordered to Siam (Thailand)

Siam had been occupied by the Japanese Army in 1941, and served as a main staging position for the invasions of Malaya and Burma. The period from 1941 to late 1944 was one of relative peace within Siam. With the American victories in the Philippines, the Japanese had prepared the forces in the region for more mobile operations by early 1945 and had shifted troops from FIC to protect Siam. With the loss of Rangoon and the Burma Area Army, the Japanese further reinforced Siam in July and August 1945. The 39th Army was supported by the remains of the 15th Army from Burma and reorganized as the 18th Area Army.[45]

SEAC Joint Planning Staff planned the movement of troops to disarm the 18th Area Army in mid-August, designated Operation Bibber. The 7th Indian Division was earmarked to move to Siam and accept the surrender of the Japanese force. It was given four tasks for its mission: (1) Secure Don Muang airfield as a staging post for the forward movement of the 20th Indian Division to FIC. (2) Locate and evacuate Allied prisoners of war. (3) Concentrate and disarm the Japanese army in Siam. (4) In all dealings treat Siam as a friendly country.[46]

On 3 September, the first elements, the 7th Division HQ, tactical HQ 114th Brigade, of the 7th Indian Division were flown from Rangoon to Bangkok. This first flight was met by a Thai guard of honor. The division HQ was set up on the Dun Muang airfield, and the first efforts to communicate with the Japanese were set in motion. Each day Japanese representatives came and met with the 7th Division HQ to outline the planning for the disarming of their troops. It was estimated that there were more than one hundred thousand Japanese forces in Siam. Over the coming days, the rest of the 7th Indian Division was flown in as Japanese representatives met and planned the transfer of power and control to the British authorities.[47]

From September to the end of the year, the 7th Indian Division disarmed thousands of Japanese soldiers and rescued more than thirty thousand military and civilian Allied prisoners, including many from the Burma-Siam railway. As law and order had been maintained and the transition in Siam had been fairly smooth, a decision was made for the 7th Indian Division to move to Malaya, starting in mid-December.[48] As the 7th Indian began to withdraw, both sides realized that the Japanese forces in Siam had not formally surrendered. On 11 January, seven Japanese lieutenant generals, eleven major generals, and two admirals formally surrendered to the 7th Indian Division. This ended the war against Japan for the 7th Indian Division.[49]

The 20th Indian Division Ordered to French Indo-China

The British were placed in charge of only part of French Indo-China (FIC); specifically, they were assigned to control the area south of the 16th parallel,[50] while the Chinese Nationalists controlled the area to the north. The British area of responsibility included not only southern Vietnam, but also Cambodia and parts of Laos, and the operation was named Masterdom.[51] The Chinese troops, having disregarded General MacArthur's orders, arrived in the area first, in early September. Their efforts were focused on pillage, rape, and looting in the northern areas of Indo-China.[52] The British mission was organized into two groups, the Control Commission[53] and the Allied Land Forces French Indo-China (ALFFIC),[54] and was headed by the seasoned and well-respected 20th Indian Division commander, Maj. Gen. Douglas Gracey.[55]

As commander of ALFSEA, General Slim issued Operational Directive no. 8 to his senior commanders for the military occupation of Malaya, Burma, the NEI, and FIC. Commanders were instructed to disarm and concentrate all Japanese forces; protect, succor, and ultimately evacuate Allied POWs and civilian internees; establish and maintain law and order; introduce food and other civil affairs supplies; and set up appropriate civil administration.[56] Gracey received further detailed orders; in addition to the points raised in Operational Directive no. 8, he was instructed to pay special attention to law and order and, more importantly, "liberate Allied territory in so far as your resources permit," which to some on his staff implied possible future operations against the Vietnamese nationalists, the Vietminh.[57] This last directive has been interpreted by later historians as General Gracey, GOC, 20th Indian Division, potentially going beyond his remit.[58] However, Slim sent a message to Gracey that the French were to be in charge of civil administration; however, in designated key areas, he would be responsible for full authority over both the military and civilians but would be working through the French administration.

By the time the British were able to send troops into Indo-China, planning was beset with difficulties. The British had minimal intelligence about the Japanese Army in the area, as well as the state of the administration and relations with the Vietminh.[59] The French had administered the area under five different colonies: Cochin-China, Tonking, Annam, Cambodia, and Laos. Until March 1945, the Vichy French had worked alongside the Imperial Japanese Army, at which point they had been ousted by Japanese occupation forces. Before the British arrived, Ho Chi Minh had declared independence from the French authorities for the new nation of Vietnam, with the tacit support of the Japanese. The resistance movement was named the League for the Independence of Vietnam, or the

Vietminh. The Vietminh provisional executive committee in the south set out to fill the political vacuum there, acting at the behest of Ho Chi Minh.[60] The Vietminh slowly started to take over governmental control in Saigon and the surrounding areas. On the same day that the Japanese surrender occurred, there were mass demonstrations in Saigon in support of the Vietminh and a declaration of independence. Violence erupted between French civilians, the Vietminh, and other political factions wishing to take advantage of the power vacuum. There were rumors of many people being killed and escalating violence.[61]

The British needed to get troops to Saigon quickly, but were hampered by acute transport shortages by air and sea. This was the start of an ongoing problem for the British and, later, the French forces. The first elements of the 20th Indian Division, 80th Indian Brigade,[62] arrived at Saigon's Tan Son Nhut airport on 8 September and immediately began to assess the situation.[63] More troops arrived on 11 September and Gracey arrived from Rangoon with his staff on 13 September.[64] Gracey immediately recognized the need for more troops, with the city and surrounding areas apparently in chaos. Ironically, Japanese troops were being used to provide security at the airfield. They would play both defensive and offensive roles under British command in the following days, weeks, and months, not just in FIC but also in the NEI.[65] And this would lead to controversy, especially with the American and British press.

While one of the chief missions for Gracey and the Indian troops was disarming the Japanese,[66] they recognized that they would need to keep a significant number in place as defensive and static forces. Indian troops were slowly starting to arrive, and the rising violence between the French and the Vietnamese communities was causing problems.[67] As the days progressed, tensions between the British/Indians and the Vietminh increased apace. The Vietminh were inciting Japanese soldiers not to surrender, but to desert with their weapons and join the Vietminh.[68] They also set out to spread anti-British propaganda among the Indian soldiers in the division, but it fell on deaf ears.[69]

Gracey and his staff viewed the Vietminh as a direct threat to law and order. On 19 September, SEAC issued contradictory directives, simultaneously ordering Gracey and the 20th Division to seize Saigon Radio and censor other broadcasts of the Vietminh and issuing a general statement about not interfering in local affairs.[70] Gracey and his staff decided on more far-reaching moves to contend with rising violence. Brigadier Maunsell,

chief of staff on the Control Commission, met with the Vietminh provisional government on 19 September, and issued a proclamation closing
all newspapers, banning provisional government seizure of buildings or
other property, banning all public meetings, all demonstrations, all proces-
sions, and the carrying of weapons, and enforcing a night curfew. He also
asked for a list of all Vietnamese police and armed units. This amounted
to declaring martial law, which Gracey then had to enforce, relying on
the equivalent of two battalions of troops.[71] Gracey advised SEAC of his
proclamation, asserting: "I would stress that though it may appear that I
have interfered in the politics of the country, I have done so only in the
interest of the maintenance of law and order and after close collaboration
with some senior French representatives."[72] Mountbatten backed Gracey
at the time, although later in life he questioned Gracey's decisions at this
point in the campaign.[73]

Gracey's proclamation was read out and in theory took effect on 21
September. In reality, however, without sufficient troops the British were
limited in their ability to enforce its tenets, particularly the curfew. On
22 September, former French POWs were released and rearmed to support the effort.[74] While at first this idea seemed like a good solution to the
manpower problems in Saigon, it was to have wider repercussions within
twenty-four hours. British and Indian troops had been moving through
the city, trying to round up and disarm the Vietminh police and armed
groups. Units of the 80th Indian Brigade also moved against the Viet-
minh-controlled administrative buildings, handing over the buildings to
the small amount of French forces after they had taken possession. The
French were able to seize control of the administrative elements of Saigon
without too much bloodshed, pushing out the Vietminh provisional government and raising the tricolor above Hotel de Ville.[75] A coup d'etat had
occurred, however, and more blood was to be spilled.[76]

The released French POWs had been guarded by the Vietminh and had
suffered at their hands. Unfortunately for Gracey and the British/Indian
forces, within twenty-four hours of the coup, French discipline began to
break down, and French troops began to kill the Vietminh and so-called
Vietminh in retaliation. The French civilian population also became involved with the ensuing mob violence. This had repercussions for the
British and Indian troops, and Gracey attempted to make the French commanders aware of the issues and to get their men back in control. These

men still fell under the command of Gracey, and he and his men would be accountable for the situation's deterioration.[77]

As a result of these developments, the Vietminh began to consider the British as part of the attempt to reimpose French colonial government in Indo-China.[78] Some authors cite this episode as the beginning of the first Indo-China war. The Vietminh launched a general strike on 24 September, paralyzing sections of the city by cutting off water or electricity. Violence also began to increase; on 25 September, more than three hundred French and Eurasian families were butchered in a northern section of Saigon by Vietminh and other paramilitary gangs. Violence escalated as the Vietminh set up roadblocks and British and Indian troops engaged them during their expanded patrols.[79] The sounds of gunfire, mortars, and other weapons were heard each night, as British/Indian, French, and Vietminh forces skirmished through the city. Many Burma veterans noted the difficulty of fighting guerrillas in an urban environment.[80]

Mountbatten praised Gracey for his actions in communicating with the Chiefs of Staff,[81] but on 24 September he cabled Gracey and asserted that British and Indian troops should be used only in designated "key areas"; the French and Japanese needed to handle sections outside of Saigon.[82] Mountbatten appeared to be growing concerned that Gracey had exceeded his orders, and began to question his ability to command. General Slim, by contrast, supported Gracey, and pushed Mountbatten to release all of the 20th Indian Division to provide support.[83] The course of action being contemplated was for British/Indian forces to take complete control of Saigon; this would require a whole division, to restore law and order and to repatriate POWs as well. General Gracey was also expected to start working to find a political solution to the problems between the Vietminh and the French, so as to allow the withdrawal of British and Indian forces.[84] It was also at this juncture that a politically fraught decision was made: to expand the use of Japanese troops. Not only would they be protecting airfields; they were also allocated to more offensive roles alongside and sometimes under the command of British officers[85] to support Gracey's efforts to impose law and order in and around Saigon, until the rest of the 20th Indian Division and the follow-on French military forces arrived.[86] The Japanese refused to work for the French, and requested that all orders and actions be directed through the British command structure.[87] In the end, however, the main French build-up of forces took longer than expected.[88]

It was at this juncture that both General Auchinleck and the viceroy, Wavell, began to note the political fallout that operations in FIC and the NEI were causing in India. Wavell stated to the secretary of state for India, Lord Pethwick-Lawrence, on 1 October 1945:

> The situation in French Indo-China and the Netherlands East Indies will give us some trouble. Indian troops are involved in both places, and we shall be attacked for allowing HMG to use them to suppress national movements. It was of course most necessary to disarm the Japanese, and to maintain law and order while this was being done. But I hope that HMG will be able to disengage the troops, both British and Indian, as soon as possible and leave the business to the French and the Dutch.[89]

General Slim was aware of and in agreement with both Wavell and Auchinleck. He advised the chief of the Imperial General Staff, Alanbrooke, that "directions we have been receiving from various sources seem to me to have been somewhat involved and at times contradictory." In the same letter, he also recounted a conversation with the British secretary of state for war, Lawson. He noted that, while Lawson intended that the British not become involved in nationalist struggles, French forces still operated under Slim's command, and that "as long as we retain this command . . . we cannot divorce ourselves from the responsibility for their actions."[90]

Meanwhile, back in Saigon, the fighting continued. On 1 October, the same day that Wavell was asking for an end to the army's commitment, the British Chiefs of Staff reversed an earlier decision, and expanded Gracey and the British and Indian troops' remit to work outside the Saigon area in support of the French. It was also on 1 October that talks were held between the British and the Vietminh. Gracey's stated position was to curb violence and restore order in Indo-China. The Vietminh expected the British to act as arbitrators, but Gracey was under strict orders not to do so, since such a role was political and outside his remit. A ceasefire was agreed on, to take effect on the evening of 2 October, and meetings between the French and Vietminh were scheduled for 2 October. Despite these efforts, sporadic fighting continued.[91] The truce ended definitively on 10 October, when the Vietminh attacked a British/Indian engineer reconnaissance party. Gracey had warned the Vietminh that they would reap the consequences of violence against his troops; he ordered his 20th Indian Division, veterans of the Burma campaign, and the newly arrived 32nd Indian Brigade to clear the areas to the north of the city.[92] Brig. D. E. Taunton of the 80th Indian Brigade recalled that "the moment rebel Annamites attacked British troops I issued orders that we would cease to use minimum force and persuasion, but would use maximum brutal force in order to effect counter-measures in the quickest way and avoid unnecessary casualties to our own troops."[93] Mountbatten had agreed to this, asserting that "I ordered strong action should be taken by the British/Indian forces to secure further key-points and so to widen and consolidate the perimeter of these areas. At the same time I insisted that further attempts to negotiate must continue."[94]

Throughout October and November, the remaining units and formations of the 20th Indian Division arrived; they set out to establish control in and around Saigon and to provide support for the French.[95] The French also began to arrive in early October; their commander, Gen. P. Leclerc, arrived on 5 October, along with the 5th Colonial Infantry.[96] Fighting continued during this period between the British/Indians and the Vietminh, and between the Vietminh and the French.[97] Japanese troops were also utilized. The British also brought in more Royal Air Force support, in the form of Spitfire fighter squadrons. These were to be used sparingly and under strict controls, but were to be called upon if necessary.[98]

By 17 October, the last units and formations of the 20th Indian Division had arrived and were ready to move against the Vietminh. It was decided to send the 100th Indian Infantry Brigade, commanded by Brig. C. H. B. Rodham, and supporting arms to the north and northeast of Saigon into the Thu Duc/Thu Dau Mot/Bien Hao areas. Intelligence reports stated that the Vietminh strength lay in these areas, and there was a clear need to break the Vietminh ring of control surrounding Saigon. Brigadier Rodham informed the Japanese command in the region that the 100th Brigade was coming to occupy the area and assume responsibility for the maintenance of law and order over the course of 23–25 October.[99] The Japanese were asked to continue disarming the Vietminh, searching for weapons, and clearing areas around the main towns. The Japanese troops now fell under the command of Brigadier Rodham and his brigade. The various units of the 100th Indian Brigade—the 1/1st Gurkha Rifles, the 4/10th Gurkha Rifles, the 14/13th Frontier Force Rifles,[100] and the 16th Light Cavalry[101]—carried out a well-planned and well-executed operation to clear the areas to the north of Saigon. The Japanese carried out the static duties of defense, while the brigade operated mobile columns to destroy any opposition and deal with any roadblocks.[102]

The units of the 100th Brigade relied upon their wartime experience and created combined arms mobile units. An example of this, an operation known as Gateforce, was established by the 14/13th FFRifles, who were based to the northeast of Saigon at Bien Hoa. Maj. L. D. Gates took his company, plus a squadron of armored cars from the 16th Cavalry, a section of mortars from the 14/13th FFRifles, a detachment of Royal Engineers, and an attachment of Japanese troops, and pushed east toward Xuan Loc. They were ordered to create a patrol base in Xuan Loc on 29 October and patrol for three days, to try to destroy and capture two thousand Vietminh and members of the HQ staff that had been reported to have fled to the area. Gates was ordered to use maximum force to clear the area and track down and destroy the Vietminh.[103] One of the most controversial aspects of this operation was the instruction to destroy any village that resisted their efforts.[104] Over the course of several days, Gateforce engaged elements of the Vietminh and succeeded in destroying various roadblocks and fortified positions. After two days of fighting, it was estimated that close to two hundred Vietminh had been killed in the Xuan Loc region, thus, in theory, breaking the back of the overt Vietminh military presence.[105] It was reported that Gateforce was also able to rescue some twenty French civilian hostages.[106]

The month of November brought about a partial shift in the campaign. As the 20th Indian Division was able to consolidate its gains, it decided to refocus on its primary operational task, disarming the Japanese Army.[107] More and more French troops were arriving in FIC and were able to start taking over key security tasks from British/Indian troops, as well as from the Japanese outside of Saigon. The various units and formations of the 20th Indian Division continued to send out mobile combined-arms patrols to show the flag and disrupt any Vietminh attempts to seize key areas within the "Saigon" area of operations, at the same time as disarming the Japanese soldiers.[108] At around this time, General Gracey made some key observations of the French army's performance in Saigon. In a report to General Slim on 5 November, he wrote: "The French troops are leaving a pretty good trail of destruction behind them, which will result in such resentment that it will become progressively more difficult for them to implement their new policy, and, I am convinced, will result in guerrilla warfare, increased sabotage and arson as soon as we leave the country."[109]

At the same time, General Auchinleck, still pressing for the withdrawal of the Indian forces in the region, sought to make clear to the British Chiefs of Staff that the Indian Army was not an open-ended resource that they could use throughout Asia: "If we continue to [send] Indian troops in Java [and FIC], as HMG apparently propose to do, for the purpose of reinstating Dutch rule in the Netherlands East Indies [and French rule in FIC], we can have no defense whatever against the accusations that these troops are mercenary troops who are acting at the bidding of the British Government against the wishes of the Indian people."[110] He followed up a similar letter to the War Office on 15 November 1945.[111]

By the end of November, units of the 100th Indian Brigade had been used in mobile columns to engage pockets of the Vietminh and had disarmed thousands of Japanese. The 14/13th FFRifles had disarmed over a thousand Japanese in one day in November.[112] At the same time, some Japanese frontline units were still being employed in battle, doing a professional job and being commended for it.[113]

The complexity of the war and the "strangeness" were staggering to many Burma veterans.[114] The 9/12th Frontier Force Regiment[115] was earmarked to set up a large Japanese internment area in Cap St. Jacques (Vung Tau) to repatriate Japanese POWs.[116] On 28 November, the 32nd Indian Infantry Brigade handed over their area of responsibility north of Saigon. The drawdown was scheduled to begin in late November, in anticipation of Mountbatten's arrival to formally accept the surrender of the Japanese general Terauchi and his forces. While in Saigon, Mountbatten met with General Gracey and the French Army commander, Leclerc, to discuss the withdrawal of the 20th Indian Division, in response to both the needs of SEAC in other areas of operation (AOs) and the political pressure being applied by the Indian National Congress against the Government of India. The 32nd Brigade was earmarked to leave by the end of the year, and the 80th Brigade to leave with the divisional HQ and General Gracey by the end of January 1946, as French forces geared up to take over.[117]

While the planning for withdrawal was in full swing, operations continued and took on a different tone during December. The 32nd Brigade carried out an operation to clear Han Phu Island of the Vietminh, which it did with minimal casualties. By 19 December, it had relinquished command of the area to the French.[118] As 80th Indian Brigade was ear-marked next, it slowly started to hand over various areas of responsibility to the French, at the same time as disarming the Japanese.[119] It became so quiet in their sector that the battalion was able to revert to peacetime training.[120] This was not true for the 100th Indian Brigade and its units, which continued to be engaged in various skirmishes with the Vietminh at the same time they were disarming the Japanese and seizing arms stocks, during December 1945 and January 1946.[121]

While the British were beginning their process of withdrawal and han-dover, French arrogance and lack of discipline, which had already caused problems in September, began to get out of hand again. General Gracey sent a letter to General Leclerc, bluntly stating his anger at the French units' arrogant and racist behavior toward both the Japanese forces and his own Indian troops. He wrote, in part:

> It might be of value for them [French troops] to realize that, had
> not the Japanese in most cases carried out my orders faithfully,
> there would have been a disaster of the first magnitude in Southern
> French Indo-China with a massacre of thousands of French people,
> and the destruction of a vast amount of French property. . . . [With
> regard to instances of disrespect toward Indian troops] the
> camaraderie which exists between officers of the Indian Army
> and their Gurkha and Indian soldiers must be explained to them.
> Our men, of whatever colour, are our friends and not considered
> "black" men. They expect and deserve to be treated in every way
> as first-class soldiers and their treatment should be, and is, exactly
> the same as that of white troops.[122]

Gracey was similarly disturbed: "There is no more fruitful source of friction between Indian Army officers and their men on one side, and French troops on the other, than when our Indian and Gurkha troops are regarded and treated as 'black' by French officers and men. I mention this point particularly as cases have occurred in which it is obvious that our Indian Army traditions have not been understood."[123] As noted previously, the 32nd and 80th brigades began to hand over control to the French and organize withdrawal, in preparation for service in British Borneo and other AOs of SEAC in December. Meanwhile, the fighting continued, in the north and northeast of Saigon, in the 100th Brigade's AO, throughout

December and early January. The brigade was stretched, due to the lack of supporting forces to the south and west. The 14/13th FFRifles carried out countless patrols in and around Bien Hoa, reverting to the term *Sher Forces*, which had originally referred to its patrolling activities in the Burma campaign. This exemplifies how many within the battalion saw this as a continuation of the Burma war, even against a different enemy.[124] While the battalion sent out "Sher Forces" to engage the Vietminh, they slowly started to see a Vietminh build-up of forces and became aware that the Vietminh controlled the night once again. Many patrols were able to surprise the Vietminh, partially due to the jungle warfare experience they had earned in Burma.

A marked similarity between the campaigns in Burma and in FIC was evident in the Vietminh attack on the patrol base at Bien Hoa. Overnight on 2/3 January 1946, a Vietminh battalion attacked the main patrol base for the 14/13th FFRifles at Bien Hoa, with attached troops from the 9th Jat Regiment. The Vietminh launched five well-coordinated, simultaneous attacks supported by heavy fire. The Indian troops were able to beat off the attacks, with heavy fire from machine guns and supporting mortars. The attack lasted for four hours and resulted in an estimated one hundred Vietminh killed, with no losses for the troops at Bien Hao, including the Japanese, who were still defending.[125] While the Vietminh lost the battle, many noted their bravery afterward.[126]

Units of the 100th Indian Brigade continued to send out patrols to keep up the pressure, before the brigade handed over responsibility to French forces.[127] The Vietminh in return kept pressure on the brigade and the various patrol bases, including Bien Hoa. The "mobile" ability provided by the 16th Light Cavalry's armored cars ended with the 16th's departure on 12 January.[128] The 80th Indian Brigade had stood down the day before, and the 20th Division HQ and General Gracey were scheduled to leave FIC at the end of the month for Malaya. The date set for the transfer of all forces, including some Indian battalions in FIC to French command, was 28 January, the day that Gracey was scheduled to leave.[129] More than fifty-four thousand Japanese soldiers had been disarmed and concentrated at Cap St. Jacques; forty soldiers from the 20th Indian Division had died and more than one hundred had been wounded between October and late January.[130] It is estimated that more than two thousand Vietminh were killed during the same period.[131] Initially the 100th Indian Brigade was assigned to support the French, but this was stopped in response to political pressures in India and objections from Auchinleck and the viceroy. The brigade left over two days, 8 and 9 February;[132] over the course of January and February close to twelve thousand troops from the 20th Indian Division withdrew from FIC.

The 9/12 FFR and 2/8 Punjab remained in FIC, the latter to guard the mission in Saigon and the former to guard Cap St. Jacques and continue the repatriation of Japanese POWs.[133] Both battalions served until the end of March under the authority of the Allied commander's Inter-Service Liaison Mission to French Indo-China, under the command of a British brigadier, F. K. S. Maunsell. Only small miscellaneous subunits remained, including one company from the 2/8th Punjab, until May 1946.[134]

Field Marshal Slim summed up the efforts of Gracey and the 20th Indian Division as follows: "Gracey was faced with the most difficult politico-military situation in Allied territory, which he handled in a firm, cool, and altogether admirable manner."[135] This assessment could serve for the whole of the Indian Army's performance in this campaign.

23rd and 5th Indian Divisions battle in the Netherlands East Indies (NEI)

As stated above, the counterinsurgency operations in the Netherlands East Indies (NEI) lasted longer than those in FIC. The deployment of Indian Army forces also entailed close to three times the numbers,[136] and the fighting in the NEI was far more costly.[137] This was partially due to the quality of the Indonesian Nationalist forces and the burden of carrying out duties longer, due to the slow progress of arriving Dutch troops. The British official historian, Major General Kirby, recalled that "they [Indonesian Nationalists] proved to be fanatical opponents and capable of fearful atrocities, as often as not against women and children."[138]

As had already occurred in FIC, the Dutch colonial troops were not as disciplined as their Indian Army counterparts; this created problems for British commanders throughout the campaign.[139] Another similarity between the two operations was the loss of focus between developing the grand strategic vision and carrying out actual operations on the ground, due to a lack of clear direction from SEAC and London. Meanwhile, units and formations in the NEI attempted to focus on their mission, in the midst of a large-scale political debate that intensified with the ending of the INA trials in late spring 1946.[140] This section will deal with the operations on the island of Java first, and then cover the operations on the island of Sumatra.

The Imperial Japanese Army and Navy did not openly support nationalist organizations during their occupation of the NEI during the Second World War, but they gradually began to allow Indonesians access to positions in government administration. The Indonesian nationalist leader, Dr. A. Soekarno (or Sukarno), was allowed to create a movement that opposed Western influence and cooperated with the occupying Japanese military authorities. From 1943, Indonesians were allowed more of a voice in running their occupied territory, although there was no question of outright independence. With the tide of war turning against the Japanese in summer 1945, a meeting was held in Singapore to discuss granting independence to the Indonesians, especially on the island of Java. Events overtook the debate, and on 17 August, Sukarno declared independence for the NEI. The Japanese began to hand over administration and dispense arms to the Nationalists.[141] By the end of August, the Japanese had given up control of law and order, and had withdrawn to camps to await the arrival of the Allies. They had also armed and trained many Nationalists, who took over the governance of much of Java, and who were openly opposed to the return of the Dutch colonial authorities and prepared to fight any landing of Dutch soldiers.

The first intelligence reports on the Japanese-raised Indonesian forces, Tentara Keamanan Rakyat (TKR), listed their strength at seven divisions. Some of the divisions were of limited value, but could operate as guerrilla bands. One division, stationed in eastern Java, had been well trained by the Japanese and, equipped with tanks and artillery, was prepared to oppose British operations in the area.[142]

The intelligence picture of what was going on in Java was not clear to SEAC. As Mountbatten noted: "I had been given no hint of the political situation which had arisen in Java. . . . Dr H. J. Van Mook [of the Netherlands East Indies Provisional Government in Australia] had given me no reason [to suppose] that reoccupation of Java would present any operational problem, beyond that of rounding up the Japanese."[143] Lieutenant General Christison stated, "there was practically no Intelligence about the state of affairs."[144] Reports came in throughout the month of September about rising levels of violence against Dutch settlers and potential colonial collaborators who were considered likely to support a Dutch return. Elements of Force 136[145] parachuted into Batavia on Java and the Royal

Navy deployed a cruiser force to the area in early September. The Royal Navy commander, Rear Adm. W. R. Patterson, specifically warned on 18 September that Allied land forces were needed in Batavia to avoid further violence and lawlessness. General Slim, commander of AFLSEA, ordered the XIV Army to release two brigades from the 23rd Indian Division, then serving in Malaya, to deploy to Batavia in the western part of Java and Surabaya in the eastern section of Java. The first brigade group sailed on 1 October.[146]

Intelligence was still sketchy in early October 1945, when Lt. Gen. Sir Philip Christison, commander of the 15th Indian Corps, was appointed the commander of Allied Forces Netherlands East Indies. When asked during a press conference what sort of reception the Indian Army was likely to receive, he indicated that he did not expect hostility, since the Indonesians liked the Dutch.[147] This underestimation and lack of intelligence were to pose a major hurdle throughout the campaign.

Campaign aims and strategy became muddled very early on: as had already happened in Saigon, the intent of the mission did not align with the expectations of Indonesian nationalists. Christison, ordered to proceed to Batavia immediately, was told initially to disarm the Japanese, rescue Allied POWs and internees, and fill the vacuum between the Japanese capitulation and returning Dutch administration. This last point proved, as it had in FIC, to be the most tricky and contentious. Mountbatten attempted to limit this aspect of the mission to "key areas," intending that Indian divisions would occupy and administer key urban areas only, maintaining law and order in the principal cities of Batavia and Surabaya on Java and Padang, Medan and Palembang on Sumatra. The hinterland was to be the responsibility of the Dutch colonial administration and military. There would be some overlap, however, when Dutch administrators and military moved through the secured "key areas" of British control into the countryside.[148]

The operation's lack of strategic focus was demonstrated in one incident that took place around this time, one that had long-term implications. Christison was ordered by the British secretary of war, Mr. Lawson, to endeavor to bring the Indonesian Nationalist leadership and the Dutch together to find a political solution.[149] Dr. C. O. Van der Plas, deputy governor of the NEI, who arrived in mid-September with the Royal Navy, had rebroadcast a message from the queen of the Netherlands from earlier in the war,[150] outlining advances in self-government. In response, Sukarno sent a message to Christison, saying that he would support the Allied mission, since it was not there to reimpose prewar Dutch colonial authority. Many moderates echoed this sentiment in indicating their cooperation to Allied staff. This turn of events greatly angered the Dutch authorities; they sent irate messages to Mountbatten and his staff, accusing Christison of mediating on their behalf and of recognizing the Indonesian Republic as a legitimate entity. They also repudiated the broadcast from Van der Plas. Within days, Sukarno contacted Christison to advise that all cooperation would cease, that he would no longer try to restrain the extremists in his organization, that he would oppose any Dutch landings, and that he and his supporters would fire on the British if they were found to be covering the Dutch landings.[151]

Western Java

The remainder of the 1st Indian Brigade, 23rd Indian Division, arrived in Batavia by 5 October. The tactical HQ of the 15th Corps (later Allied Forces Netherlands East Indies) and 23rd Indian Division arrived on 6 October; the rest of the unit followed and were in place by 10 October.[152] For the first few days, the units of the brigade were made responsible for law and order and guarding the internment camps. The Indonesian police force was brought under British control. Indonesian nationalists did not harass Indian and British forces at first, although they did begin to establish roadblocks. It was noted that, initially, British and Indian troops were able to visit cafes without arms.[153] On 10 October, the first violent engagements began between Indonesians and British/Indian forces; from that day forward, daily clashes were the norm.[154]

Similar issues arose in Batavia that the 20th Indian Division troops had already encountered in Saigon. First, Dutch nationals living in the area began to make false reports of looting or armed Indonesian nationalists, in order to force British/Indian forces to patrol constantly. Indian battalions noted their frustration with this practice in their war diaries.[155] Second, Dutch "Colonial Forces" in the area, the Koninklijk Nederlands-Indisch Leger (KNIL), were reraised following the arrival of British forces and quickly gained a reputation for lack of discipline and overreaction.[156] The British commanders recognized that they were potentially a rallying call for the Indonesian nationalists. It was decided to redeploy them to the southern sector of the city and put them under Dutch command.[157]

British command soon discerned a need to extend its reach further into the interior in order to safeguard the internment camps.[158] In haste, a company from the 1/16th Punjab Regiment deployed to the town of Buitenzorg, a railway center one hundred miles to the south of Batavia. The decision to extend the British area of administration necessitated additional troops,[159] whose arrival exacerbated growing tensions.[160] Tactical intelligence concerning numbers of internees and armed nationalists was lacking.

The company was to be relieved as quickly as possible by the arrival of the 37th Indian Infantry Brigade. The 3/3rd Gurkhas arrived on 15 and 16 October and was sent to Buitenzorg immediately as replacement troops. Once established, the Gurkhas quickly identified an impending humanitarian crisis, due to the larger number of Allied POWs and civilian internees in the area. Coordinating with Japanese forces already stationed in the area, the Gurkhas undertook to maintain law and order and evacuate the internees. Tensions continued to rise as Indonesian extremists massacred hundreds of Eurasians. Gurkha forces had to rely upon the moderate Nationalist authorities for electricity and water supplies, and continued, whatever else was happening, to carry out patrols in order to rescue as many internees as possible and ship them back to Batavia. Their mission continued through the end of 1945 and into 1946, when the 1/16th Punjab returned to the area.[161]

While it appeared that most Japanese soldiers and officers were supportive of imposing law and order under the authority of British and Indian forces,[162] this was not always the case. As noted previously, some within the IJA had provided weapons and training to the Indonesian Republican forces before the British/Indian forces arrived. This did not go unnoticed, and resulted in the arrest of Major General Nakamura, Japanese commander of all forces in Central Java, along with some of his HQ. They were shipped to Singapore for trial, accused of disobedience to their orders to surrender.[163]

The 3/5th Royal Gurkhas were sent to Bandoeng in October 1945, and almost immediately began active patrolling against insurgents in and around the area to liberate as many internees and POWs as possible. The 3/5th Gurkhas had less difficulty reestablishing law and order, due to the fact that Japanese forces, obeying orders, took back the town from the extremists.[164] Japanese forces in the area supported the Gurkhas in their efforts to create a bubble of security in and around the town, and Japanese tanks were used to destroy roadblocks and extremist positions that threatened the mission.[165]

Central Java

The lack of accurate intelligence within SEAC about numbers of camps and internees in the areas targeted for occupation was conclusively demonstrated by the campaign to land troops in Semarang. Originally, operations in central Java were not a priority: Surabaya in the east was supposed to be the second major operational area for the 15th Corps. As with the rest of the operation, there were minimal forces available for the mission. The 3/10th Gurkhas from the 37th Brigade were reembarked on transports and shipped to Semarang, 250 miles east of Batavia, in response to reports of fighting between Nationalists and Japanese, with many internees still in camps that needed to be rescued.[166] On 19 October, the battalion landed in an almost-deserted harbor; as they moved into the city they could hear sporadic gunfire, and were shortly fired upon themselves. In the aftermath, Indonesian Nationalist officials came to claim that the firing had come from Japanese soldiers, while the apologetic Japanese commander characterized the incident as fighting that had erupted between insurgents and Japanese troops, resulting in a mistaken attack on the Gurkhas.[167]

Japanese troops in the area had been stationed to the south near some of the large internment camps in Ambarawa and Magelang. The Japanese commander had decided to move toward Semarang in an attempt to reimpose order, but had found his unit repeatedly engaging with insurgents. The Japanese helped the Gurkhas to reestablish control inside Semarang and to escort small detachments to Ambarawa and Magelang to support the feeding and repatriation of the allied POWs and civilian internees.[168]

It was clear that the 3/10th Gurkhas could not hold the areas for which they had been given responsibility, and the decision was made to send the 3rd Brigade or the Royal Artillery Brigade, which had close to two battalions of infantry, to support the Gurkhas. Troops began arriving on 22 October. Upon arriving into Semarang, the 3/10th Gurkhas were ordered to move the whole battalion to Magelang. The battalion lacked transport and had to fight their way through numerous roadblocks. As the Gurkha battalion arrived, close to five thousand extremists attacked their positions, bolstered by artillery and mortars. Japanese forces in the area came once again to support the Gurkhas; after a few days of heavy fighting, members of the Indonesian Republican government sought to negotiate a truce. After a series of talks, it was agreed that as soon as the British had gathered up all the internees and POWs in the area, they would withdraw back to

Semarang. In the end, more than twenty-five hundred internees were evacuated and the British withdrew from Magelang on 21 November.[169]

The extremists were slowly gathering strength as British and Indian forces began to withdraw from parts of central Java. Gurkhas, Japanese, and internees arriving from Magelang into Ambawrawa witnessed chaos. While there had been a cease-fire in effect in Magelang, it was constantly being violated. As the Gurkhas and the internees moved toward and into Ambarawa, they had to fight their way through a series of roadblocks and ambushes.[170] The RAF was being used to destroy Indonesian positions, including artillery positions, which were bombarding the British lines. One internee camp was attacked and many British troops and woman and children were killed. The Allied Forces Netherlands East Indies (AFNEI) began to pull the 23rd Indian Division back toward Batavia and central Java, after the heavy fighting in Surabaya and the arrival of more Indian Army reinforcements. The fighting in eastern Java, at Surabaya, is discussed more below.

On 27 November, elements of the 49th Brigade arrived and pushed out toward Ambarawa, to support the withdrawal of Gurkhas and internees to Semarang. British and Indian troops began to evacuate POWs and internees to Semarang; they completed this task on 8 December, and pulled out of Ambarawa a week later.[171] As reinforcements began to arrive in Semarang and the withdrawal from Ambarawa began, Indonesian insurgents closed in on Semarang. Violence in and around the town began to increase during mid-November. Some of the fighting became so intense that naval gunfire support was called in. As at Semarang, the brigade was reinforced with troops from Ambarawa. The 49th Brigade began to sweep the areas around the town, clearing out large numbers of insurgents.[172] On 11 January 1946, the 5th Parachute Brigade arrived to relieve the 49th Brigade, who then proceeded to move to Batavia to the west, where the 23rd Indian Division was concentrating its brigades. The 5th Parachute Brigade remained in Semarang for just over a month, until additional Dutch forces arrived and were able to take over responsibility.[173]

Eastern Java

Before considering the difficult campaign in eastern Java, in and around Surabaya, it is necessary to provide a general picture of the 23rd Indian Division as of October 1945. The AFNEI and 23rd Indian Divisional HQ, along with the 1st Indian Brigade and the 37th Indian Infantry Brigade, were in the west, in the Batavia-Buitenzorg-Bandoeng area; the divisional troops or the Commanding Royal Artillery (CRA) Brigade were in and around the Semarang-Ambarawa-Magelang area in central Java. There was continuous fighting in and around the British/Indian formations. Over the course of October and November, fighting increased in severity in some locations. Royal Navy ships were brought in to provide naval gunfire support. British and Indian forces did their best to track down and evacuate all Allied POWs and civilian internees, rounding up thousands and pulling them back to various harbors for repatriation.[174]

The last remaining brigade from the 23rd Indian Division, the 49th Indian Infantry Brigade, under the command of Brig. A. W. S. Mallaby, were ordered to land at Surabaya, in eastern Java. They arrived on 25 October, encountering some of the best-armed and best-trained Indonesian Nationalist forces operating in the NEI. Lieutenant General Nagano, commander of the IJA 16th Army, reported to General Christison that "We have been training 7 divisions of Indonesian soldiers who never saw the Dutch. Most of these divisions are not formidable but the one in East Java is tough and well led. They will give you much trouble."[175] The practice of deploying a brigade into a volatile area of operations was not new to either the 23rd Indian Division or General Christison, but eastern Java was a different matter. It rapidly became clear to SEAC that more troops would be necessary. On 17 October, even before the 49th Brigade had arrived in Surabaya, more units, including Indian cavalry regiments, had been requested from Malaya and other regions to support the overstretched 23rd Indian Division. By the end of October, two brigades from the 5th Indian Division[176] were also en route to Java to provide additional support.[177]

Brigadier Mallaby[178] and his 49th Indian Brigade were ordered to carry out the same mission as other brigades and units: evacuate internees and disarmed Japanese military personnel and maintain law and order. The possibility of reestablishment of Dutch control was not specifically discussed with Indonesian Republicans at any point in the campaign. Upon their arrival into the harbor of Surabaya, brigade staff noted the number of "hostiles" in and around the area, and the British sent two officers to arrange to meet with Dr, Moestopo, commander of the Indonesian (Japanese-trained and -equipped) Republican Army, TKR, and Dr. Soerio, Indonesian governor of East Java. Tensions were high; Dr. Moestopo wanted to kill the small British delegation and throw their bodies into the harbor, while the British officers insisted that they had come in peace, and Dr. Soerio tried to act as mediator. Mallaby's staff received a signal not to land troops without Dr Moestopo's permission, but Brigadier Mallaby and his staff made it clear that they were not going to wait for permission to land troops. The British and Indian forces landed with fixed bayonets and loaded weapons, and began to seize key areas of the harbor and town. This bold action initially appeared to pay off as the Indonesians sent a small delegation to meet with Mallaby and his staff regarding arrangements for the future.[179] By this point, the British were in control of the port and most of the facilities, but not the power station and one of the key bridges.[180]

In the first round of talks, the British stressed that they had come to evacuate internees and maintain law and order, not to interfere in the internal politics of Indonesia. They also confirmed that there were no Dutch officials serving on brigade staff. A meeting between Dr. Moestopo and Mallaby on 26 October focused on the issues of arming and disarming the civilian population. Mallaby and Moestopo agreed that Indonesian uniformed soldiers and police were to remain armed and carry out law-and-order operations alongside British and Indian forces. Armed civilians, meanwhile, were to be disarmed.[181] The Indonesians remained suspicious and continued to insist on British confirmation that no Dutch were to be landed. The British and the Indonesians moved quickly to set up boundaries of areas of responsibility and arrangements for internees to be processed.[182]

What happened next highlighted the disconnect between orders emanating from SEAC and the 23rd Divisional HQ and the situation on the ground. On the morning of 27 October, an RAF Dakota transport flew over the town and dropped leaflets; this was part of an RAF operation that had been going on for several weeks, moving from the western part of Java to the east. The problem was that the leaflets did not account for any changes to the environment on the ground: they stated that the British Military Administration would supersede the Indonesian Republican Government in the area and, more crucially, that all arms were to be surrendered and that anyone bearing arms illegally would be shot by British and Indian troops. Many Indonesian nationalists considered this high-handed, and that they had been "duped" by the British. This failure to communicate essentially negated all the hard work that had been done on 26 October. Dr. Moestopo met with Brigadier Mallaby, but there was no consensus on what the future held. Brigadier Mallaby did assert that he had not been made aware that the leaflets were going to be dropped, but also confirmed that he was obligated to follow the orders of his superior officer, Major General Hawthorn from the 23rd Indian Division.[183] As a result, negotiations broke down.

On 29 October Indonesian forces, TKR, supported by artillery and tanks, attacked all the British and Indian positions in and around Surabaya,[184] as well as internees' camps and convoys. Hundreds were killed, and several British officers and Indian VCOs were caught, tortured, and killed, and their bodies mutilated. Some British and Indian positions ran out of ammunition and were overrun and massacred by Indonesian forces. It is estimated that the four thousand British and Indian forces stationed in the area were attacked by twenty thousand armed soldiers of the TKR and supported by another fourteen thousand armed civilians.[185] The intensity of the fighting is best conveyed by an officer from the division:

> 49 Bde. were fighting for their lives and for the lives of the internees they had come to protect, with the odds weighed heavily against them. . . . There had been no time to move up reserves of ammunition and food which lay useless in the docks. . . . Fight they did with magnificent gallantry—in some cases until their ammunition was gone. . . . There were desperate battles all over town.[186]
>
> The brigade HQ sustained over 25 percent casualties, and two platoons of the Rajputana Rifles were wiped out to the last man.[187] It was estimated that the Indonesians lost close to six thousand men.[188]

Mountbatten sent Sukarno to Surabaya to broker a cease-fire. Sukarno met with Mallaby and members of the Indonesian Republican Government and succeeded in doing so. On 30 October, General Hawthorne arrived to meet with Sukarno and Mallaby; he ordered the brigade to pull back to positions in the harbor, take the airfield, and maintain some positions in the south, where there were internees, while the Indonesians held the city. Sukarno agreed to this plan, and he and Hawthorne flew back to Batavia. However, fighting broke out afresh within twenty-four hours; moderate voices in the Indonesian government were sidelined by extremists, who called for attacking British and Indian troops in and around Surabaya, disregarding the orders of Sukarno.[189]

The almost-immediate return to open warfare was partially due to the
fact that many Indonesians believed that the British had caved in and surrendered. As a result, several units and subunits were caught inside the
city; one company from the 6/5th Mahrattas, tasked with defending the
International Bank Building, was ordered by the Indonesians to surrender
their weapons. They refused and fighting erupted.

Not only was Mallaby unsuccessful in his attempts to negotiate an end
to the fighting, but two of his officers who had been working with Sukarno and attempting to negotiate a cease-fire were captured; they were
killed and their bodies were mutilated. Mallaby and some of his staff returned to Bank Square in another attempt to end the fighting; they were
ambushed and the brigadier was killed on 30 October.[190]

The actions of the Indonesian forces in Surabaya further exacerbated
problems in other parts of Java. The 3/10th Gurkhas encountered difficulties at Magelang and withdrew to Semarang at the end of November.
Tensions continued to rise in Batavia, and in eastern Java, the Indonesian
extremists requested the 49th Brigade in Surabaya to lay down their arms.
The brigade had pulled back to a smaller perimeter that had been agreed
on before Mallaby's death; internees were evacuated, and a limited cease-
fire prevailed for the first few days of November.[191] General Christison
issued a warning to all Indonesian extremists that "unless those responsible for Mallaby's murder were handed over, [he] would bring the whole
weight of my land, sea and air forces to bear on Surabaya."[192] Royal Navy
ships arrived into the Surabaya harbor to add support to the besieged 49th
Brigade. During this period, some captured British and Indian troops were
returned to the brigade HQ.[193]

On 2 and 3 November, the 9th and 123rd Indian Infantry brigades, from
the 5th Indian Division, fresh from occupation duties in Singapore and
southern Malaya, began disembarking in Surabaya as reinforcements for
the 49th Brigade. The concentration of the two brigades was kept secret,
and the 49th Brigade continued to hold the new perimeter.[194] Maj. Gen.
E. C. Mansergh, a highly respected divisional commander from the Burma
campaign, assumed command of the three brigades in Surabaya. Mansergh
attempted to meet with moderates in Surabaya on 7 November, in order
to find a political solution. However, it rapidly became clear to divisional
staff that the extremists were in charge and thought they were winning.[195]
An ultimatum was delivered that the criminals involved in the killing of
Mallaby and other British and Indian officers and men were to be handed

over to British authorities. By 9 November, the two brigades had completed their disembarkation and were ready for offensive operations. On
the same day, leaflets were dropped stating that the British were going to
take action against the extremists in the town, and that no political settle-
ment would be forthcoming.[196]

Meanwhile, opposition and tension in New Delhi were steadily increasing. On 7 November, Wavell telegraphed Pethick-Lawrence, warning that
"serious repercussions likely to arise here [India] if Indian troops are used
to suppress Indonesian movement and reinstate the Dutch."[197] Pethick-
Lawrence responded on 11 November that "the position we have to deal
with is one of extreme difficulty. . . . Our object has throughout been to
avoid being involved in any hostilities with the Indonesians. . . . To aban-
don Java might lead to much wider withdrawals, facing us with serious loss
of prestige in Malaya and Burma and leading to similar troubles there."[198]

At the same time, the 5th Indian Division was poised to mount a major
offensive in Surabaya, with General Mansergh and his staff making plans
to seize back the town and gain access to the nearby internee camps. When
the ultimatum regarding the handover of those who had killed Mallaby
and other British and Indian personnel went unanswered, the order was
given to move into the city. The offensive to take back the town began
early on the morning of 10 November;[199] British and Indian troops were
attacked almost immediately by a considerable Indonesian force, supported
by artillery and surrendered Japanese tanks. Within a few hours it was clear
that the troops would need more support,[200] and both naval gunfire and
RAF air cover were provided as British and Indian troops fought their way
back into the town against stiff and heavy opposition. Both artillery and
naval gunfire support were to be used only when needed, in an attempt
to avoid too much damage, and tank support could be used only with the
permission of the divisional commander.[201]

Taking back Surabaya was a slow and bloody process;[202] the town was
not cleared until 29 November, and even then sporadic fighting and house
searches continued and the town was not declared fully secure until late
December.[203] By the end of November, British and Indian troops had suffered more than eight hundred casualties, including just under one hundred
killed, but had also recorded nearly two hundred personnel missing.[204]

The units and formations of the 5th Indian Division (the 49th Indian
Brigade having moved back to Semarang and then on to Batavia in late
November to consolidate all of the 23rd Indian Division in one area) set

out to continue in their mission of repatriation of internees and surrendered Japanese soldiers throughout the last months of 1945 and into early 1946. The British and Indians commanded the town and continued forays into the countryside to disrupt any build-up of Indonesian forces; the resulting actions employed more guerrilla tactics than before. British and Indian troops successfully foiled all Indonesian attempts at seizing key locations in and around the town.

General Mansergh and his divisional staff set up a military government and began to lay the foundations of a civil administration, including police, law, education, and broadcasting. Dutch troops began to arrive in early February 1946, and the divisional staff began the handover process. On 23 April 1946, General Mansergh left the division to take up the command position of GOC Allied Land Forces Netherlands East Indies (ALFNEI). The various brigades began to withdraw by sea from Surabaya in April, and the handover of control to the Dutch was completed on 8 May.[205]

The End of the British and Indian Presence in Java

Fighting intensified in western Java in late November and December 1945 as the British/Indian offensive in Surabaya continued. The extremists made a concerted effort to sever communications between Batavia and Bandoeng during this period; however, as more and more units from central and eastern Java made their way back to Batavia (during consolidation of the 23rd Indian Division), pressure on the British began to decrease. As 1946 began, it was clear that the situation in Java had changed. British and Indian troops had secured Surabaya and its environs; they had been successful in extricating numerous internees and Japanese POWs from central Java; and they were consolidating forces in Batavia and in the western interior.[206]

At the end of 1945, a meeting was held in Singapore to discuss the current and future situation in the area. Lieutenant General Christison sent a staff officer, a lieutenant colonel, to present on the final plans to deal with extremists in western Java to Lord Mountbatten and Lord Alanbrooke, chief of the Imperial General Staff. In discussing the possibility of casualties, Mountbatten made a specific request that Indian troops be used, saying that he did not want to see British wives widowed so long after the war's official end. The lieutenant colonel, greatly angered and offended by this, responded, "Sir, do you really think it is different if Mrs Poop Singh is made a widow?"[207]

As of February 1946, large-scale violence had lessened significantly, but sniping, looting, and murder continued. AFNEI had been forced to redeploy forces in and around Java as the Dutch began to arrive to take over;[208] the 23rd Indian Division had consolidated outside Batavia and was attempting to control lines of communications into the interior and the key towns of Bandoeng and Buitenzorg.[209] There was some serious fighting in mid-March, but units of the 23rd Indian Division, notably the 1st Patialas (Indian State Forces), were able to control the situation.[210] Over the next months, British and Indian troops pulled back to Batavia as more and more Dutch troops came in to take over their positions. The 50th Indian Tank Brigade and the 161st Indian Infantry Brigade (5th Indian Division) remained in Batavia and the 5th Parachute Brigade held Semarang in central Java until the Dutch relieved them in the second half of February. Two brigades from the 5th Indian Division stayed in Surabaya until April. British and Indian forces did not control much outside the coastal enclaves in central and eastern Java, but in western Java they did control portions of the interior. Throughout this period, and until the last British and Indian troops withdrew, they continued to undertake the withdrawal of Japanese soldiers, sailors, and airmen, as well as the rescue of Allied civilian and military internees.[211]

The year 1946 also brought major changes in the command structure. On 1 February, Christison was sent home to the United Kingdom to take up Northern Command; he was replaced first by Lt. Gen. Sir Montagu Stopford as GOC ALFNEI, and later, in April, by the recently promoted Mansergh, from the 5th Indian Division. Mountbatten was replaced on 1 June as commander of SEAC by Stopford, who was made acting commander of ALFSEA.[212] By summer 1946, the 23rd Indian Division was the last formation left in Java. The division was withdrawn in four stages, throughout October and November, coinciding with the departure of the 26th Indian Division from Sumatra (see below). With the final Indian divisions evacuated from the NEI, both SEAC and ALFSAE ceased to exist as of midnight 30 November 1946.[213] Thus, the final elements and connection to the Burma campaign came to end.

Final counts for British and Indian units show approximately six hundred killed, fourteen hundred wounded, and 320 missing during the thirteen months of operations in Java.[214] The number of missing is the total from both the 23rd and the 5th Indian divisions, and records indicate that some of these soldiers were deserters. Attempts by Indonesian nationalists to subvert the authority of the Indian and British commanders, and to entice Muslim soldiers to desert to their cause, have been documented. Colonel Condon, writing the 13th Frontier Force Rifles's regimental history, refers to this: discussing the role of the 8/13th FFRifles, working in and around Buitenzorg, in Java, under the command of the 36th Indian Infantry Brigade (Independent), he writes that

> service in Java, coming as it did after a World War when all were hoping for release, put a very great strain on discipline and *esprit de corps*. Indeed, it would be difficult to find a situation containing more temptations to a soldier or a role calling for the use of more tact, patience and self-control. It is only fair to record that the conduct of the 8th Battalion was such that it was held up as an example to other troops in Java. General Stopford, in a letter . . . circulated to all units on 6th March [1946] . . . [said] that the checking of the increase in desertion and preventable disease was a matter of unit discipline and *esprit de corps*.[215]

The 26th Indian Division Moves to Sumatra

At the same time as operations moved into both FIC and Java, SEAC earmarked the 26th Indian Division to proceed to the NEI island Sumatra,[216] and disarm the Japanese 25th Army and rescue the various POWs and civilian internees.[217] As with the other occupation duties, the division was also to maintain law and order. As in Java, the British intended to limit their presence to specific areas of the island and not seek to administer the whole island. Three chief towns were chosen as the main focus for the 26th Division. Medan in the north would serve as the focus for the division HQ and the 4th and Royal Artillery brigades. The town of Padang on the south east coast would have a composite brigade of two battalions, while the southern town of Palembang would have the 71st Brigade.[218] SEAC had a clearer picture of the number of POWs and civilian internees, as well as the potential numbers of armed Indonesians. The number of armed Indonesian nationalists and TKR was estimated between fifteen thousand and twenty thousand men.[219] Motorized "all arms columns" were created as mobile reserves in case violence erupted or if the Japanese troops caused issues. In the end, while there were tensions and fighting on Sumatra, the level of violence was not as high as it was on Java.

By early October 1945, the first elements of the 26th Division started to arrive on Sumatra, under the command of Maj. Gen. H. M. Chambers.[220] Upon arrival, the various units and formations found that there were much civil unrest and armed youths. At first, the Indonesians did not take much notice of the Indian and British soldiers. As with Java, a political vacuum had been created. The nationalists on Sumatra were clearly linked with the nationalist movement on Java. There was an additional issue for the 26th Division: there were racial divides on the island, between Chinese and Ambonese on one side and the Indonesians on the other. Throughout the rest of the months of 1945, political and ethnic tensions were rising; however, clashes between the 26th Division and armed militia were minimal. One veteran from the 2/13th FFRifles stated: "The first few weeks the Sumatrans gave no trouble. Nor did they seek or welcome any contacts with us. . . . It gave one an uncomfortable feeling. . . . In the countryside people would melt away but there was a sense of being watched all the time."[221] Sniping was a distraction at times, but no serious injuries occurred. The division carried out major efforts to collect and evacuate POWs and civilian internees and the disarming of the Japanese soldiers. The first major escalation in violence occurred in Padang, when the brigade major of the 71st Indian Brigade and a female Red Cross worker were kidnapped and killed. British and Indian troops attacked the two villages where the bodies were found. Various armed members of the villages were killed and captured,[222] and curfew was imposed after another serious incident. Curfew was a serious matter. The commanding officer of the 1st Lincolns stated: "In future, during the hours of curfew, any local who, acting in a suspicious manner, fails to halt on being challenged by a sentry or patrols or who runs away on being approached, will be shot."[223] These draconian actions appeared to work, as there were no more violent attacks in the Padang for the next two months.[224]

Tense moments occurred in February 1946, in Palembang. The Dutch had landed troops on an offshore island, Bangka. The Indonesian nationalists viewed this as a precursor to future Dutch landings on Sumatra itself. Three Royal Navy officers were attacked and killed and wounded on 25 February. Tensions increased, and by mid-March, elements of the 71st Brigade in Padang were flown to Palembang to reinforce. A British battalion, the 1st Lincolns, had a company attacked by armed Indonesians on 30 March. A fierce battle erupted and the COY was able to extricate itself, with casualties. Things would quiet down in Palembang, after the fighting on 30 February; however, things had become more tense and violent in Medan and Padang, as the Indonesian nationalists and the TKR became better organized in March.[225]

In both Medan and Padang, the extremists sniped and ambushed British and Indian forces at times in February. The 26th Division responded with battalion- and brigade-sized sweeping operations in and around the two towns. The first use of British/Indian artillery occurred on 12 February in support of the 2/7th Rajputs outside Medan.[226] A reconnaissance patrol from the C Coy, 2/13th FFRifles, was attacked on 9 March, and a major and two jawans were killed.[227] In the minds of the British and Indian troops, the Indonesian forces "became the enemy and we had a guerilla war on our hands."[228] The Japanese troops provided some troops for static duties as British/Indian mobile columns swept areas. The extremists were not as much of a threat as they were on Java. Things remained tense throughout the summer months in the three locations as more and more Japanese were rounded up and returned home to Japan. There was constant patrolling and countersniping activities against extremists, who wished to fight.[229] Unlike in Java, there was more success in British cooperation with moderate Indonesian nationalists. Various military commanders worked with local leadership in attempts to lessen tensions and carry out the duties earmarked by SEAC.[230]

Tensions rose in September as more and more Dutch started to return to Sumatra and took over the responsibility for law and order from the 26th Division. Any threats of violence were met fiercely by the 26th Division, and casualties were light for the British and Indian units.[231] By the end of November 1946, the 26th Division had handed over control to the Dutch forces in Medan, Palembang, and Padang. In the end, more than sixty-eight thousand Japanese surrendered and were returned home; more than thirteen thousand POWs and civilians were liberated, while the violence cost the division fifty-five KIA and 303 WIA.[232]

Occupation Duties in Japan

The deployment of the 268th Indian Brigade as part of the larger Allied occupation force in Japan is a fitting end to this story for a few reasons.

The larger force was to be named the British Commonwealth Occupation Force (BCOF).[233] The elements from the Burma campaign were part of the BRINDIV (British-Indian Japan). The division was made up of the 268th Indian Infantry Brigade and the British 5th Infantry Brigade, from the 2nd British Division, as well as the 7th Light Cavalry, from recent Burma fame. The commander was Maj. Gen. D. T. "Punch" Cowan. As noted previously, he had commanded the 17th Indian Division since the withdrawal from Rangoon in 1942 and had led the division during the decisive battles of the campaign in 1945 on the road to Rangoon. The 268th Indian Brigade[234] had fought well in 1945 and would be commanded by an Indian commissioned officer, Brig. K. S. Thimayya,[235] highlighting how far the reforms of the XIV and larger Indian Army had come since 1919 and the defeats of 1942. This final peaceful mission was a fitting testimony to the XIV Army and the larger Indian Army and the payback it had inflicted upon the IJA in Burma in 1945. The return of the 268th Indian Infantry Brigade Group in the summer of 1947 also signaled the end of the XIV Army's presence in the post-1945 occupation duties.

As with the deployments throughout SEAC, the political wrangling to deploy the 268th Brigade was equally confusing and delayed.[236] After a series of meetings in Washington, DC, in late 1945, it was agreed that the British Commonwealth would provide an occupation force that would serve under the command of the Gen. Douglas MacArthur, as Supreme Commander for the Allied Powers (SCAP). The overall mission for both SCAP and the BCOF was fairly straightforward:

> The ultimate objective of the United Nations with respect to Japan is to foster conditions which will see the greatest possible assurance that Japan will not again become a menace to the peace and security of the world and will permit her eventual admission as a responsible and peaceful member of the family of nations. . . . Certain measures considered to be essential for the achievement of this objective have been set: . . . abolition of militarism and ultra-nationalism in all their forms; the disarmament and demilitarization of Japan, with continuing control over Japan's capacity to make war; the strengthening of democratic tendencies and processes in governmental economic and social institutions; and the encouragement and support of liberal tendencies in Japan.[237]

The US occupation included two armies, initially the 6th and the 8th. BCOF was to supplement the effort, hence the long delay in the deployment of the force until early 1946. Some of the delay was due to the need to clarify where the BCOF would serve. The US State Department and SCAP opposed the idea of "national zones" of occupation, as this would cause tensions with the Soviets and Chinese. The occupation of Japan was going to be led by the United States and policy would be directed by Washington, DC. The specific directives for the BCOF were worked out and clarified:

> BCOF will constitute a component of occupation forces in Japan under the command of the Supreme Command for the Allied Powers . . . military control of the Hiroshima Prefecture. These areas do not constitute a National Zone. . . . General Officer Commanding, BCOF will have the right to direct access to the Supreme Commander for the Allied Powers on matters of policy affecting the operational capabilities of the Force.[238]

The first elements of the BRINDIV were to start arriving by early March 1946. The BCOF would serve under the command of the US 8th Army and slowly replace the USA 1st Corps in the Hiroshima area. As with the overall SCAP mission, the BCOF mission was the same. They were to safeguard Allied installations, take military control of Japanese installations, and demilitarize the Japanese in their area of responsibility.[239]

As the units and formations began to organize for their deployment, General Auchinleck visited the 268th Infantry Brigade and the 7th Light Cavalry in India. He specifically stated in a speech on parade,

> I am very glad that you are going to Japan to represent the Indian Army there. The Indian Army did much to bring about the defeat of the Japanese and all the world knows how well it fought in Assam and Burma. . . . Your Commander is the first Indian Officer to command a brigade in war[240] and I have much pleasure in presenting this flag to him and I know you will guard it well.[241]

The BCOF and in particular BRINDIV moved troops and stores by air and sea. Over the coming months, the division took over from the USA 24th Infantry Division. By June, the division was able to report that all was settled in terms of accommodation and HQs had been set up. The BCOF and BRINDIV set out to carry out their duties within SCAP's remit.

Throughout the coming months the BCOF and BRINDIV carried out their duties with professionalism.[242] At the end of 1946, Brigadier Thimayya was to hand over command and return to India to take up another high-level appointment.[243] In early January 1947, Brig. S. M. Shirnagesh took over command of the 268th Brigade. The role of the 268th Brigade was expanded and was renamed as a brigade group due to the withdrawal of the British 5th Brigade for Malaya. In early March, BRINDIV was disbanded and the 268th Brigade Group took over the previous responsibilities of BRINDIV. It was at this juncture that Major General Cowan also departed. With Indian and Pakistan independence on the horizon, decisions were made to start to withdraw the 268th Indian Brigade Group. By October 1947, the various units of the 268th Indian Brigade had returned to either India or Pakistan, both newly independent states. Thus, the final connection to the old victorious XIV Army hence came to an end.[244]

Conclusion

The XIV Army and GHQ India were asked to carry out occupation duties throughout Asia at the end of the Second World War in a major political vacuum that would take time to organize and maneuver. The Japanese military needed to be disarmed. Some of these operations in Burma, Malaya, Singapore, Siam, and Japan were quiet and fairly peaceful. Some of the formations from the quiet sectors were shifted to the NEI to deal with the violence and insurrection. In both FIC and the NEI, British and Indian army units were sent into difficult political situations and left to contend with a muddled and shifting strategy. Despite this, as the 23rd Indian divisional history stated: "We came to Java as soldiers, as soldiers we went away, and we cherished the thought that in performing our duty with steadfast courage and disciplined restraint we had played our part in averting what was so nearly a great human tragedy and had, perhaps, helped bring peace to a troubled land."[245] Units and individual officers provided various perspectives in their assessments, including statements such as "it was a relief when it became known that the sojourn was nearing an end. The role of the British/Indian forces had been a distasteful one."[246] One veteran of the campaign later recalled: "I believe that in 1945 and 1946 through much of South-East Asia the old Indian Army did a difficult job with humanity and success."[247] Lieutenant Colonel Bristow wrote that "the loss of life in Java seemed unnecessary and was deeply deplored. Veterans and heroes of Eritrea, the Western Desert, Imphal and Burma were killed in a futile conflict which was forced on us."[248]

The 5th, 23rd, 20th, and 26th Indian divisions' violent experiences in FIC and the NEI highlighted the complexity that underlies even the apparently simplest military engagement. These postwar deployments resoundingly contradict the common assertion that the Second World War was not politically complex. HMG's government was never quite clear about what role the British and the Indian armies should play in supporting their European allies in the restoration of their former colonies. The uneven and continually evolving strategy within SEAC also highlights some of the issues that had arisen between India Command and SEAC. While both the XIV and the XII armies fell under the command of SEAC, their formations were predominantly Indian. It was one thing to have forces working in former British colonies, such as Burma and Malaya—which Indian Army units did. Their roles in FIC and the NEI, on the other hand, created a major political issue in India.[249]

The lack of clear strategy, and contradictory advice from both SEAC and London, left Indian Army and SEAC commanders to develop planning and strategy on their own, from the perspective of the unit on the ground. While this resulted in some mistakes, particularly in the early days, Indian Army commanders and troops were able to recover, regain the initiative to secure key areas, and repatriate thousands of Allied POWs and civilians as well as disarm hundreds of thousands Japanese soldiers, airmen, and sailors. The divisional and corps staffs set out to carry out their mission, at first with minimal support; along strict military lines, they did a professional job. The officers, VCOs, NCOs, and soldiers of the 5th, 20th, 23rd, and 26th Indian divisions carried out this difficult mission with the same level of professionalism and ability as they had shown in Burma from 1943 to the end of the war. Many Burma veterans had remained with the divisions and applied their experiences and knowledge to the campaigns in FIC and the NEI. Many of the officers, VCOs, NCOs, and jawans considered themselves professional soldiers and recent victorious veterans of Burma, and their job was to carry out the orders of their commanders professionally—even when lack of strategy and political awareness at the highest levels left them in the middle of a series of difficult political and combat situations.

The concluding remarks in the 5th Indian divisional history on the fighting in the NEI state:

> To the individual Indian soldier this task must have presented serious problems. Their propagandists at home missed no opportunity of comparing the duties that had to be carried out in Indonesia with what they, in India, were fighting against in their efforts to rid India of British occupation. . . . The soldiers had been away for years and were longing to return home. Yet, despite these important facts, they carried out their duty to their regiments, their officers and their Commander in the loyal, patient and self-sacrificing way so characteristic of the Indian soldier.[250]

The war in Asia for the XIV Army was finally over.

Conclusion
The Last of Its Kind

The XIV Army's campaign in 1945 has been analyzed and described in many ways. It demonstrated Slim's inspired leadership, flexible and innovative planning by his staff, improvisatory logistics that rapidly overcame every obstacle that arose. It showed the formidable skills Slim's army had developed and honed since the dark days of 1943. The XIV Army was one of the great fighting forces of the war—indeed, of the twentieth century. But it was something else as well. A British officer who had served with the Indian Army in Burma, looking back three decades later, told an inquiring historian with admiration in his voice that he had served with "the last great mercenary army." What he meant was that the Indian Army of the British Raj was the last in a line of polyglot, multiethnic professional armies created by the demands of empire. The legions and auxiliaries of imperial Rome were such forces, as were the armies of early modern Europe's great powers—like the Army of Flanders that sustained Spanish Hapsburg power in the Low Countries for several generations. But the intellectual currents of the eighteenth century, then the French Revolution and the rise of the nation-state and its military embodiment, the "nation in arms," changed armies. To soldier for any country but your own now became suspect. "Mercenary" ceased to be a job description and became a value judgment. A few such forces lingered on, like France's Foreign Legion, but the citizen soldier became the norm, the "hireling" an object of scorn.[1] In India, however, an older form of soldiering lived on. The East India Company built its armies on an amalgam of European military and administrative technique and Mughal practices and that fusion created the army that conquered India for the merchants of Leadenhall Street and then, given mobility by the company's navy and the Royal Navy, projected British power everywhere from Egypt to China. The Crown Raj inherited this army in 1858 and, although tweaked, it remained until 1947 what the company had created—polyglot, multiethnic, paid professionals.

World War I and its aftermath began to slowly, gingerly, change the Indian Army. Military modernity required different skills and a different type of recruit. Political concessions to Indian nationalism required a military counterpart: Indian officers. World War II turned a cautious embrace of change in a torrent of rapid adaptation. By 1945 the Indian Army was a modern force, in its equipment, doctrine, tactics. Now of its forty-three thousand officers, fifteen thousand were Indians. Its commander-in-chief said, as the XIV Army wrapped up its brilliant campaign, that every one of those Indian officers "worth his salt" was a nationalist. The campaign of 1945 was the final act for the last of the old-style imperial armies, something John Masters (4th Gurkha Rifles) memorialized as he remembered "Sea or Bust" jumping off: "this was the old Indian Army, going down to the attack, for the last time in history, exactly two hundred years after the Honourable East India Company had enlisted its first ten sepoys on the Coromandel Coast."[2] Masters saw in that moment the coming end of empire. The XIV Army's victory was, ironically, the prelude to the end not only of the "last great mercenary army" but of the empire it had served so well. Perhaps that is why Winston Churchill showed so little interest in it.

Notes

1. Field-Marshal Viscount William Slim, *Defeat into Victory* (London: Cassell, 1956), 369.

2. Max Hastings, *Nemesis: The Battle for Japan, 1944–45* (London: Harper, 2007) points out in his usual forceful style how marginal XIV Army's campaign was to Japan's defeat. Chris Bayly and Tim Harper in *Forgotten Armies: The Fall of British Asia, 1941–45* (London: Allen Lane, 2004) painted, brilliantly, the big picture into which XIV Army's story must be fitted.

Introduction

1. The best brief account of the retreat in 1942 from Burma is Alan Warren, *Burma 1942: The Road from Rangoon to Mandalay* (London: Continuum, 2011).

2. Maj. Gen. J. G. Smyth, VC. Smyth won his VC on the Somme but in late 1941 he was seriously ill. Anxious to take the division he had commanded since its formation into action he persuaded army doctors first in India, then in Burma, to certify him fit. Perhaps the VC weighed a bit too heavily with the doctors.

3. The best one-volume treatment of the war in Burma as a whole is Louis Allen, *Burma: The Longest War, 1941–1945* (London: Dent, 1984).

4. This battle is well covered in Allen, 150–191.

5. The whole Stilwell enterprise put a heavy burden on the Raj machine, which had to house, feed, and support Stilwell's units, find armies of laborers to build airfields for the American airlift to China, and yet more follow American road engineers and road-building machinery into Burma. This was a huge commitment for a governmental machine never designed for total war but already committed to mobilizing India for one. See appendix 1 to this chapter for a summary of this herculean effort.

6. Wingate chose the "chinthe," the mythological beast that guards Burmese temples, as the symbol of his 77th Indian Infantry Brigade. Turned by war correspondents into "chindit," it became the name by which Wingate's troops would be known to history. See appendix 2 to this chapter.

7. The rebuilding of the Indian Army in 1943 and after is covered in detail in the

next chapter. The key texts are Daniel Marston, *The Phoenix from the Ashes: The Indian Army in the Burma Campaign* (Westport, CT: Praeger, 2003); and Alan Jeffreys, *Approach to Battle: Training the India Army during the Second World War* (Solihull, UK: Helion, 2017).

8. Mutaguchi had a second objective beyond Imphal—the Raj itself. At the beginning of the war, Subhas Chandra Bose, a Bengali radical and sometime rival of Gandhi and Nehru, had escaped house arrest in India and made his way to Berlin. The Germans were uninterested in his plan for an invasion of India. They shipped him by U-boat to the Japanese, who were happy to let him form a government in exile—a propaganda asset for them. Bose's "Free India" government had its own army—the Indian National Army, made up of Indian Army POWs and recruits from the large Indian population of Malaya. Bose convinced Mutaguchi that if he unfurled his banner on Indian soil, the Indian Army would desert to him en masse, leading to the collapse of the Raj. This fantasy took root in Mutaguchi's mind and affected his planning for the Imphal-Kohima battle.

9. It is interesting to note that Slim, himself a Gurkha Rifles officer, had, in the 4th Corps, numerous Gurkha officers as key subordinates: Punch Cowan came from the same regiment, the 6th Gurkhas, as Slim. Gracey and Scoones were Gurkha Rifles officers and Ouvry Roberts, a British Army sapper, had been Scoones's deputy as director of military operations and intelligence at Indian Army headquarters in 1939–1941 before joining Slim's 10th Indian Infantry Division Staff in Iraq. From there he rejoined Scoones at the 4th Corps as Brigadier General Staff (in effect Corps chief of staff) before taking over the 23rd Indian Infantry Division from Savory. He might be considered Gurkha Rifles by adoption. Slim fought the great battle with a group of subordinate commanders from the same tightly knit military clan, surely an important asset.

10. Starting with the restructuring of the Indian Army following the Mutiny of 1857, every Indian brigade normally included a British battalion—a safeguard for sepoy loyalty and an example to them, it was thought, of good soldiering. This rule began to collapse as the Indian Army steadily expanded after 1940 while the British began to experience manpower constraints, which, after 1943, became a manpower crisis. The reinforcement pipeline was producing only a trickle by 1944. The only XIV Army division, at the opening of the Imphal battle, that had its full complement of British battalions was Gracey's 20th Indian, and many of those units were understrength. The situation got steadily worse thereafter. The fact that this development was inevitable did not stop the prime minister from complaining about it.

11. A summary of the Imphal-Kohima battle is Raymond Callahan, *Triumph at Imphal-Kohima: How the Indian Army Finally Stopped the Japanese Juggernaut* (Lawrence: University Press of Kansas, 2017).

12. Martin Gilbert and Larry Arnn, eds., *The Churchill Documents*, vol. 20, *Normandy and Beyond May–December 1944* (Hillsdale, MI: Hillsdale College Press, 2018), 731. Churchill made this remark at a meeting of the War Cabinet's Defence Committee on 6 July 1944.

13. Gilbert and Arnn, 731. This remark was made at the same meeting. See appendix 3 to this chapter for further discussion of this point.

14. Simultaneously planners at SEAC headquarters at Kandy in Ceylon (Sri Lanka) were working out their latest amphibious design—Dracula. This would be a seaborne assault on Rangoon, which had replaced northern Sumatra as a way station on the way to Singapore. Unlike most SEAC amphibious plans, a version of this one would be carried out—but as an auxiliary to the XIV Army's overland drive.

15. The story of India's mobilization is a subject only now attracting scholarly attention. Excellent surveys are Yasmins Khan, *The Raj at War: A People's History of India's Second World War* (London: Bodley Head, 2015); and Srinath Raghavan's *India's War: The Making of Modern South Asia, 1939–1945* (London: Allan Lane, 2016). Ashley Jackson's *The British Empire and the Second World War* (London: Hambledon, 2006), chap. 12, provides a succinct introduction.

16. In March 1944, US Army railroad operating units took over substantial control of part of the Bengal and Assam railway in the interests of larger deliveries to both Stilwell's Chinese-American combat units and his road-builders. The Americans had long been dissatisfied with the rate at which supplies reached them and had been pressing this measure for some time. Eventually the balance of power in the alliance allowed the Americans to prevail. The carrying capacity of the portion of the railroad they took over did increase—given the number of specialized personnel and amount of equipment (unavailable in India) they deployed, this is not very surprising. The various American enterprises in far Northeast Assam were, of course, part of the logistic problem—they consumed as much as the XIV Army.

17. The only study to tackle the logistic history of the XIV Army's campaigns is Graham Dunlop, *Military Economics, Culture and Logistics in the Burma Campaign, 1942–1945* (London: Routledge, 2009). It is excellent and can be supplemented by the detailed appendices on "administration" (i.e., logistics) in volumes 2–4 of the official history: S. W. Kirby et al., *The War against Japan* (London: Her Majesty's Stationery Office, 1957–1969). The official history is not sprightly reading but there is a huge amount of information, clearly conveyed. Neither Dunlop nor the official historians tackled the larger Indian background covered in the books cited in note 15 in this chapter. Slim's logistics manager, Maj. Gen. Arthur ("Alf") Snelling, wrote a short but very informative article, "Notes on Some Administrative Aspects of the Campaign of the Fourteenth Army, 1943–44," which appeared in *Army Quarterly* 80 (April–July 1965): 176–197.

18. Wingate and the Chindits have produced an impressive library of writing. There is a discussion of it in Raymond Callahan, *Triumph at Imphal-Kohima: How the Indian Army Finally Stopped the Japanese Juggernaut* (Lawrence: University Press of Kansas, 2017), 145–149. The best guide to the tangled arguments about the Chindit campaign in 1944—Operation Thursday—is Shelford Bidwell, *The Chindit War: Stilwell, Wingate, and the Campaign in Burma* (New York: Macmillan, 1980). The Indian official history's verdict can be found in Bisheshwar Prasad, ed., *The Reconquest of Burma*, vol. 1 (Calcutta: Orient Longmans, 1958), 402. In an interesting, generally favorable, revisionist account of Wingate—Simon Anglim, *Orde Wingate and the British*

Army, 1922–1944 (London: Pickering & Chatto, 2010)—the author stops short of analyzing the Chindit operations of 1944.

19. Martin Gilbert and Larry P. Arnn, eds., *The Churchill Documents*, vol. 20, *Normandy and Beyond May-December 1944* (Hillsdale, MI: Hillsdale College Press, 2018). Cited hereafter as "CP20."

20. Churchill to Hollis, 7 May 1944, CP20, p. 106.

21. Chiefs of Staff Committee Minutes, 6 July 1944, CP20, p. 731.

22. War Cabinet Minutes, 8 August 1944, CP20, p. 1012. It would appear that no one had briefed him on the actual climate and terrain in Burma's dry belt, where XIV Army would fight in 1944–1945. It is interesting that when writing his memoirs after the war he complained to his "Syndicate" of assistants that there had been inadequate knowledge in London about Malayan weather in 1941, especially the impact of the northeast monsoon.

23. Churchill to Smuts, 3 December 1944, CP20, p. 2002. Once again the prime minister's ignorance of the geography and climate of north Burma is on display. He was served by a highly competent staff. Did no one correct his misunderstanding? Of course no one in 1940–1941 corrected his belief that Singapore was a true fortress. Perhaps they understood that on some issues it was best not to argue.

24. When Capital did come to his notice, Churchill dismissed it as "ruinous and costly." He still wanted an amphibious operation for which the resources were simply not available. Churchill to Ismay, 11 September 1944, CP20, p. 1329. The operation he wanted was Dracula, a major amphibious assault on Rangoon before the 1945 monsoon, which, he felt, allow the shutting down of the XIV Army's campaign. Confusingly, although this operation was dropped for lack of resources, the name was resurrected for the smaller operation mounted in May 1945 to ensure that if the XIV Army's drive on Rangoon was balked by the monsoon, as turned out to be the case, the port would still be taken since it was the only solution to supplying the XIV Army through the monsoon.

25. Casey to Churchill, 20 May 1944, CP20, p. 522. Churchill circulated Casey's letter to the War Cabinet.

26. Chiefs of Staff Committee Minutes, 8 August 1944, CP20, p. 1021.

27. Anderson to Churchill, 6 September 1944, CP20, p. 1291. Anderson estimated that the cost of the bonuses involved would be about one hundred million pounds—a very large sum for a bankrupt country.

1. A Professional Force: The XIV Army at the End of 1944

1. See Alan Jeffreys, *Approach To Battle: Training The Indian Army During The Second World War* (Solihull, UK: Helion, 2017), in particular chapter 7, "Training in India at the End of the Second World War," which highlights the level of sophistication of training within the Indian Army by the end of 1944.

2. The performance of the Indian divisions in the North African campaign remains largely unexamined. A comparative analysis with other Commonwealth forces is needed.

3. This image of the Indian Army in Indian society had significant political weight, as even members of the Indian National Congress came to recognize.

4. Raymond Callahan, *Churchill and His Generals* (Lawrence: University Press of Kansas, 2007), 211 and 239. See also Callahan, "Were the Sepoy Generals Any Good? A Re-Appraisal of the British-Indian Army's High-Command in the Second World War," in *War and Society in Colonial India*, ed. Kaushik Roy (New Delhi: Oxford University Press, 2006).

5. S. L. Menezes, *Fidelity & Honour: The Indian Army from the Seventeenth to the Twenty-First Century* (New Delhi: Viking, 1993), 370.

6. Questions were raised in certain quarters about whether the Indian Army needed to be expanded. Prime Minister Winston Churchill in particular denigrated the efforts of the Indian Army throughout the war, even after it had undertaken significant reforms, conclusively defeated the Imperial Japanese Army, and played an important supporting role in the successful East African, North African, and Italian campaigns. See Raymond Callahan's work in *Churchill and His Generals* for a detailed discussion of the tensions between Churchill and his Indian Army commanders, chiefly Gens. Claude Auchinleck and William Slim.

7. See Daniel Marston, *The Indian Army and the End of the Raj* (Cambridge: Cambridge University Press, 2014), for a much more in-depth discussion of martial races and recruitment.

8. Tan Tai Yong, *The Garrison State: Military, Government and Society in Colonial Punjab, 1849–1947* (New Delhi: Sage, 2005), 290–291.

9. Claude Auchinleck to Leo Amery 17/3/1941, Auchinleck Papers, University of Manchester.

10. When he was commander-in-chief, Middle East, the Assam, Bihar, Chamar, and Afridi regiments were raised.

11. Auchinleck to Amery 17/3/1941, Auchinleck Papers, University of Manchester.

12. Amery stated that he was sad to lose him due to his great work for the Indian war effort and his point of view on certain issues relevant to the army. Amery to Auchinleck 25/6/1941, Auchinleck Papers, University of Manchester.

13. There were other infantry units besides the Sikh Light Infantry and the Madras Regiment raised from the new classes: four battalions of the Bihar Regiment, of which the 1st Battalion saw active service in Burma; three battalions of the Assam Regiment, of which the 1st Battalion saw service in Burma; five battalions of the Mahar Regiment, of which none saw active service; four battalions of the Ajmer Regiment; and two battalions of the Chamar Regiment, of which one served in Burma. John Gaylor, *Sons of John Company* (Tunbridge Wells, UK: Spellmount, 1992), 207–213. None of these units saw active service until 1944 and 1945; prior to this they were all held in reserve.

14. 1/2/42 L/WS/1/456 Class Composition of the Army in India, Oriental and India Office Collection, British Library (hereafter abbreviated as OIOC, BL).

15. 3/11/42 L/WS/1//968 42–44 Expansion, OIOC, BL.

16. 3/11/42 L/WS/968 OIOC, BL.

17. Interview with Major Barton, Madras Regimental Centre and 4/3rd Madras, 5/7/2000.

18. 17/2/43L/WS/1/136 OIOC, BL.

19. 21/7/43L/WS/1/136 OIOC, BL.

20. Even Leo Amery stated, in a letter to Linlithgow on 27 August 1942, the following point: "Congress has nothing in common with the fighting races of India of whom well over a million have volunteered for the Army during the present war." Nicholas Mansergh, ed., *The Transfer of Power, 1942–1947*, 12 vols. (London: HMSO, 1970–1983), vol. 2, 637, p. 830; hereafter abbreviated as *TOP* with the volume number.

21. Auchinleck to Wavell, "Size and Composition of the India Army," 2/8/43, Auchinleck Papers, University of Manchester.

22. Auchinleck to Wavell 2/8/43, Auchinleck Papers, University of Manchester.

23. L/WS/1/136 No 1175/1/LB, November 1943, OIOC, BL.

24. This was to prove crucially important later, when British Army units in the Burma campaign in 1945 were being forced to withdraw due to lack of reinforcements and their places were being filled by Indian units.

25. Persia (Iran) and Iraq Force. They were Indian and British units and formations carrying out line of communication duties to supply Russia from the Persian Gulf and occupation duties.

26. L/WS/1/707 Indian Army Morale, OIOC, BL.

27. Interview with Major Delafield, 2/13th FFRifles, 23/1/2001.

28. Army Reorganization Committee (Wilcox Report) Part II, L/WS/1/1030 OIOC, BL.

29. Wilcox Report, Part II, L/WS/1/1030 OIOC, BL.

30. Interviews with officers of the 1st Punjab, Baluch, FFR, FFRifles, and Probyn's.

31. In cavalry units, the establishment was doubled. The Emergency British and Indian Commissioned Officers (ECOS and EICOs) would command troops. In infantry battalions the numbers also doubled; extra officers were not platoon leaders but extra company officers. VCOs remained in all units.

32. Bishenwar Prasad, *Official History of the Indian Armed Forces in the Second World War Expansion of the Armed Forces and Defence Organisation* (New Delhi: Orient Longmans, 1956), 182; and Gautum Sharma, *Nationalisation of the Indian Army* (New Delhi: Allied, 1996), 194.

33. There were 274 Hindus, 138 Muslims, seventy-five Sikhs, and seventy others. Sharma, *Nationalisation*, 174.

34. A series of letters in late 1939 and early 1940. L/MIL/7/19157 Emergency Commissions for Indians OIOC, BL.

35. Auchinleck took a keen interest during the prewar years in the careers of some of the ICOs. He persuaded his Indian friends to have their sons join up as officers, notably in two instances. Major General D. K. Palit's father served with Auchinleck as the Indian medical officer of the 1/1st Punjab. Auchinleck was present at the selection board for D. K. Palit in the 1930s. He sat in the back of the room. (Interview with Major General Palit, 4/11/2000.) During the first years of the war he influenced

his old Munshi to have his son Ibrahim Quereshi join as an ECIO in the 1st Punjab Regiment. Interview with Brigadier Quereshi, 10/10/2000.

36. He was responding to Mr. Amery's questions regarding Indianization.

37. Auchinleck to Amery, 12/10/1940, L/MIL/7/19156, OIOC, BL.

38. Auchinleck to Amery, 12/10/1940, L/MIL/7/19156, OIOC, BL.

39. In the 4/12th FFR, Cap. S. H. J. F. Manekshaw was the commader of A Company with various British ECOs junior to him. He went on to win the MC (Military Cross) during the campaign. 1/29/1942 WO 172/932 War Diary NA. The 7/10th Baluch provides a further two examples; Captain Siri Kanth Korla, commander of C Company, was awarded the DSO during the campaign. The second-in-command of the 7/10th Baluch was an Anglo-Indian named Major Dunn. January 1942 WO 172/928 War Diary National Archives (NA).

40. The official order was published as File No. B/59865/AG-1 (6) of 3 August 1940.

41. L/MIL/7/19156 OIOC, BL.

42. The issues of the power of punishment of British personnel would not be resolved until early 1943. See Marston, *Indian Army and the End of the Raj* for more detail.

43. 21 November 1940.

44. Philip Warner, *Auchinleck: The Lonely Soldier* (London: Buchan & Enright, 1981), 70. See also letters of Amery to Linlithgow, 4/12/42, *TOP*, 3:251, and *TOP*, 3:351.

45. Army Instruction (India) No. 76 of 1941 L/MIL/17/5/531 OIOC, BL.

46. Auchinleck to Amery 17/3/1941, Auchinleck Papers, University of Manchester.

47. In 1940 it was 25 to 75 percent. By 1941 it had risen to 29 to 71 percent. Sharma, *Nationalisation*, 180.

48. There were some within the Indian Army as well as the British Government who did not want to see the numbers of British cadets dry up. Other senior Indian Army officers, such as Auchinleck, General Savory and Maj. Gen. Punch Cowan, supported dismantling the prewar Indianization model.

49. The one prejudice that all officers, British and Indian, did express was that they considered the class of soldier that they commanded, Pathan, PM, Dogra, Madrassi or Gurkha, and so on, to be the best soldiers in the Indian Army.

50. As with prewar Indian cadets, these came from both martial and nonmartial race backgrounds. There tended not to be distinctions made regarding the Indian cadets' background. British cadets also represented many different classes of their society, including NCOs promoted to the officer ranks. Some British cadets felt that they would not have been welcomed by the prewar Indian Army officer class, as they came from working- or lower-middle-class backgrounds.

51. See Jeffreys, *Approach to Battle*, 199–203, for a description of the OTS in India.

52. There are a few reasons for this. First, the British Army, both at home and abroad, also needed to fill officer positions. A program was begun to recruit NCOs from British battalions in India, but this was a failure and was admitted as such by the War Office. Another effort was launched to attract "white" cadets from the

Commonwealth, but demand in their home countries limited these as well. Americans were also sought from the American Field Service Corps. These efforts netted twenty to thirty Americans. Interviews with three "American" Indian Army officers, Scott Gilmore, 4/8th Gurkhas, 22/7/1999; Pat Pattullo, 13th FFRifles, 26/7/1999; and Wendell Nichols, 18th Garwhal Rifles, 18/7/1999. It became clear that Indians were needed to fill the spots. L/WS/1/799 Provision of Officers for the Indian Army, OIOC, BL.

53. Prasad, *Expansion*, 181–182 and Sharma, *Nationalisation*, 183–184. However, by 1945 there were problems attracting enough Indian officers of "sufficient quality." (There were also problems attracting British officers of "sufficient quality.") This was an issue that Auchinleck felt was going to create major headaches unless confronted. Secret Telegram from Viceroy to Secretary of State for India, 21/12/44, L/WS/1/799 OIOC, BL.

54. Telegram from India Command to the War Office London, 1/5/1945, L/WS/1/707 OIOC, BL.

55. Some officers that Daniel Marston interviewed, from 1999 to 2007, noted that many of the participants mixed socially, at the OTS (Officer Training School) and during leave periods as well. Some British officers spent time at the family homes of Indian officers, according to interviews with officers. There would still be some teething issues such as pay equality and powers of punishment over British officers and soldiers. These issues would be worked out by 1944. See Marston, *Indian Army and the End of the Raj*, for a more detailed discussion.

56. L/MIL/17/5/2225 Lectures for Officers Joining the Indian Army, OIOC, BL.

57. L/MIL/17/5/2330 Notes for Guidance of Commanding Officers, Staff and Regimental Officers, OIOC, BL.

58. This was the same report that recommended the formation of the training divisions and tactical reforms for the Indian Army. It also included a section on morale, which dealt with officers. L/WS/1/1371 Report of the Infantry Committee, India 1–14 June 43 OIOC, BL.

59. The rest of the report considered other, more specific problems. One issue raised was that the war in Burma required younger and more fit COs to command battalions. The committee recommended, as a general rule, that commanding officers should be replaced after two years' service, as remaining with any one battalion for too long made them stale. In reality, most COs did not spend this long with their units. The officers were either promoted or sent to other units, and probably did not have the opportunity to become stale. L/WS/1/1371 OIOC, BL.

60. D. K. Palit, *Major General A. A. Rudra* (New Delhi: Reliance, 1997), 269–272.

61. Sharma, *Nationalisation*, 180.

62. Palit, *Rudra*, 274. One example of the continued persistence of discrimination that existed in some places also shows the efforts of some senior commanders to stamp it out. It involves Captain M. Nair, who had been serving with the 16th Light Cavalry. When he was posted to the XIV Army HQ as GSO 3, the staff was expecting an Irishman after hearing his name and his accent when he spoke on the phone. Captain Nair was not Irish but an Indian, and his arrival astonished the HQ, which promptly

sent him back to Delhi with excuses. Upon hearing of these, Auchinleck immediately signaled General Slim, who had not been present, to register his complaint about such behavior. Slim agreed with Auchinleck and immediately advised all units and formations within the XIV Army that this type of incident would not be tolerated again. Palit, *Rudra*, 279–84.

63. Auchinleck to Wavell, 19/12/1944, L/WS/1/924 Post-war Officering of the Indian Army.

64. *Indian Army List*, 1940.

65. *Indian Army List*, 1942.

66. *Indian Army List*, 1944.

67. L/WS/1/824 Staff College Quetta, OIOC, BL.

68. Auchinleck ordered a committee to report on the future size and needs of the Indian Army in early 1945. It was named the Army in India Reorganisation Committee (Wilcox Committee). The section dealing with the future size of the officer corps was largely drafted by Brig. Enoch Powell (Rt. Hon. Enoch Powell). It stated that, considering future needs and problems with recruitment of Indian officers, the Indian Army would need to recruit British officers for the next twenty-five years. The secretary of the Chiefs of Staff Committee, India, Phillip Mason, noted that Powell had based this conclusion on certain axioms, completely failing to recognize the human aspect and reality of the political situation in India in 1945. As Mason noted, "Auchinleck dismissed this chapter as altogether off the mark." Phillip Mason, *A Shaft of Sunlight* (London: Andre Deutsch, 1978), 197–198.

69. See "Future Provision of Officers for the Indian Armed Services," memo by secretary of state for India, 24/4/45, *TOP*, 5:407, for clear direction for the ending of entry of British officers and the further Indianization of the Army.

70. Wavell to Amery, 5/3/45, *TOP*, 5:297. See also 298, which highlights the initial debates, but also reinforces the notion that the army performed well during the war, even during the Quit India movement.

71. War Cabinet, 27/3/45, *TOP*, 5:346; see pages 775–776, for specific numbers. Although in a later memo, the time period was decreased to ten to fifteen years; see War Cabinet, 23/4/45, *TOP*, 5:405, p. 933.

72. John Masters, *The Road Past Mandalay: A Personal Narrative* (London: Michael Joseph, 1961), 312–313.

73. Slim, *Defeat into Victory* (London: Cassell, 1956), 386. The 11th Army Group Commander, Gen. Sir George Giffard, stated similar sentiments. See Timothy Moreman, *The Jungle, the Japanese and the British Commonwealth Armies at War, 1941–1945* (London: Frank Cass, 2005), 170. See Marston, *Phoenix from the Ashes*, for a wider discussion the tactical reform.

74. Quoted in Moreman, *Jungle*, 147 (battle instructions for jungle fighting, 4 September 1944, NA WO 203/2475).

75. This report was exhaustive and extremely well organized, with excellent analysis. This was done during the war, in a time without computers and other so-called modern conveniences. The authors recommend that readers who are interested should read the report in its entirety. It is two volumes, each of which is about two hundred

pages. It is an impressive document on learning and adaptation across multiple allied commands. See the Lethbridge Papers, LHCMA, Kings College London.

76. 19th and 25th Indian Divisions.

77. 5th, 7th, 20th, 23rd, and 26th Indian Divisions.

78. 17th Light Indian Division.

79. 36th British Division.

80. 2nd British Division.

81. Commander of the 11th Army Group.

82. By the end of 1943, the Indian Army had established a central system to handle training and reinforcements for the coming jungle war. The War Office in London as late as December 1943 still failed to recognize the need for specialized jungle warfare training. A committee had been created to deal with the needs of British troops being deployed to the East after the war in Europe had ended. It noted that the War Office stated the need for only three sorts of divisions: airborne, air assault, and amphibious. The committee noted that the listing of these formations "takes no account of the necessity for a normal infantry division or an infantry division organized properly with a view to jungle warfare." The committee attached a copy of the organization for an Australian Jungle Division. It also noted that 220 Mission was in India at the time and that their report would be published soon. 16/12/1943. L/WS/1/650 Committee on Organization for War against Japan, OIOC, BL.

83. Maj. Gen. J. S. Lethbridge Papers, 220 Military Mission Report, 2 vols., Liddell Hart Centre, Kings College, London.

84. Each stage of the report was dealt with by the War Office, London, comparing different training methods, organizational tables, and so on. March 1944 L/WS/1/650 OIOC, BL.

85. He accepted a demotion to brigadier to remain on the HQ staff.

86. A letter from GHQ India emphasized that the report by 220 Military Mission focused on the need for standardization as well as on recent operations. 18/4/1944 GHQ India to War Office, L/WS/1/616 Army in India Divisional Organization, OIOC, BL.

87. Including Auchinleck, Giffard, and Slim.

88. This was held during the Imphal battles.

89. Minutes of Meeting, 26–27/5/1944, L/WS/1/650 OIOC, BL.

90. Some divisions fighting in 1944 still did not have a divisional HQ battalion attached.

91. The 2nd British Division did not have one due to lack of British reinforcements in Burma.

92. The 2nd Manchester Regiment was a machine gun battalion of four companies. One company would be attached to each brigade and support them in defense and offense. For a full account of their actions, see R. King-Clark, *The Battle for Kohima, 1944: The Narrative of the 2nd Battalion—the Manchester Regiment* (Cheshire: Fleur de Lys, 1995).

93. The 26th Indian Division did not have a MMG battalion.

94. The 99th Indian Infantry Brigade was formed as the third infantry brigade

for the 17th Indian Division with 6/15th Punjab, 1/3rd Gurkhas and 1st Sikh Light Infantry. 17/7/1944 L/WS/1/1365 Reorganization of the Indian Infantry, OIOC, BL.

95. Minutes of Meeting, 26–27/5/1944, L/WS/1/650 OIOC, BL.

96. 17/7/1944 Organization of the Infantry, L/WS/1/1365 Reorganization of the Indian Infantry, OIOC, BL.

97. The 50th Armored Brigade was with the 15th Corps, the 254th Brigade with the 4th Corps, and the 255th Brigade was sent to Ranchi in the summer of 1944.

98. Sherman or Grant/Lee Tanks.

99. Stuart Light Tanks or Humber armored cars.

100. 30/6/1944 Protection of tanks in Far East L/WS/1/650 OIOC, BL.

101. Scott Gilmore, *A Connecticut Yankee in the 8th Gurkha Rifles: A Burma Memoir* (London: Brassey's, 1995), 173.

102. *Jungle Omnibus* (London: HMSO, 1945), January 1945, 11–19.

103. This may have arisen from the vulnerability of the 7th Divisional HQ. It did not have a formal protection force larger than thirty men. It was not properly protected within any other formation box when the Japanese arrived north of the Admin Box. The 4/8th Gurkhas saw copied extracts of No. 24 distributed in April 1944. See Marston, *Phoenix from the Ashes*, for a more detailed discussion of the 4/8th Gurkhas at the Admin Box.

104. AITM No. 24, 18–21.

105. This highlights the need for time to infiltrate properly. The 7/10th Baluch, when attacking "Red Hill," did not have the time to send out infiltrating patrols. The Japanese were threatening the divisional HQ from the heights and it was critical to clear them quickly. It does not consider the problems of very difficult positions such as Point 551, where all routes in or around were covered by the sheer terrain of the region. It would seem that the only appropriate measure in this circumstance would be to ring the area and starve and bomb the position into defeat.

106. This reiterates that reconnaissance patrols should be no more than three or four men under the command of an officer or NCO. Fighting patrols should not be less than a platoon or more than a company.

107. AITM No. 25. (*Jungle Omnibus*, 24–26.)

108. It underlines this stricture with a few politically incorrect suggestions: (a) do not fire until you see the yellow of the enemy's eyes; and (b) one round, one Jap.

109. This meant that ordinary infantrymen would not be required to protect Admin personnel.

110. AITM No. 25.

111. Headed by Lt. Gen. Reginald Savory.

112. These were distributed throughout India Command, including the jungle schools, two training divisions, regimental centers, officer training centers, and rest, reinforcement, and training camps in Ranchi, Chittagong, and Shillong.

113. L/WS/1/764 DMT Monthly Training Reports, March–November 1944 OIOC, BL.

114. L/WS/1/778 GHQ, India Infantry Committee Letters, No. 1–15 1944 and 1945 OIOC, BL.

115. See L/WS/1/777 Study Period on Burma, for more details on the discussion points and lessons.

116. Only the units of the 26th Indian Division, 2/13th FFRifles, received formal amphibious training. The rest continued along the lines of A & MT divisions. When the strategic situation changed in the autumn of 1944, both the 17th and 5th Indian divisions were reorganized once more. See the section dealing with these two divisions in this chapter.

117. There were numerous delays in the establishment of a training battalion for the 3rd Madras Regiment, and eventually the regimental training center decided to set up its own jungle warfare training ground. Interview with Major Barton, 5/7/2000, 4/3rd Madras.

118. Anthony Brett-James, *Ball of Fire: The Fifth Indian Division in the Second World War* (Aldershot, UK: Gale & Polden, 1951), 392. See the Divisional War Diary, WO 172/4281, NA, for more details on the training regime and the various training directives.

119. The lessons of the Tiddim Road operation had been covered during the "Post Mortem" at 123rd Indian Brigade HQ on 11 November. WO 172/4939 11/11/1944 NA. These were reprinted by 123rd Brigade HQ and distributed to all units of the brigade. The main points raised were that units needed to harass the enemy with flanking patrols and ambushes, while trying to avoid outright frontal attacks. WO 172/4449 November 1944 (123 Ind Brig) NA.

120. Interview with Major Arthur, 21/3/2000.

121. Training instruction number 15, 1/1945, WO 172/6963 (5th Indian Div.) NA.

122. See the Brigade War Diary entries, WO 172/4449, NA, for the month of November 1944. There is a detailed discussion of the key lessons from recent operations on the Tiddim Road.

123. WO 172/6963 January 1945 (5th Indian Div.); and Brett-James, *Ball of Fire*, 391–392.

124. See WO 172/7693, NA, specifically the months of January and February, for entries in training in the motorized role and with tanks. It was also during this time that many dignitaries visited the division and the various formations and units.

125. Interviews with Majors Arthur, 21/3/2000, and Kerr, 24/1/2001.

126. 7th Indian Division Training Instruction 1944 No. 2, 3 July 1944, WO 172/4290 NA.

127. Lt. Gen. Frank Messervy Papers, Liddel Hart Centre Military Archives, King's College London (LHCMA), May–December 1944 and January 1945.

128. The brigade drew up seven training instructions from August to December 1944. WO 172/4439 August–December 1944 (89th Indian Brigade) NA.

129. As noted earlier, Messervy was divisional commander during the retraining efforts. In August 1944, he outlined the overall plan of training and retraining the division's units. He emphasized weapons training, field craft, patrolling, map reading, physical fitness, and battle inoculation. Messervy Papers, File 5/14, LHCMA, as well as WO 172/4439 (89th Indian Brigade), "Lessons from Operations," September 1944 NA. He specifically highlighted the lessons from the 4/8th GR as "Lessons from

Operations," operational note number 15 and distributed it to the rest of the division. See Messervy Papers, File 5/15, LHCMA, for more details.

130. Walker had been second in command of the battalion as well as GSO 1 of the 7th Indian Division under Major General Messervy.

131. An officer who had recently joined the battalion commented that most officers and men who had participated in the recent fighting did not require much training, but that Walker had indicated that there were lessons to be learned from the fighting. Interview with Cap. Patrick Davis, 17/1/2000, and Patrick Davis, *A Child at Arms* (London: Hutchinson, 1970), 62–63.

132. All officers of the 4/8th Gurkhas noted that there were discussions among the officers regarding the problems and lessons of the recent fighting.

133. Walker drew up his own training instructions and noted AITM No. 24 and 25. His "Lessons from Operations" was distributed throughout the division. He specifically stated what training should be carried out, as well as listing innovations drawn from AITM No. 25 regarding patrols. Messervy Papers, File 5/15, LHCMA. See the War Diary for 4/8th GR, WO 172/5029 and the entries for November and December for exhaustive listing of the training. There were quite a few references to combined-arms training as well as air-landing exercises.

134. Interviews with Brigadier Myers, 23/9/2000, Majors Wickham, 4/12/1999, Seaman, 1/4/2000, and Gilmore, 1/8/1999, and Captain Davis, 17/1/2000.

135. WO 172/5029 October–December 1944 NA.

136. Davis, *A Child at Arms*, 62–63.

137. 26/7/1944 L/WS/1/1511 OIOC, BL.

138. With the threat of Ha-Go and U-Go, various units on the North-West Frontier of India were called up for possible duty in the Arakan or Assam.

139. J. D. Hookway, ed., *M & R: A Regimental History of the Sikh Light Infantry* (Oxford: Oxford University Computer Services, 1999), 31 and correspondence with Colonel Maling.

140. On 23 June, the Mazhbi and Ramdasia Sikh Regiment formally changed its name to Sikh Light Infantry. It was renamed by General Savory. Hookway, *A Regimental History of the Sikh Light Infantry*, 31.

141. WO 172/4465 May–August 1944 (99 Ind Brig) NA and correspondence with Colonel Maling.

142. Hookway, *A Regimental History of the Sikh Light Infantry*, 32, and correspondence with Colonel Maling.

143. Major Baldwin mentioned that there was only one day when an issue of discipline arose. This was resolved quickly and the reinforcements progressed well during the training. Interview with Major Baldwin, 7/9th Jats, 13/8/2000.

144. Hookway, *A Regimental History of the Sikh Light Infantry*, 34–35.

145. There were three of these, all extremely detailed documents, highlighting the lessons of the recent fighting and ways to train the men in revised tactics. Correspondence with Colonel Maling. See the War Diary, WO 172/4972, NA, specifically the month of August for a detailed description of the various training directives as well as lessons identified. It is pretty exhaustive.

146. WO 172/4972 July–October 1944 NA.

147. Interviews with Brigadier Randle, 10/4/2000, and Major MacLean, 22/3/2000. Brigadier Randle set up his own company school for his VCOs, developing the lessons based upon his experiences of the fighting in Assam.

148. WO 172/4972 August–November 1944 NA.

149. 6/7th Rajput Regiment became the new HQ protection battalion.

150. WO 172/4979 July–December 1944 NA.

151. WO 172/6986 (17th Ind) January 1945 NA and Slim, *Defeat into Victory*, 321.

152. WO 172/7736 January–February 1945 and WO 172/7729 January–February 1945.

153. Interviews with Brigadier Randle, 10/4/2000, Majors Martin, 12/1/2000, MacLean, 22/3/2000, and Barrett, 12/8/2000, and Captains Murtough, 17/6/2000, and King, 13/3/2000. The commando platoons from both the 7/10th Baluch and 4/12th FFR were to be used in patrolling to determine if a given area was suitable for tanks.

154. Training Instruction, 23/1/45. Also noted: "[This] will form the basis for training from now on in our present location and forward. It is not comprehensive and many gaps are left for brigade and battalion commanders to fill in." WO 172/6986 (17th Indian Div.) NA.

155. The 98th Indian Brigade included the 8/12th FFR, 4/4th Gurkha Rifles, and the 2nd Royal Berkshire Regiment, which we will see more of in the chapter on 1945.

156. WO 172/4980 1944, WO 172/4866 1944 (2 Royal Berkshire Regiment) NA and interview with Major Williams, 26/4/2001.

157. See Lt. Col. Hamilton Stevenson, LHMCA, for more details.

158. For a unique personal account, see John Hill, *China Dragons: A Rifle Company at War, Burma 1944–5* (London: Blandford, 1991), 27–30.

159. Quote in Moreman, *Jungle*, 167.

160. The HQ of the 20th Indian Division drew up five "Battle Instructions" from August to November, underlining the need for lessons to be learned from the recent fighting. These specifically called for all battalion officers to discuss the lessons learned in their own units and how training could incorporate these lessons. WO 172/4319 (20th Indian Division) August–November 1944 NA.

161. Following earlier analysis of lessons to be learned during the Ukhrul road operations. On 10 June a report written by battalion HQ assessed current tactics and lessons from operations. WO 172/7743 June 1944 NA and 8012–63 TS History 14/13th FFRifles NAM.

162. WO 172/7743 August–November 1944 NA.

163. See references in November 1944, WO 172/7743 NA.

164. Interview with Major Coppen, 1/11/2000.

165. Cipher Commander-in-Chief, India to War Office, London 3/8/1944 L/WS/1/1511 Burma Assam Operations OIOC, BL.

166. It also included the Royal Deccan Horse, the 6/7th Rajputs, and later the 16th Light Cavalry.

167. The main armament was a 75mm gun and two or three coaxial machine guns.

168. Major B. H. Milne, ed., *An Account of Operations in Burma Carried Out by Probyn's Horse* (privately published, 1945), 3.

169. The regiment had forty-two Sherman tanks, Milne, 5.

170. Interview with Major H. E. I. C. Stewart, 11/7/2000.

171. WO 172/4608 19/9/1944 NA.

172. See his papers, 8208–213, National Army Museum (NAM), for a detailed description of his thinking and training regime for his Brigade.

173. Brigadier Pert's Papers NAM.

174. WO 172/4461 September-December 1944 (255 Arm Brig.) NA.

175. WO 172/4608, NA (5th Probyn's), September 1944, Training Instruction No. 1.

176. WO 172/4608 October–December 1944 NA. Specifically see Training Instruction No. 2 for a detailed discussion of Harbours and Protection of Harbours.

177. Interviews with Majors Stewart, 11/7/2000, and Chiles, 8/5 2000, and Brigadier Riaz Khan, 15/10/2000.

178. WO 172/4608 December 1944 NA.

179. Miles Smeeton, *A Change of Jungles* (London: Hart-Davis, 1962), 80.

2. Endless Frustration: The Arakan

1. The Admin Box Battle is described in Slim, *Defeat into Victory* (London: Cassell, 1956), 223–243 as well as in the official history, S. W. Kirby et al., *The War against Japan* (London: Her Majesty's Stationery Office, 1957–1969), 2:133–159. The infantry combat in the Arakan was grueling, intense small-unit action very well described in Michael Lowry's *Fighting through to Kohima: A Memoir of War in India & Burma* (Yorkshire: Leo Cooper, 2003). Lowry, a British officer of the Queen's Royal Regiment (part of the 7th Indian Division), served in the Arakan during the "Admin Box" fight and subsequent counterattack.

2. See appendix 1 to this chapter, which deals with Slim's African divisions.

3. The composition of the 15th Corps Indian divisions underscored the ever-intensifying British manpower shortage. The 25th Indian had only one British battalion and the 26th Indian had two. All British battalions in SEAC were, by this time, chronically understrength.

4. Kirby et al., *War against Japan*, 345n3.

5. Major General Hugh Stockwell had served for five years with the Royal West African Frontier Force (1930–1935) and so was no stranger to African forces.

6. Kirby et al., *War against Japan*, 351.

7. Kirby et al., 351.

8. The only overall survey is Ashley Jackson's *The British Empire and the Second World War* (London: Hambledon, 2006), although, of course, individual parts of the empire have been studied by specialist historians. Oddly, the "Oxford History of the British Empire" made no real attempt to present a synthesis of the empire at war, devoting one short anodyne chapter to the culminating episode in imperial history.

9. Africa ultimately contributed five hundred thousand men to the imperial

military effort—two hundred thousand from West Africa. Most served in support and pioneer (construction) units, which, for the most part, were unarmed. (The Union of South Africa, a self-governing dominion whose prime minister, Jan Smuts, was a close friend of Churchill's, was very hostile to the raising of "black armies" of fully trained soldiers, especially in territories abutting on South Africa.)

10. In the advance on Addis Abbaba, Nigerian units led the way, only to be halted on the outskirts of the city to allow it to be "liberated" by white South African troops.

11. Although Slim did not mention it, the need for European officers for the expanding West African forces had produced one of the most unusual expedients of the empire's war. The Polish army that had reassembled itself in Britain had a surplus of officers (who would have had a very strong incentive to escape Poland's Nazi and Soviet conquerors). The British borrowed four hundred of them, who were posted to West African units, which must have produced some mind-boggling linguistic complications.

12. John A. L. Hamilton, *War Bush: 81 (West African) Division in Burma, 1943–1945* (Norwich, UK: Michael Russell, 2001).

13. It is worth remembering how few British divisions actually served east of Suez in 1939–1945. The 18th Division was made up of East Anglian Territorials and en route to the Middle East when it was diverted to Singapore, landing only weeks before the surrender. The 2nd Division reached India in late 1942, played a small role in the debacle of the first Arakan campaign, and then spent a year training for SEAC amphibious operations that never took place before becoming part of the XIV Army during the Imphal-Kohima battle. It remained with Slim until after Mandalay fell when it was withdrawn to India—it was impossible to keep its infantry battalions up to strength and it required far more logistic support than any Indian or African division. The 36th Division, originally an Indian division, was restructured as a British division in 1944. It had only two brigades and like all British formations in SEAC had trouble replacing casualties. In 1944–1945 it was committed to action in Stilwell's Northern Combat Area Command. It was withdrawn to India early in 1945 for the same reasons as the 2nd Division was. Finally, there was the 70th Division, almost as star-crossed as the 18th. Originally formed in the Middle East as the 6th Division at war's outbreak, it became the 70th Division, moved to India, and became part of Slim's 15th Corps in 1942. Slim thought very highly of the division but it was destined never to fight as a division, being broken up in late 1943 to provide the manpower for Wingate's "Special Force," a decision about which Slim was sharply critical. There were, of course, British battalions in some Indian brigades, understrength by 1944–1945 and destined during the campaign of 1945 to be replaced by Indian battalions, which were easier to keep up to strength and which made fewer demands on the XIV Army logistics. There were, in addition, other British units not embodied in brigades or divisions—antitank and antiaircraft units, garrison battalions in India, and so on. It is no criticism of any of these units to point out that there were never many of them and that by 1944–1945 they were attenuating fast. Slim's last campaign was waged largely by Indians and Africans. Britain had run out of men.

14. Slim, *Defeat into Victory*, 356.

15. The 3rd Nigerian Infantry Brigade had a strange war. As soon as it reached India it was detached from the 81 West African Division and handed over to Orde Wingate's Special Force. As Wingate put Special Force together in India after the Allied summit at Quebec had gifted him with it, his ideas of what he could do steadily expanded, and so did his demand for resources. He developed the concept of defended airheads ("strongholds") that would serve as bases for his roving columns. This meant that he needed garrison units. An attempt to raid Slim's 26th Indian Infantry Division was stopped cold by Slim. Wingate would only take British or Gurkha units, but not Indian (the 26th Indian had two of the former and one of the latter). At that point he was offered Nigerians and took them. They were intended as stronghold garrisons (and despite nearly provoking a crisis with Slim over the issue, Wingate failed to produce training guidance for stronghold defense until a week before the operation began).

The detail of the 3rd Nigerian Brigade's service in Operation Thursday is carefully laid out by the 81st West African Division's very precise historian: Hamilton, *War Bush*, 261–309. Only three points call for notice here. The carriers, once again, were invaluable, capable of moving with loads in terrain and weather where mules failed. Then there is the virtual neglect of the Nigerians in the many Chindit accounts. Finally a vignette of Wingate: on 20 March he flew in by light plane to "Aberdeen," the stronghold of Brig. Bernard Fergusson's 16th Brigade (which the Nigerians were to garrison). Fergusson had already laid out a Dakota strip but Wingate insisted on resiting it. The result: a strip very dangerous for Dakotas (there were several crashes) and one whose dangers could only be mitigated by reducing their loads, hence their efficiency, and thus increasing the number of runs they had to make. Comment seems superfluous.

While it is true that none of 3rd Nigerian Brigade's British officers wrote accounts as widely read as those by Chindit commanders like Michael Calvert, Bernard Fergusson, and John Masters, Charles Carfrae's *Chindit Column* (London: Kimber, 1985), by a British regular officer who served with the Nigeria Regiment, is a very readable account of the Nigerians' service with the Chindits.

16. A. Haywood and F. A. S. Clarke, *The History of the Royal West African Frontier Force* (Aldershot, UK: Gale & Polden, 1964); H. Moyse-Bartlett, *The King's African Rifles: A Study in the Military History of East and Central Africa, 1890–1945* (Aldershot, UK: Gale & Polden, 1956).

17. A copy of this memoir is in the Churchill Archives Center at Churchill College, Cambridge.

18. While there is almost no writing by, or about, the Africans who served in Burma, two titles deserve mention: Barnaby Phillips, *Another Man's War: The Story of a Burma Boy in Britain's Forgotten African Army* (London: Oneworld, 2014), a remarkable piece of historical detective work, tells the story of Isaac Fedoyebo, who enlisted at sixteen in the Nigeria Regiment and fought in the Arakan. Separated from his unit, he survived in hiding, with local help, until he could reunite with his division. Biyi Bandele's *Burma Boy* (London: Jonathan Cape, 2007) is a novel based on the experiences of his father and other African veterans of the 3rd Nigerian Brigade's service

in Wingate's Special Force. "Burma Boy" was a colloquialism used in West Africa to describe veterans of the war in Burma.

3. Operation Capital to Operation Extended Capital

1. Earl Mountbatten, *SEAC Report to the Combined Chiefs of Staff by the Supreme Allied Commander South-East Asia* (London: His Majesty's Stationery Office, 1951), 76.

2. See chapter 1 for a more detailed discussion.

3. S. W. Kirby et al., *The War against Japan* (London: Her Majesty's Stationery Office, 1957–1969), 4:101–102.

4. Mountbatten, *Report*, 77.

5. Mountbatten, 83.

6. Mountbatten, 83.

7. Kirby et al., *The War against Japan*, 4:106–108; and John Ehrman, *Grand Strategy* (London: HMSO, 1956), 6:167.

8. Ehrman, *Grand Strategy*, 6:174.

9. Kirby et al., *The War against Japan*, 4:108–109.

10. See chapter 2 for the full description of this part of the campaign.

11. See Raymond Callahan, *Triumph at Imphal-Kohima: How the Indian Army Finally Stopped the Japanese Juggernaut* (Lawrence: University Press of Kansas, 2017) for more details.

12. At the end of the Imphal-Tamu-Sittaung road, which had originally been built by the 20th Indian Division before U-Go.

13. Ehrman, *Grand Strategy*, 6:176.

14. Really the size of a British/Indian corps.

15. British intelligence estimated more than two hundred thousand soldiers, NCOs, and officers. The Burma Area Army far outnumbered other IJA garrisons in South-East Asia. See *Grand Strategy*, 6:174.

16. *Burma Operations Record: 15th Army Operations and Withdrawal to Northern Burma*, Japanese Monograph, No. 134 (Tokyo: US Army HQ, 1957), 167.

17. *Burma Operations Record*, No. 134, 171.

18. Brian Bond, ed., *British and Japanese Military Leadership in the Far Eastern War, 1941–1945* (London: Frank Cass, 2004), 50.

19. SEATIC Bulletin No. 242, reproduced in Bisheshwar Prasad, ed., *The Reconquest of Burma*, vol. 2 (Calcutta: Orient Longmans, 1958), appendix 5.

20. *Burma Operations Record*, No. 134, 175–176.

21. An open plain between the Chindwin and Irrawaddy rivers.

22. Under the command of Lt. Gen. Frank Messervy: 19th and 7th Indian divisions, plus the 255th Armoured Brigade.

23. Under the command of Lieutenant General Stopford: 2nd British and 20th Indian divisions, supported by 254th Armoured Brigade and 268th Indian Brigade.

24. The 19th Indian Division would see its first actions of the war during Operation Capital/Extended Capital. It was one of the most highly trained divisions and its stellar performance in 1944/1945 would bear this fact out.

25. Slim, *Defeat into Victory* (London: Cassell, 1956), 321–322.

26. See the description of the 8/12th FFR advance in this chapter.

27. This was originally the 11th Army Group, renamed in November 1944. General Giffard was replaced and succeeded by Lt. Gen. Sir Oliver Leese. The 15th Corps was placed under direct command of ALFSEA, with the XIV Army to comprise only the 4th Corps and the 33rd Corps.

28. Kirby, *The War against Japan*, 4:163–164.

29. "The new plan was thoroughly discussed [by] Slim's staff but not cleared in advance with either ALFSEA or SEAC." Bond, *British and Japanese Military Leadership*, 50.

30. Kirby, *The War against Japan*, 4:164–165.

31. Radio contact between units of the 4th Corps was to be kept to a minimum. If they came upon large Japanese forces, they were to go around them and allow the 28th East African Brigade to deal with them. The Japanese were to think that a unit of brigade size only was operating on the western side of the Irrawaddy so far south. Interviews with officers of the 1/11th Sikh and 4/8th Gurkhas.

32. This was the main admin area for both the Japanese 15th and 33rd armies. There were five airfields, major road and railway connections, and a supply depot.

33. Lieutenant General Kimura noted in an interrogation report that he had no intention of fighting a major battle on the Shwebo Plain, planning instead to hold a line along the Irrawaddy River. SEATIC WO 106/5897 NA and Kirby et al., *The War against Japan*, 4:165–167.

34. Slim, *Defeat into Victory*, 327.

35. Kirby et al., *The War against Japan*, 4:165.

36. Kirby et al., 4:167.

37. Kirby et al., 4:173–174.

38. Ehrman, *Grand Strategy*, 6:178.

39. Mountbatten, *Report*, 103.

40. Six squadrons of Hurricanes, three squadrons of Thunderbolts, four squadrons of Spitfires, three squadrons of Beaufighters and Mosquitoes, two squadrons of recce aircraft.

41. Kirby et al., *The War against Japan*, 4:254 and Mountbatten, *Report*, 126 and 128.

42. Raymond Callahan, *Churchill and His Generals* (Lawrence: University Press of Kansas, 2007), 211 and 239; see also Callahan, "Were the Sepoy Generals Any Good? A Re-Appraisal of the British-Indian Army's High-Command in the Second World War," in *War and Society in Colonial India*, ed. Kaushik Roy (New Delhi: Oxford University Press, 2006).

43. The 33rd Indian Corps Account of Operations, vol. 3, 16 December 1944–20 March 1945, WO 203/2685, NA.

44. Kirby, *The War against Japan*, 4:184.

45. *Burma Operations Record*, No. 134, 183.

46. WO 172/4980 December 1944 NA.

47. WO 172/7737 January 1945 NA.

48. 33rd Indian Corps Account of Operations, vol. 3, 16 December 1944–20 March 1945, WO 203/2685, NA. See a very descriptive account of the crossings at

Kyaukmiyaung in John Prendergast, *Prender's Progress: A Soldier in India*. (London: Cassell, 1979), 200–204.

49. Kirby, *The War against Japan*, 4:178–179.

50. At Thabeikkyin and Kyaukmyaung.

51. The 11th Sikh Machine Gun battalion was surrounded by the Japanese crossing at Kabwet and required extrication. Correspondence with Lieutenant Colonel Schaefli, 11th Sikh Machine Gun Battalion.

52. Prendergast, *Prender's Progress*, 206–207.

53. WO 172/7737 February 1945 NA.

54. 12/2/45 WO 172/6996 (19th Indian Div) NA.

55. 33rd Indian Corps Account of Operations, vol. 3, 16 December 1944–20 March 1945, WO 203/2685, NA.

56. *Burma Operations Record*, No. 134, 186.

57. John Masters, *The Road Past Mandalay: A Personal Narrative* (New York: Harper, 1961), 286.

58. Masters, 291. John Masters gives much more detailed accounts relating to the leadership and professionalism of General Rees in chapter 23.

59. Prendergast, *Prender's Progress*, 219. See his description of the advance of the Stiletto Force for more details.

60. *Burma Operations Record: 33rd Army Operations*, Japanese Monograph, No. 148 (Tokyo: US Army HQ, 1957), 51.

61. Masters, *The Road Past Mandalay*, 300.

62. WO 172/7737 February–March 1945 NA.

63. Masters, *The Road Past Mandalay*, 300.

64. For more detail regarding the decision making and debates, see Prendergast, *Prender's Progress*, 220–222; and John Hill, *China Dragons: A Rifle Company at War, Burma 1944–45* (London: Blandford Press, 1991), 112.

65. Hill, *China Dragons*, 112.

66. Kirby et al., *The War against Japan*, 4:289–290; and Hill, *China Dragons*, 115.

67. Masters, *The Road Past Mandalay*, 302–303.

68. The fort encompassed twenty thousand square yards. The wall protecting the fort was about twenty-three feet high and two to three feet thick, with a moat surrounding all sides.

69. WO 172/7737 10/3/45 NA.

70. WO 172/7737 10/3/45 NA.

71. See descriptions in Prendergast, *Prender's Progress*, and Hill, *China Dragons*.

72. WO 172/7737 11–16/3/45 NA.

73. Further breaches in the wall were created by 5.5-inch howitzers.

74. WO 172/7737 17/3/45 NA.

75. Interview with Major Williams, 26/4/2001.

76. WO 172/7737 17/3/45 NA.

77. WO 172/7737 17–30/3/45 NA.

78. Kirby et al., *The War against Japan*, 4:300. Prendergast listed the date as the 22nd. Prendergast, *Prender's Progress*, 227.

79. See Hill, *China Dragons*, 121–123 for a more detailed description of the fighting in the streets of Mandalay.

80. WO 172/7737 March Appendix NA. Also see Hill, *China Dragons*, 124, where General Rees stated, "My congratulations on your further fine fighting round the South West of Mandalay. KEEP IT UP."

81. "Minutes of conference, 20 December 1944," 33rd Indian Corps Account of Operations, vol. 3, 16 December 1944–20 March 1945, WO 203/2685, NA.

82. A Bailey pontoon bridge was constructed across the Chindwin River at Kalewa. It was 1154 feet long, then the longest Bailey in the world.

83. The battalion had used the network of "Sher Forces" in the recent fighting in the Imphal Plain of 1944. See Daniel Marston, *The Phoenix from the Ashes: The Indian Army in the Burma Campaign* (Westport, CT: Praeger, 2003), for a more detailed description.

84. WO 172/7743 1–23/1/1945 NA and interview with Major Coppen, 1/11/1999.

85. WO 172/7743 January 1945 NA.

86. The only major action of the battalion before it reached the Irrawaddy River was at Wunbye. B Company, over the course of two days, infiltrated the Japanese rearguard in the village, killing fifty Japanese with a loss of two men. WO 172/7743 20–24/1/1945 NA.

87. Interview with Major Coppen, 1/11/1999.

88. WO 172/7743 January 1945 NA.

89. January 17, 1945, 33rd Indian Corps Account of Operations, vol. 3, 16 December 1944–20 March 1945, WO 203/2685, NA.

90. This would apply pressure on the Japanese to release and deploy troops opposite the 19th Indian Division to the south to attack the bridgeheads of the 20th Indian and 2nd British divisions. Kirby et al., *The War against Japan*, 4:183–184.

91. 2 February 1945, "steps will be taken to protect the outer flank of the division from counter-attacks that might develop." 33rd Indian Corps Account of Operations, vol. 3, 16 December 1944–20 March 1945, WO 203/2685, NA.

92. WO 172/7743 1–7/2/1945 NA.

93. Kirby et al., *The War against Japan*, 4:260–261.

94. 14/13th FFRifles, 4/10th Gurkhas, and 2nd Border Regiment.

95. Kirby et al., *The War against Japan*, 4:261.

96. WO 172/7743 12/2/1945 NA.

97. A flight of Allied planes was ordered over the crossing. Their engines were to drown out the noise of the outboard motors of the boats. Captain Wallis, who was the 100th Indian Brigade liaison officer, noted that the planes had flown too high to drown out the noise of the boats, and feared that the Japanese would easily be able to hear the crossing. Interview with Captain Wallis, 29/11/1999.

98. C Company commander Major Coppen noted that it was difficult to dig in properly in the area because of the sandy terrain. Slit trenches filled in with any movement of men in the position. He also noted, however, that any sort of cover was important. Interview with Major Coppen, 1/11/1999.

99. During the day and night, as the companies consolidated and moved, they sent

a number of reconnaissance and fighting patrols to locate and destroy any roaming Japanese forces in the area. WO 172/7743 13/2/1945 NA.

100. WO 172/7743 14–15/2/1945 NA.

101. Kirby et al., *The War against Japan,* 4:261.

102. WO 172/7743 16/2/1945 NA.

103. Jemadar Parkash Singh was instrumental in the defense of C Company's position. He rallied the men and carried ammunition between the posts. He had been wounded three times before a grenade killed him. He died in the arms of his company commander, Major Coppen, after telling him not to worry about him, that he was all right. He was awarded the VC posthumously for his action in the defense, while Major Coppen received the MC. Interview with Major Coppen, 1/11/1999.

104. During the battle, the two companies were under the command of Maj. Akbar Khan, due to the fact that communications with battalion HQ were poor. He received a DSO for his command during the battle.

105. WO 172/7743 17/2/1945 NA.

106. WO 172/7793 20/2/1945 NA.

107. Quote in Bryan Perrett, *Tank Tracks to Rangoon* (London: Robert Hale, 1992), 185–186.

108. Perrett, 186.

109. WO 172/7743 18–20/2/1945 NA.

110. Kirby et al., *The War against Japan,* 4:261–262.

111. WO 172/7743 March–May 1945 NA.

112. 20 December 1944, 33rd Indian Corps Account of Operations, vol. 3, 16 December 1944–20 March 1945, WO 203/2685, NA.

113. 2 February 1945, 33rd Indian Corps Account of Operations, vol. 3, 16 December 1944–20 March 1945, WO 203/2685, NA.

114. *Burma Operations Record,* No. 134, 186.

115. Kirby et al., *The War against Japan,* 4:262–263; and 33rd Indian Corps Account of Operations, vol. 3, 16 December 1944–20 March 1945, WO 203/2685, NA.

116. Under the command of Maj. Gen. Geoffrey Evans.

117. 19 January 1945, 4th Corps Narrative of Operations, October 1944–May 1945, WO 203/2679, NA.

118. WO 172/7732 1 January–4 February 1944 NA.

119. Interview with Major Farrow, 1/11th Sikh, 21/2/2000.

120. See Prasad, *The Reconquest of Burma,* vol. 2, appendix 11, for the specific details of Cloak.

121. The XIV Army culture of constant assessment continued during this phase. The GOC of the 7th Indian Division, Major General Evans, specifically wrote up a series of "lessons on the crossings." He specifically stated that while things went well, things could still be improved. Lt. Gen. Geoffrey Evans Papers, Imperial War Museum, "Crossing of the Irrawaddy."

122. WO 172/7732 4–10/2/1944 NA.

123. The INA soldiers reported that the Japanese troops had moved north to deal with the main 7th Indian Division's landing at Nyaungu. The INA company was ordered to remain at Pagan.

124. WO 172/7732 13/2/1944 NA.

125. More than one hundred men surrendered. Kirby et al., *The War against Japan*, 4:265.

126. WO 172/7732 14–15/2/1944 NA.

127. WO 172/7732 17–18/2/1944 NA.

128. They had dug themselves in and allowed B Company to move forward without opposition. Interview with Farrow, 21/2/2000.

129. Major Farrow was with battalion HQ when it was attacked. He noted that B Company troops should have patrolled the area before advancing. He also pointed out that while battalion HQ lacked a large number of men, they all fought as infantry. This was one reason why the HQ was able to survive. Interview with Major Farrow, 21/2/2000.

130. WO 172/7732 18/2/1944 NA.

131. Interview with Major Farrow, 21/2/2000.

132. WO 172/7732 19–21/2/1944 NA.

133. Slim, *Defeat into Victory*, 359–360. See Lt. Gen. Geoffrey Evans Papers, Imperial War Museum, Interrogation reports with Japanese commanders, "Irrawaddy River Fighting," for detailed comments from Japanese senior commanders and their lack of understanding and identification of the XIV Army's main effort.

134. They lost eight men killed and seven wounded out of fifteen men.

135. Although the attack was successful, it was apparent that the patrols had not properly reconnoitered the area. They had attacked without proper information, and if the Japanese had been more heavily dug in, the outcome could have been very different. WO 172/7732 23 February–11 March 1944 NA.

136. Maj. Gen. "Punch" Cowan had commanded the division since the fighting north of Rangoon in March 1942.

137. The 48th and 63rd Indian brigades moved south as lorry-transported infantry. The 99th Indian Brigade was to be air-transported into Meiktila to support the rest of the division.

138. 4th Corps OP Instruction, No. 125, 5 February 1945, reproduced in Prasad, *The Reconquest of Burma*, vol. 2, appendix 13.

139. *Burma Operations Record*, No. 134, 186.

140. Kirby et al., *The War against Japan*, 4:267.

141. Under the command of Lieutenant Colonel McLeod, who had arrived to command the battalion in April 1944.

142. The Brigade was commanded by Brig. C. Pert. He had spent a lot of time in Imphal, getting his brigade trained up with infantry and artillery, to create mobile teams for the coming fight in the central plains of Burma. He laid out a training package that was divided into five phases and was collated as a written document named "Infantry and Tanks in Attack." Many units from the 17th Indian Division worked with units from the 255th Armoured Brigade. When the call came on the race to Meiktila, both formations were ready. See Major General Pert papers at the National Army Museum, 8208–213, for more details.

143. WO 172/7736 1–26/2/1944 NA.

144. Kirby, *The War against Japan*, 4:269–270.

145. The railway line ran west-east and bisected the town north-south.

146. WO 172/7736 1–5/3/1944 NA and WO 172/7347 4/3/1945 (Probyn's) NA.

147. Minus A and B companies, who were detached for patrolling activities to the south of the town.

148. WO 172/7736 5–8/3/1944 NA and interviews with Majors Barrett, 12/8/2000, and Murtough, 17/6/2000.

149. Kirby et al., *The War against Japan*, 4:273.

150. *Burma Operations Record*, No. 148, 51.

151. 4th Corps Deception Scheme "CONCLAVE," reproduced in Prasad, *The Reconquest of Burma*, vol. 2, appendix 16.

152. The Japanese troops earmarked to destroy the 17th Indian Division far outnumbered the British/Indian garrison.

153. Cowan was one of the main architects of jungle warfare training after suffering the defeats of 1942. He realized that a different approach to the defense of Meiktila was needed and adapted and combined some of the main principles of jungle and open-style warfare.

154. The 4/12th FFR, 7/10th Baluch, and 5th Probyn's took part.

155. The 1st Sikh Light Infantry was initially part of this plan.

156. Kirby et al., *The War against Japan*, 4:286.

157. The troops were to make contact with B echelon units of 17th Indian Division who were moving toward Meiktila.

158. During the evening, Japanese patrols were encountered and destroyed by 4/12th FFR. Miles Smeeton, *A Change of Jungles* (London: Hart-Davis, 1962), 97.

159. WO 172/7736 10–11/3/1944 NA.

160. WO 172/7736 12/3/1944 NA.

161. The battalion was commanded by Lieutenant Colonel Wright until 22 March, when command was given to Lt. Col. D. S. Dutt, an Indian commissioned officer.

162. It was during one of the sweeps on 2 March that Naik Fazal Din of 7/10th Baluch won a posthumous VC.

163. WO 172/7729 February–3 March 1944 NA; WO 172/7347 (Probyn's) 1–3 March NA.

164. Interviews with Brigadier Randle, 10/4/2000; Major Maclean, 22/3/2000; Captain Bruin, 1/3/2000; and Lieutenant King, 13/3/2000.

165. WO 172/7729 3–11/3/1944 NA.

166. Interview with Major Randle, 10/4/2000.

167. It had operated with A Squadron, 5th Probyn's, on 1–3 March when moving into Meiktila from the west.

168. WO 172/7729 10–23/3/1945 NA.

169. Interviews with Majors Randle, 10/4/2000, and Maclean, 22/3/2000, and Captain Bruin, 1/3/2000.

170. Less B Company.

171. WO 172/7729 24–30/3/1945 NA.

172. Interviews with officers of the 4/12th FFR and 7/10th Baluch.

173. Quoted in Timothy Moreman, *The Jungle, the Japanese and the British Commonwealth Armies at War, 1941–1945* (London: Frank Cass, 2005), 193.

174. Under the command of Lieutenant Colonel Barlow-Wheeler until 19 March, when Maj. (Col.) J. D. Maling took over.

175. WO 172/7134 (99th Ind Brig.) January-February 1945 NA.

176. Maling's diary, in J. D. Hookway, ed., *M & R: A Regimental History of the Sikh Light Infantry* (Oxford: Oxford University Computer Services, 1999), 40.

177. Maling's diary, in Hookway, 40–41.

178. Correspondence with Colonel Maling.

179. Maling's diary, Hookway, *M & R*, 41–42; and interview with Brigadier Riaz Khan, 15/3/2000, 5th Probyn's.

180. "Static" in the sense that patrols were sent just outside the perimeters and not in a combined tank/infantry force.

181. The men carried out some patrols in trucks as well as on foot.

182. WO 172/7134 (99th Ind Brig.) 3–13/3/1945 NA.

183. Maling's diary, in Hookway, *M & R*, 43.

184. The 9th Indian Brigade, 5th Indian Division, had been flown in over the course of 15–17 March to reinforce Meiktila and the airstrip. This released the 99th Indian Brigade from static defense for offensive actions.

185. WO 172/7134 (99th Ind Brig.) 13–17/3/1945 NA; and Maling's diary, in Hookway, *M & R*, 43–47.

186. The 9/13th FFRifles was the MMG battalion for the 17th Indian Division. Two officers who served with the battalion noted that the numbers of dead Japanese soldiers outside their box perimeters piled up over the course of March 1945. One company counted over 250 dead outside its perimeter location. Interviews with Majors Lamond, 27/10/1999, and Wright, 20/12/1999, 9/13th FFRifles.

187. WO 172/7134 (99th Ind Brig.) 19–30/3/1945 NA; and Maling's diary, in Hookway, *M & R*, 47–50.

188. Colonel Maling noted that the battalion dug all-round defenses and carried out local patrols at all times without being ordered to do so by the 99th Brigade. Correspondence with Colonel Maling.

189. Cowan: "I can best describe them by saying that, in my opinion, the Sikh LI are absolutely first class. . . . [I] never had any doubts about their fighting abilities, but I was afraid that junior leadership was going to let them down, owing to a lack of training and experience. Taken by and large the junior leaders have done extremely well. I am delighted with the Battalion and proud to have them in my division . . . They have killed a large number of Japs and their morale is terrific. Their casualties have been comparatively heavy, but that has not deterred them in any way." Reproduced in Hookway, *M & R*, 59–60.

190. Auchinleck: "I have been more than delighted to hear very good accounts of your first battalion from General Messervy. He writes, 'I thought you would like to know how wonderfully well the 1st Sikh LI have done in battle.'" Reproduced in Hookway, *M & R*, 50.

191. Hookway, *M & R*, 59–60.

192. Interviews with officers of the 4/12th FFR, 7/10th Baluch, 9/13th FFRifles, and 5th Probyn's Horse.

193. Under the command of Lieutenant Colonel Miles Smeeton.

194. WO 172/7347 23 February–10 March 1945 NA.

195. Interviews with Major Stewart, 11/7/2000, Captain Chiles, 8/5/2000, Brigadier Riaz Khan, 15/10/2000, and correspondence with Lt. Richard Jones.

196. Mentioned in the section on the 4/12th FFR.

197. Commanded by Lt. Col. J. N. Chaudhuri, the first Indian officer to command an Indian cavalry regiment.

198. *An Account of the Operations in Burma Carried Out by Probyn's Horse,* June 1945, pp. 22–3; and WO 172/7347 10–12 March 1945 NA.

199. WO 172/7347 14/3/1945 NA.

200. He was wounded in the nose, which was reputed to be prominent. His driver, Risaldar Major Mohammad Arif, noted that Smeeton, since he was a brave man, took many risks when leading the tanks into attack. Arif was also wounded during the attack. Interview with Risaldar Arif, 12/10/2000.

201. WO 172/7347 14/3/1945 NA; and *Operations in Burma Carried Out by Probyn's Horse,* 27–28.

202. WO 172/7347 14–29/3/1945 NA; and interviews with Major Stewart, 11/7/2000, Brigadier Riaz Khan, 15/10/2000, Captain Chiles, 8/5/2000, Brigadier Amarjit Singh, 22/10/2000, and Risaldars Arif and Nawaz, 12/10/2000.

203. Interviews with officers and VCOs of 5th Probyn's Horse.

204. Pert papers, NAM 8208–213, 22 March 1945.

205. Pert papers, NAM 8208–213, 7 April 1945.

206. Major General Mansergh took over on 22 February, after Maj. Gen. D. F. W. Warren was killed in a flying accident.

207. R. C. B. Bristow, *Memories of the British Raj* (London: Johnson, 1974), 132–133. The Havildar was awarded the IDSM for his bravery.

208. "Story of the Japanese 33rd Division," by Lieutenant General Hanaya (GOC), Evans Papers, IWM.

209. *Burma Operations Record,* No. 148, 52.

210. *Burma Operations Record,* No. 148, 53.

211. Kirby et al., *The War against Japan,* 4:298.

212. Kirby et al., 4:284–286.

213. Kirby et al., 4:305–306. See M. R. Roberts. *Golden Arrow: The Story of the 7th Indian Division in the Second World War, 1939–1945* (Aldershot, UK: Gale & Polden, 1952), 193–214, for a much more detailed description of the battles the 89th and 114th brigades were engaged in over these days.

214. Kirby et al., *The War against Japan,* 4:311.

215. *Burma Operations Record,* No. 148, 58–60.

216. If the road were cut by Japanese troops, divisions would be supplied exclusively by air.

217. It was also withdrawn because of the problems of trying to reinforce British battalions in the theater. At this point, many Indian Divisions also lost their British battalions due to lack of reinforcements.

218. Slim, *Defeat into Victory,* 395–403.

4. The Race to Rangoon

1. Slim, *Defeat into Victory* (London: Cassell, 1956), 485–486.

2. Earl Mountbatten, *SEAC Report to the Combined Chiefs of Staff by the Supreme Allied Commander South-East Asia* (London: His Majesty's Stationery Office, 1951), 142 and 150.

3. S. W. Kirby et al., *The War against Japan* (London: Her Majesty's Stationery Office, 1957–1969), 4:322.

4. See Kirby et al., *The War against Japan*, 4:323 and Mountbatten, *Report*, 151, for more details.

5. See Kirby et al., *The War against Japan*, 4:328–329 and Mountbatten, *Report*, 145–146, for more details.

6. Reproduced in Bisheshwar Prasad, ed., *The Reconquest of Burma*, vol. 2 (Calcutta: Orient Longmans, 1958), appendix 18, p. 519. See also the 4th Corps War Diary for 1945, WO 172/6895, NA. These loss rates were confirmed in the postwar period and noted in Kirby et al., *The War against Japan*, 4:357; and *Burma Operations Record: 15th Army Operations and Withdrawal to Northern Burma*, Japanese Monograph (Tokyo: US Army HQ, 1957), No. 134 and 148.

7. Kirby et al., *The War against Japan*, 4:356.

8. Reproduced in Prasad, *The Reconquest of Burma*, vol. 2, appendix 18, p. 520. See also the 4th Corps War Diary for 1945, WO 172/6895, NA.

9. Including both the 254th and 255th Armoured brigades.

10. *Burma Operations Record*, No. 148, p. 61.

11. B. H. Mylne, ed., *An Account of the Operations in Burma Carried out by Probyn's Horse during February, March & April 1945* (privately published, 1945), 46.

12. *Burma Operations Record*, No. 148, pp. 62–63.

13. Quoted in Bryan Perrett, *Tank Tracks to Rangoon* (London: Robert Hale, 1992), 220.

14. Kirby et al., *The War against Japan*, 4:358–359.

15. 4th Corps Narrative of Operations October 1944–May 1945, WO 203/2679, NA.

16. Mylne, *Account*, 55.

17. Slim, *Defeat into Victory*, 496.

18. The battalion participated in the taking of Taungtha and the protection of Mahlaing. The battalion formed into boxes each evening and easily repelled any Japanese attacks. WO 172/7693 29 March–4 April 1945 NA.

19. Lieutenant Colonel Appleby was still in command of the battalion.

20. The second-in-command, Major Meraj-ud-Din, was killed by a Japanese air attack while at the 5th Division HQ. The HQ was a properly sighted box to deal with any Japanese land attacks, but was unable to contend with the Japanese air attack. Interview with Major Kerr, who was a liaison officer with the division, 25/1/2001.

21. WO 172/ 7693 8–14/4/1945 NA; see also Mohammed Ibrahim Qureshi, *The First Punjabis* (Aldershot, UK: Gale & Polden, 1958), 338 for more details.

22. *Burma Operations Record*, No. 148, 68–69.

23. Many Japanese troops were trying to retreat toward Thailand. WO 172/7693 15 April–28 May 1945 NA.

24. *Burma Operations Record*, No. 148, 69 and 73.

25. Kirby et al., *The War against Japan*, 4:389.

26. Quoted in Perrett, *Tank Tracks*, 229.

27. Slim, *Defeat into Victory*, 502.

28. 4th Corps Narrative of Operations, October 1944–May 1945, WO 203/2679, NA.

29. The history of the INA is outside the purview of this monograph. There are many sources on the origins and employment of this organization. See Daniel Marston, *The Indian Army and the End of the Raj* (Cambridge: Cambridge University Press, 2014), for a wider discussion of the impact of the INA in the postwar period.

30. Mylne, *Account*, 60–62.

31. *Burma Operations Record*, No. 148, 70.

32. Kirby et al., *The War against Japan*, 4:392.

33. Orders reproduced in Mylne, *Account*, 63–64.

34. 4th Corps Narrative of Operations, October 1944–May 1945, WO 203/2679, NA.

35. See Slim's description of his mistake of seeking to see the battle at Pegu on 1 May. He specifically stated, "I had no business as Army Commander to go where I did, and, if I was so stupid to go, I had no excuse for taking Messervy or others with me." Slim, *Defeat into Victory*, 505.

36. Kirby et al., *The War against Japan*, 4:365–366.

37. 33rd Corps Op Order 21, 33rd Corps Account of Operations, vol. 4, 20 March 1945–28 May 1945, WO 203/2686, NA; M. R. Roberts, *Golden Arrow: The Story of the 7th Indian Division in the Second World War, 1939–1945* (Aldershot, UK: Gale & Polden, 1952), 219–221; and Kirby et al., *The War against Japan*, 4:371–372.

38. 33rd Corps Op Order 21, 33rd Corps Account of Operations, vol. 4, 20 March 1945–28 May 1945, WO 203/2686, NA and also reproduced in Prasad, *The Reconquest of Burma*, 2:522.

39. WO 172/7787 15 April–10 May 1945; Scott Gilmore, *A Connecticut Yankee in the 8th Gurkha Rifles: A Burma Memoir* (Washington, DC: Brassey's, 1995), 214–219; and interviews with officers of 4/8th Gurkhas. For a more detailed account of the battle, see Gilmore's book, as well as Maj. Denis Sheil-Small (B Company commander), *Green Shadows: A Gurkha Story* (London: William Kimber, 1982); and Patrick Davis, *A Child at Arms* (London: Buchan & Enright, 1985).

40. WO 172/7732 (1/11th Sikh) 1–10/5/1945.

41. Quoted in Roberts, *Golden Arrow*, 233.

42. See Roberts, 233.

43. Patrick Davis was a B Company officer who noted that the company felt that if it gave up its position, the Japanese would be able to move through at night without observation. Interview with Patrick Davis, 17/1/2000; and Davis, *A Child at Arms*, 202.

44. Roberts, *Golden Arrow*, 234.

45. WO 172/7787 11–12/5/1945 NA.

46. Rifleman Lachhiman Gurung won the VC when he and his platoon, C Company, held out against an attack by more than two hundred Japanese soldiers.

47. WO 172/7787 12–13/5/1945 NA.

48. WO 172/7787 13–15/5/1945 NA.

49. Quoted in Roberts, *Golden Arrow*, 235.

50. WO 172/7787 22/5/1945 (order of the day) NA.

51. WO 172/7743, May 1945, NA and quoted in W. E. H. Condon, *Frontier Force Rifles* (Aldershot, UK: Gale & Polden), 421.

52. WO 172/7743, May 1945, NA.

53. Perrett, *Tank Tracks*, 217.

54. See the various war diaries, as they continued to list the number of killed Japanese in the areas.

55. Mountbatten, *Report*, 163.

56. Kirby et al., *The War against Japan*, 4:328–332.

57. Mountbatten, *Report*, 146.

58. Quoted in Kirby et al., *The War against Japan*, 4:353.

59. Kirby et al., 4:332.

60. Mountbatten, *Report*, 156.

61. Kirby et al., *The War against Japan*, 4:352.

62. Mountbatten, *Report*, 156.

63. Kirby et al., *The War against Japan*, 4:395.

64. See Kirby et al., 4:395–396, for an interesting account of an RAF Wing Commander who flew into Rangoon on 2 May and was able to confirm that the Japanese had withdrawn by 30 April.

65. 2/13th FFRifles, WO 172/7740, May 1945, NA.

66. Slim, *Defeat into Victory*, 507.

67. Slim, 510–511.

68. WO 172/7732 NA; and see P. G. Bamford, *1st King George V's Own Battalion: The Sikh Regiment* (Aldershot, UK: Gale & Polden, 1948), 142–145 for more details.

69. John Hill, *China Dragons: A Rifle Company at War, Burma 1944–45* (London: Blandford Press, 1991), 138.

70. Sheil-Small, *Green Shadows*, 15.

71. Slim, *Defeat into Victory*, 543.

72. Slim, 539.

73. John Masters, *The Road Past Mandalay: A Personal Narrative* (New York: Harper, 1961), 311–313.

5. The Final Battles

1. This may seem to slight the achievement of Lt. Gen. Richard O'Connor and the Western Desert Force in Operation Compass, the offensive (December 1940–February 1941) that swept the Italians from the borders of Egypt back to Tripoli, taking 130,000 prisoners while suffering less than a thousand fatal casualties. However,

the Italian Army, at its best (which it seldom was) was nothing like as formidable as the Imperial Japanese Army. O'Connor's logistics were of the shoestring variety but nothing like the mix of Dakotas, trucks, improvised watercraft, mules, elephants, and porters with headloads that carried the XIV Army from Imphal to Rangoon.

2. There is a copy in the Slim papers housed in the Churchill Archive Center, Churchill College, Cambridge: Slim Papers 2/3. It is written with Slim's trademark good humor, but the underlying anger peeps out.

3. Arthur Bryant, *Triumph in the West, 1943–1946* (New York: Doubleday, 1959). Eventually Brooke's full diaries would be published: Alex Danchev and Daniel Todman, eds., *War Diaries 1939–1945: Field Marshal Lord Alanbrooke* (London: Weidenfeld and Nicolson, 2001). This barely improves on the silence in Bryant's version.

4. Kirby et al., *The War against Japan*, vol. 5, *The Surrender of Japan* (London: His Majesty's Stationery Office, 1951), 27n2. See also appendix 1 to this chapter.

5. Slim, *Defeat into Victory* (London: Cassell, 1956), 164, emphasis in original.

6. Mountbatten's official biography, by Philip Ziegler—*Mountbatten: A Biography* (New York: Knopf, 1985)—is one of the better examples of the genre, sympathetic but far from uncritical. Adrian Smith's brilliant *Mountbatten: Apprentice Warlord* (London: I. B. Tauris, 2010) is much more searching and critical but stops at the point where Mountbatten becomes SACSEA. A second volume is promised.

7. In fact, the Americans were quite correct as far as Churchill himself was concerned. The prime minister had little patience with the American fixation with China and little enthusiasm for the overland reconquest of Burma—"going into the water to fight a shark." He wanted a maritime/amphibious strategy to reclaim Singapore and the empire's badly battered prestige in Asia.

8. Danchev and Todman, *War Diaries*, 582, entry for 19 August 1944. This entry reflects a conversation Brooke had with Gen. Sir Henry Maitland Wilson, the Allied Supreme Commander in the Mediterranean theater.

9. Danchev and Todman, *War Diaries*, 613, entry of 21 October 1944.

10. Danchev and Todman, 551, entry of 26 May 1944 and appended postwar note.

11. A baronetcy is a hereditary knighthood.

12. Slim, *Defeat into Victory*, 384–385. In all his published references to Leese, Slim was impeccably polite.

13. Robert Lyman, *Slim: Master of War* (London: Constable, 2004), 236–237. This is the best assessment yet written of Slim's generalship.

14. Brig. Michael Roberts to Slim, 8 June 1955, Slim Papers, 5/1, Churchill Archives Center. Roberts commanded a brigade in Burma, did research for Slim during the writing of *Defeat into Victory*, and was part of the team that wrote the official history.

This was not the first time this historic rivalry had threatened Slim. When Burcorps reached India in May 1942, the command controlling eastern India, Eastern Army, was led by Lt. Gen. Noel Irwin, a British regular who also disliked the Indian Army, particularly disliked Slim, and tried to scapegoat him for his own errors directing the disastrous first Arakan campaign. Slim's career survived; Irwin's did not. Leese might have taken note.

15. W. J. Slim, *Unofficial History* (New York: David McKey, 1959), 127–148. This

chapter, titled "Counsel of Fears," should be read by anyone interested in how Slim's command style evolved.

16. Slim to Brig. Michael Roberts, 22 October 1959, Slim Papers, 5/3, Churchill Archive Center.

17. Roberts to Ronald Lewin, 11 June 1976, Roberts Papers, MRBS 1/4, Churchill Archive Center.

18. Smith's *Mountbatten* is a rich source for this character trait.

19. Slim, draft chapter on events of May 1945, Slim Papers, 2/3, Churchill Archive Center.

20. Ziegler, *Mountbatten*, 293.

21. Slim's official biographer pointed out that as a captain, Slim wrote an essay on amphibious operations that garnered a prize and was subsequently published in the British Army's professional journal, *Army Quarterly*. Ronald Lewin, *Slim: The Standard Bearer* (London: Leo Cooper, 1976), 238n.

22. Quoted in Ziegler *Mountbatten*, 293–294.

23. Ziegler, 293.

24. "The Life and Times of General Sir Philip Christison, Bt., G.B.E., C.B., D.S.O., M.C., B.A., D.L.: An Autobiography." This typescript memoir written between 1947 and 1981 can be faulted on details and certainly bathes Christison in a flattering light but Christison apparently showed the sections on the command crisis in May 1945 to Leese and Leese and agreed it was accurate. A copy, catalogued as CHIE 1, is in the Churchill Archive Center.

25. The material in the foregoing paragraphs is based on Slim's own account (Slim Papers 2/3, Churchill Archive Center). Lewin, *Slim*, 237–246. Lewin corresponded with or interviewed all the surviving participants in the episode. Ziegler, *Mountbatten*, 293–295; and Raymond Callahan, *Churchill and His Generals* (Lawrence: University Press of Kansas, 2007), 231–233 and the sources cited there.

26. Slim Papers 2/3; Lewin, *Slim*, 244.

27. Mountbatten to Brooke, 23 May 1945, quoted in Ziegler, *Mountbatten*, 294.

28. This exchange is printed in General Sir David Fraser, *Alanbrooke* (London: Collins, 1982), 496–497, drawing on the Alanbrooke Papers. Fraser, like Leese, was an Etonian and a Grenadier. In Fraser, *And We Shall Shock Them: The British Army in the Second World War* (London: Hodder and Stoughton, 1983), he said this about the XIV Army's campaign: their victory "require[d] leadership of a transcendant quality" (376).

29. Lewin, *Slim*, 245.

30. Fraser, *Alanbrooke*, 498. Danchev and Todman, *War Diaries*, 703, print the diary entry but not the later gloss by Lord Alanbrooke (as he had become). Brooke's sympathy took concrete form: he made Leese general officer commanding, Eastern Command, a distinctly second-tier appointment but a face-saving prelude to retirement. He was never appointed full general, shortly retired from the army, and took up horticulture, writing a book on cacti.

Leese never wrote a memoir and left no papers. The closest thing we have to his version is what he told Christison at the time: "Brookie went to Churchill and told him the Indian Army wouldn't fight without Slim. 'Who sacked Slim,' said Churchill. 'Leese,' said Alanbrooke [*sic*]. 'Well, sack Leese.'" Christison memoir, CHIE 1, Churchill Archive Center. Leese maintained to the end of his life that he, not Mountbatten, was the responsible party in the episode.

31. If there was credit going, Dickie tended to annex it, or try to. Ronald Lewin, for instance, had to remind Mountbatten that the documents showed that Slim, not he, was the source of the idea of campaigning through the monsoon. Mountbatten's skill in manipulating the record was considerable. He persuaded Churchill to scrap the draft chapter on Dieppe that had been prepared for *The Hinge of Fate*, the fourth volume of his war memoirs, and to substitute for it Mountbatten's own draft, which diffused the blame very widely, an exercise described in David Reynolds, *In Command of History: Churchill Fighting and Writing the Second World War* (London: Allen Lane, 2004), 354–358. Professor Callahan experienced Mountbatten's careful curation of history's record of his career when he was commissioned to write a brief volume on the Burma campaign in the 1970s. He received an unsolicited letter from a former member of Mountbatten's SEAC staff, offering assistance, but clearly fishing for the "line" that would be followed by Professor Callahan in writing about Mountbatten.

32. Roberts to Lewin, 8 February 1973, Roberts Papers, MRBS 1/4, Churchill Archive Center.

33. Lewin, *Slim*, 128.

34. Julian Thompson, *The Imperial War Museum Book of the War In Burma, 1942–1945* (London: Sidgwick and Jackson, 2002), 388. Ronald Lewin, Slim's official biographer, exonerated Mountbatten, who was still alive when he wrote, but had private doubts. He told Professor Callahan that a sealed pattern Guardsman like Leese was very unlikely to take a step like sacking Slim without orders, or what he believed to be such—and totally unlikely afterward to fail to show loyalty to the superior who gave, or allowed Leese to believe he had been given, those orders. Leese himself told Christison afterward, "I gather I'm carrying the can for Dickie over this" (Ziegler, *Mountbatten*, 294). If so, he did it faithfully the rest of his life.

It is worth noting that the proof of Mountbatten's innocence—Browning's letter to Brooke—was written by a very ambitious officer who had been the commander of the Airborne Corps that mounted Operation Market Garden, an epic disaster. Finished as a field commander, but still well connected, Browning was found a safe harbor with Mountbatten, whose very competent chief of staff, Henry Pownall, had left due to illness. Nothing in Browning's previous record marked him as a gifted staff officer. Brooke's actions, and his postwar musings on the episode, indicate that he did not find the exculpations flowing from Kandy entirely convincing.

35. There were, of course, numerous independent brigades and unbrigaded battalions, many intended for static defense and garrison work and often comprising "lower category," i.e., older and less physically fit, men. Many British troops in India Command by 1945 fell into this group.

36. There is a good analysis of the mood of the British troops in India in Alan Allport, *Browned Off and Bloody-Minded: The British Soldier Goes to War, 1939–1945* (New Haven: Yale University Press, 2015), 166–179 and passim.

37. On his visit to Chequers, Slim told Churchill that the British troops in the XIV Army would not vote Conservative. The late Dr. W. J. Reader, then a young Royal Signals subaltern attached to the Indian Army, told Professor Callahan that he knew how the general election would go when he realized that every British sergeant in his unit was voting Labour.

38. Churchill, distracted by the impending general election and preparation for the Potsdam Conference, had to ask Gen. Sir Hastings Ismay, his personal chief of staff, on 16 June, "Please remind me what is 'Zipper.'" Martin Gilbert and Larry Arnn, eds., *The Churchill Documents*, vol. 21 (Hillsdale, MI: Hillsdale College Press, 2018), 1724.

39. Lacking radio links, Sakurai had to pass orders via liaison officer—a time-consuming, and insecure, process.

40. The final operations in Burma and the Japanese breakout across the Sittang are covered by the official history, Kirby et al., *The War against Japan*, 5:1–47; and the Indian official history, Bisheswar Prasad, ed., *The Official History of the Indian Armed Forces in the Second World War: The Reconquest of India* (Calcutta, 1959), 2:454–460. Louis Allen, who, as a young Japanese-speaking intelligence officer, took part, wrote a fascinating account from Japanese materials: Allen, *Sittang: The Last Battle* (New York: Ballantine, 1974). Allen also covered it in Allen, *Burma: The Longest War, 1941–1945* (London: Dent, 1984), 488–534. Slim, *Defeat into Victory*, 527–28, describes it briefly. (Slim, of course, was on leave in England during this battle.)

There is some dispute over how many Japanese died in the breakout attempt. The Japanese figure for the 28th Army before the breakout was 27,764, a suspiciously precise number in the circumstances. They report fourteen thousand reached safety. British intelligence estimated at the time that Sakurai had about nineteen thousand, of whom seven thousand survived. Whatever the true numbers may be, it is clear that over half of the 28th Army died trying to cross the Sittang. The British took 660 prisoners—a huge haul by previous standards—yet the British official history admits that "most . . . were taken, only because they were incapable of further effort" (46–47). Between the fall of Rangoon and the war's end, the 4th Corps lost only 435 men.

41. Kirby et al., *The War against Japan*, 5:27n2. Kirby had died the year before the volume appeared.

6. The XIV Army's Last Campaigns

1. See the volume 5 of the British official history, Kirby et al., *The War against Japan*, vol. 5, *The Surrender of Japan* (London: His Majesty's Stationery Office, 1951); Earl Mountbatten of Burma, *Post Surrender Tasks; Section E of the Report to the Combined Chiefs of Staff by the Supreme Allied Commander South-East Asia, 1943–1946* (London: Her Majesty's Stationery Office, 1969); Bisheshwar Prasad, *Official History of the Indian Armed Forces in the Second World War, 1939–1945: Post-War Occupation Forces Japan and South-East Asia* (New Delhi: Historical Section [India & Pakistan], 1958), and the various regimental histories for more detailed discussions of the peaceful occupation duties in the former British colonies and Siam.

2. There has been considerable research into this period in the last twenty-five years, mostly within the context of the post–Second World War political environment; there has not been much specific emphasis on the Indian Army's role as distinct from the larger strategic context of British decolonization and the impending conflict in French Indo-China that would engulf the French (and later the Americans) in two costly wars, as well as the Indonesian war of independence. For further details on the larger issues surrounding this chapter, see the following: John Springhall "Kicking Out the Vietminh: How Britain Allowed France to Reoccupy South Indo-China, 1945–6," *Journal of Contemporary History* 40, no. 1 (January 2005): 115–130; Ronald Spector, "After Hiroshima: Allied Military Occupations and the Fate of Japan's Empire, 1945–7," *Journal of Military History* 69, no. 4 (October 2005): 1121–1136; Peter Neville, *Britain in Vietnam: Prelude to Disaster, 1945–6* (London: Routledge, 2007); Peter Dennis, *Troubled Days of Peace: Mountbatten and South East Asia Command, 1945–6* (Manchester: Manchester University Press, 1987); Geraint Hughes, "A 'Post-War' War: The British Occupation of French-Indochina, September 1945–March 1946," *Small Wars & Insurgencies* 17, no. 3 (2006); Louis Allen, *The End of the War in Asia* (London: Hart-Davis MacGibbon, 1976); Peter Dunn, *The First Indo-China War* (London: C. Hurst, 1985); F. S. V. Donnison, *British Military Administration in the Far East, 1943–6* (London: Her Majesty's Stationery Office, 1956); Kirby et al., *The War Against Japan,* vol. 5; Mountbatten, *Report to the Combined Chiefs of Staff* (vol. 5); *Post Surrender Tasks* (vol. 6); and *Transfer of Power* (vol. 7, hereafter abbreviated *TOP*) (London: Her Majesty's Stationery Office, 1969); as well as the papers of Gen. Sir Douglas Gracey, Liddell Hart Centre for Military Archives, King's College London. For more details on the Netherlands East Indies, see John Springhall, "Disaster in Surabaya: The Death of Brigadier Mallaby during the British Occupation of Java, 1945–6," *Journal of Imperial and Commonwealth History* 24, no. 3 (September 1996): 422–443; Richard McMillan, *The British Occupation of Indonesia, 1945–1946* (London: Routledge, 2005); papers of Lt. Gen. Sir Philip Christison, Imperial War Museum, London; and the papers of Lt. Col. A. J. F. Doulton, National Army Museum, London.

3. Interview with Major G.C. Coppen, 1/11/1999.

4. See Kirby et al., *The War against Japan,* vol. 5, appendix 30, for a detailed discussion regarding the numbers of POWs in SEAC AO.

5. A sad commentary regarding this point was the death of Lt. Col. Sarbjit Singh Kalha of the 2/1st Punjab Regiment at Surabaya in Java, the NEI. As noted in chapter 1, he had risen to command the battalion during the Burma campaign and was highly respected. According to the 5th Indian divisional history, he was "calm and unruffled in battle, fearless, and with delightful manners, he had won the DSO and Bar. His remarkable ability included that of commanding both British and Indian officers, and there was no one in his battalion or in the Division who did not hold him in the highest regard. He was one of those senior Indian Army officers whom India could least to afford to lose." Antony Brett-James, *Ball of Fire: The Fifth Indian Division in the Second World War* (Aldershot, UK: Gale & Polden, 1951), 463.

6. All the senior officers mentioned in this chapter were Indian Army, except for Generals Christison, Dempsey, and Mountbatten.

7. See Hughes, "A 'Post-War' War," 276: "Indian and Gurkha troops who provided 20th Division with nearly all of its frontline soldiers, and who showed no qualms about treating local nationalists as the new enemy." See also NA, WO 172/7218, 80th Brigade security intelligence report, 23 October 1945.

8. A. J. F. Doulton, *The Fighting Cock: Being the History of the 23rd Indian Division, 1942–1947* (Aldershot, UK: Gale & Polden, 1951), 311.

9. See Richard McMillan, *The British Occupation of Indonesia, 1945–1946* (London: Routledge, 2005), for a detailed study.

10. See Dening to Foreign Office, 31 July 1945, *Documents on British Policy Overseas*, series 1, vol. 1 (1945) (London: HMSO, 1984), calendar 1 to no. 599, also quoted in Dennis, *Troubled Days*, 11–12.

11. Saigon was placed high on the list due to the fact that the Japanese HQ for their Southern Army was housed there. Dunn, *The First Indo-China War*, 119. See below for a description of Zipper.

12. Slim, *Defeat into Victory* (London: Cassell, 1956), 529–530.

13. HMG made an announcement in February 1945 that all British soldiers, NCOs, and officers who had served in the Far East for three years and eight months would be repatriated to the United Kingdom and released from service. In June 1945 this was amended to three years and four months. This policy decision created significant difficulties for SEAC and GHQ India in manning British battalions in the Indian Army, as well as British divisions, during the final phases of the Burma campaign. Decisions made about expanding SEAC's area of responsibility extended its impact into the postwar period. See Kirby et al., *The War against Japan*, 5:83–91, for a full description of its effects.

14. As Professor Ronald Spector noted: "Mountbatten suffered from the most critical shortage of troops as well as the worst timing. . . . [A] large proportion of Mountbatten's non-British forces were divisions of the Indian Army. . . . [A] good number of the Indians were career soldiers and many of the rest were in no hurry to be discharged." Ronald Spector, "After Hiroshima: Allied Military Occupations and the Fate of Japan's Empire, 1945–1947," *Journal of Military History* 69 (October 2005): 1128–1129.

15. It is interesting to note that, in Mountbatten's private diary, he never alludes to any tension regarding the use of Indian Army troops or to Auchinleck's and Slim's concerns, despite mentioning both men numerous times. See Philip Ziegler, ed., *Personal Diary of Admiral the Lord Louis Mountbatten: Supreme Allied Commander, South-East Asia, 1943–1946* (London: Collins, 1988).

16. Slim, *Defeat into Victory*, 530–531; and Dunn, *The First Indo-China War*, 124.

17. See Daniel Marston, *The Indian Army and the End of the Raj* (Cambridge: Cambridge University Press, 2014), for a more in-depth and detailed discussion of the issues in India in 1945–1947 in terms of communal violence and the impact of the Indian National Army trials.

18. Dennis, *Troubled Days*, 7.

19. Dunn, *The First Indo-China War*, 123.

20. Dennis, *Troubled Days*, 13.

21. It was feared that many Japanese soldiers would still fight on until they heard

that the emperor had actually surrendered. It was estimated that there were close to five million Japanese soldiers in the empire, and their impression was that they had not been defeated.

22. General Wedemeyer had been the chief of staff to Mountbatten in SEAC, but in October 1944, he replaced General Joseph Stillwell, to assume command of all US forces in China and to serve as Chiang Kai-shek's chief of staff.

23. See Earl Mountbatten of Burma, *Post Surrender Tasks*; WO 172/1778, Gairdner to Mountbatten, 21 August 1945, NA, and Dunn, *The First Indo-China War*, 123. See Albert Wedemeyer's very interesting memoir, *Wedemeyer Reports! An Objective, Dispassionate Examination of World War II, Postwar Policies, and Grand Strategy* (New York: Henry Holt, 1958), for more details.

24. Dennis, *Troubled Days*, 14–15. See also Field Marshal Slim's critical comments regarding this issue in Slim, *Defeat into Victory*, 530–531.

25. See WO 203/5444, 28 August 1945, ALFSEA Operational Directive No. 12, "Masterdom," NA and Springhall, 119.

26. Slim, *Defeat into Victory*, 530–531.

27. Doulton, *The Fighting Cock*, 219. While the Japanese would not oppose the British/Indian forces, they still were brutal right up to the end of the occupation. In the town of Malacca, the staff from the local Chinese newspaper were arrested and killed. Their crime was that the Japanese accused them of making outspoken comments regarding the collapse of Japanese resistance. See Doulton, 226–227, for more details.

28. Mountbatten, *Post-Surrender*, 300.

29. Kirby et al., *The War against Japan*, 5:267.

30. 224 Group RAF report, quoted in Kirby et al., 5:268–269.

31. Doulton, *The Fighting Cock*, 220.

32. Unlike in other occupied areas, the Japanese forces in Malaya had not attempted to fill a political vacuum or stir any anticolonial feelings. The three weeks between the Japanese surrender and the arrival of the 34th Corps were a quiet period. The Japanese had withdrawn to the towns and waited for the British arrival.

33. J. P. Lawford, *Solah Punjab: The History of the 16th Punjab Regiment* (Aldershot, UK: Gale & Polden, 1967), 275.

34. Violence increased between the Malays and the Chinese resistance forces; however, Indian and British troops were not involved in suppressing the violence. By early 1946, the violence had subsided, but political agitation continued to increase. See Mountbatten, *Post-Surrender*, 302–307, for a detailed description of the tense phase of the Military Administration, between September 1945 to April 1946, as well as appendices I–K. The British-sponsored Chinese resistance movement, Malayan People's Anti-Japanese Army, would adhere initially to disarming; however, it hid most of their caches in the jungle. They would be reraised by 1948 and begin a serious and violent insurgency in Malaya. This next war was named the Malayan Emergency, a conflict that has been written about extensively. Ironically, many former XIV Army veterans would play central and key roles in the eventual defeat of the insurgency.

35. Doulton, *The Fighting Cock*, 229.

36. See Brett-James, *Ball of Fire*, 429, for a detailed description of the meeting.

37. WO 172/6965, September 1945, NA.

38. Lt .Col. Sarbjit Singh Kalha, an Indian commissioned officer, and the CO of the 2/1st Punjabis, was one of the escorting officers for the Japanese generals.

39. Quoted in Kirby et al., *The War against Japan*, 5:272.

40. Reproduced in Brett-James, *Ball of Fire*, 439–440.

41. Kirby et al., *The War against Japan*, 5:273. See appendix 20 for the full instrument of surrender.

42. Reproduced in Brett-James, *Ball of Fire*, 431–432.

43. Quoted in Brett-James, 437.

44. Brett-James, 443.

45. Kirby et al., *The War against Japan*, 5:292.

46. WO 172/6975 September 1945, NA. Ironically, Siam had declared war on Great Britain in 1941.

47. M. R. Roberts, *Golden Arrow: The Story of the 7th Indian Division in the Second World War, 1939–1945* (Aldershot, UK: Gale & Polden, 1952), 265–267.

48. WO 172/6975 September–December 1945, NA.

49. Roberts, *Golden Arrow*, 268–289.

50. In the end, the 20th Indian Division spent most of its time and effort in and around Saigon.

51. See WO 203/5444, Operational Directive, No. 12, 28 August 1945, NA and Springhall, p. 119.

52. See Springhall, "Kicking Out the Vietminh," 119; and Dunn, *The First Indo-China War*, 139.

53. This organization was made up of resources from SEAC and reported directly back to SEAC HQ in Kandy, Ceylon. General Gracey had an extensive list of tasks to fulfill for SEAC: assume control of HQ Japanese Southern Army; supervise the surrender; transmit SEAC orders to the Japanese; obtain information regarding Japanese dispositions and supplies; control Japanese communications; study the Recovery of Allied Prisoners of War and Internees (RAPWI) problem and render all possible aid; report on Indo-China's lines of communication, airfields, and the port of Saigon; open river and sea approaches to Saigon; using Japanese resources, reduce size of Japanese HQs as soon as possible; and maintain liaison with the French local government, keeping Mountbatten informed. Gracey Papers, file 4/2, Liddell Hart Centre, KCL, 30 August 1945.

54. This was a larger organization than the commission; it included French military forces and directly reported back to Gen. Sir William Slim and ALFSEA.

55. Springhall, "Kicking Out the Vietminh," 119.

56. General Gracey Papers, file 4/2, Liddell Hart Centre. ALFSEA Op Directive no. 8, 23 August 1945.

57. Gracey papers, Operational Directive no 12, Liddell Hart Centre, 28 August 1945.

58. See debate in Dunn, *The First Indo-China War*, 140–147.

59. Dunn, 134; and General Gracey Papers, file 4/2. More information started to trickle out to the British, but it was not of a high quality.

60. Kirby et al., *The War against Japan*, 5:290.

61. Springhall, "Kicking Out the Vietminh," 117–118.

62. It would not be in fully in country until the 26th, due to the many transport issues.

63. There is some discrepancy on the date: some authors such as Springhall state the first troops arrived in the 8th. The first detachment was a company minus from the 1/19th Hyderabad Regiment. Kirby states that the first troops arrived on the 8th.

64. Upon arriving, Gracey and his staff walked past the small Vietminh delegation and met with the Japanese contingent. This action specifically stated that the Allies did not recognize the Vietminh as a legitimate government.

65. Interestingly, many Indian Army veterans recalled, from their command of Japanese POWs, the professionalism and discipline that the Japanese displayed. Some even indicated their preference for commanding Japanese over their own Indian jawans. Interviews with Indian Army officers, 1999–2007. The CO from the 3/8th Gurkha Riles, Lt. Col. E. H. Russell, noted in a letter to his wife upon arrival in Saigon that "the most incredible thing—really incredible thing—is to see the Japs. As we came down the gangplank, a Jap fatigue party took the men's kit from them, and loaded it onto lorries. They did it at the double. My right arm will fall off soon, as every Jap, even if he is 500 yards away, salutes, and one has to the return the salutes." Cited in 8th Gurkha Rifles Association, *Red Flash* 15 (February 1992): 6.

66. The process of disarming and rounding up soldiers and weapons was complicated. The British and Indian soldiers would do it first and then hand over the weapon stores to the French authorities and military, as the Japanese refused to deal with them.

67. Kirby et al., *The War against Japan*, 5:298–299.

68. It was estimated that more than two thousand Japanese soldiers did desert before and after the arrival of the British and Indian troops. Springhall, "Kicking Out the Vietminh," 119.

69. Gracey Papers, "Report on Ops 80 Ind Inf BDE," Box 5/4, see page 6, "propaganda to suborn Indian soldiers were freely posted up by Annamites. These had no effect at all."

70. It was stressed by Mountbatten in a communiqué: HMG's goals in sending British troops into FIC were fourfold—to control Field Marshal Terauchi's headquarters, which commanded the Japanese armies in the southern regions; to disarm the Japanese; to release and repatriate Allied POWs and internees; and to maintain law and order until the arrival of French Forces. He stressed that HM Government had no intention of using British forces in FIC to crush resistance movements. Dunn, *The First Indo-China War*, 167.

71. WO 172/1784 NA, Gracey to Mountbatten.

72. WO 203/5562 NA Gracey to Mountbatten, 21 September 1945; Dennis, *Troubled Days*, 39; and Springhall, "Kicking Out the Vietminh," 120.

73. See Mountbatten, *Post Surrender Tasks*, Section E, as well as Dunn, *The First Indo-China War*, 173; and Dennis, *Troubled Days*, 41.

74. The French 9th DIC (Colonial Infantry Division) was still not in Vietnam, but was to be released soon, to relieve the 20th Indian Division.

75. See Gracey papers, Saigon Control Commission, Political Report, 13 September to 9 October 1945, Liddell Hart Centre, for a more detailed account, as well as Dunn, *The First Indo-China War*, 183–189.

76. Throughout this period, a series of debates was ongoing in both SEAC and London, where the British mission began and ended. "Mission creep" had been occurring since mid-August and there was at times a lack of clear strategy and end goal. General Gracey felt that he had to carry out the coup to allow for law and order to be restored, and that the French forces and administration were best placed to carry this out, since the Vietminh was not a recognized organization. For a much more detailed account of the higher-level issues regarding strategy and joint British and French planning and thinking on Indo-China, see Dennis, *Troubled Days*, Springhall, "Kicking Out the Vietminh," and especially Dunn, *The First Indo-China War*. An interesting document is the "Report on Ops 80 Ind Inf BDE" found in General Gracey's papers. It clearly outlines the need and planning for the seizure of key administrative buildings and centers in Saigon, stating: "the stage was now set for the coup d'état by the French to take over the civil administration in Saigon" (4). Gracey Papers, "Report on Ops 80 Ind Inf BDE," Liddell Hart Centre, 23 September 1945.

77. See Dunn, *The First Indo-China War*, 195–197; and Dennis, *Troubled Days*, 43–48.

78. As noted, "On September 23, armed and protected by the British forces, the French colonialists launched their attack and occupied Saigon. Our people replied by force of arms, and from that moment, our heroic resistance began." Truong Chinh, *Primer for Revolt, the Communist Takeover in Viet-Nam: A Facsimile Edition of the August Revolution and the Resistance Will Win* (New York: Praeger, 1963), 17; and Dunn, *The First Indo-China War*, 202–203.

79. The first American casualty in the history of US intervention in Vietnam occurred during this period. Lt. Col. Thomas Dewey of the OSS was killed in a Vietminh ambush. The role and position of the US OSS during this period is controversial; see Dunn, *The First Indo-China War*, and Dennis, *Troubled Days*, for a more detailed discussion of their stance in relation to the British and French activities.

80. See war diaries from the 20th Indian Division for more information; see also Dunn, *The First Indo-China War*, 200–201.

81. Dennis, *Troubled Days*, 50.

82. See Dunn, *The First Indo-China War*, 200–210; and Dennis, *Troubled Days*, 50–54.

83. Springhall, "Kicking Out the Vietminh," 124, as well as Hughes, "A 'Post-War' War," 271; and Dunn, *The First Indo-China War*, 229–230. At a meeting in Singapore on 28 September, Slim backed Gracey against Mountbatten in the view that the whole division was needed to restore law and order in and around Saigon. See Hughes, "A 'Post-War' War," 270.

84. Dennis, *Troubled Days*, 59–61.

85. Interviews with Indian Army veterans, 1999–2007, and 1/1 Gurkha Rifles, WO 172/7769, October 1945, NA, as well as Dunn, *The First Indo-China War*, 204.

86. The Japanese forces followed a multifaceted approach to the campaign. Some units clearly did not want to support the British and French, and actively aided the

Vietminh with weapons and lack of support to the British and Indian troops. Other units actively worked with British and Indian troops and fought and died alongside them in battle with the Vietminh. See Dunn, *The First Indo-China War*, for a more in-depth discussion.

87. General Gracey reiterated this in a letter to General Slim on 5 November: "It is most necessary that I should continue to run the whole Japanese side of things as long as we are here. The Japanese will take anything from us, but will do nothing for the French." Later in the letter, he noted a request from the Japanese command: "We respectfully submit a request that all orders to our forces should be passed by a British officer and not a French officer, as we find it increasingly difficult to carry out the orders resulting from their shameless plans." Gracey Papers, Gracey to Slim, Box 5/4, Liddell Hart Centre, 5 November 1945.

88. The 9th DIC was not formally in place until the end of November 1945, although other forces started to arrive in October and early November. General Philippe Leclerc, commander of the French Forces, arrived on 5 October. See WO 203/5608, NA, 19 November 1945, SACSEA Joint Planning Staff, "Turnover of Command," and Dennis, *Troubled Days of Peace*, 59–61.

89. *TOP*, VI, London: HMSO, 127, Wavell to Lord Pethick-Lawrence, 1 October 1945, 306. Wavell would reiterate this point in a follow-on letter to Lord Pethick-Lawrence on 9 October 1945. See *TOP*, VI, 135, p. 323.

90. Slim to Brooke, 6 October 1945, annex to COS 9450 607 (o), CAB, 80/97, and cited in Dennis, *Troubled Days*, 165.

91. Gracey to Mountbatten, WO 172/1786, 1 October, NA, and Dennis, *Troubled Days*, 66–67. See also Dunn's chapter "Truce" in *The First Indo-China War* for a very detailed discussion of the truce talks and the higher-level political issues that occurred.

92. Gracey was quick to point out that it was not going to be wanton killing; there would be no provocative use of force, and troops would cause minimal disturbance to law-abiding citizens. However, this did not mean he would not use all of his weapon platforms against the violent elements of the Vietminh. Dunn, *The First Indo-China War*, 259–260.

93. Gracey Papers, "Report on Ops 80 Ind Inf BDE," Box 5/4, Liddle Hart Centre, Kings College London.

94. Mountbatten, *Post Surrender Tasks*, Section E, 282, and Dunn, *The First Indo-China War*, 257. See Marston, *Indian Army*, for more details on the negative impact of the use of Indian troops within India and the political fallout with the various Indian Nationalist parties.

95. Lieutenant Colonel Russell, 3/8th Gurkhas, noted some of his frustration with the mission in a letter to his wife. On 23 October, after his battalion had lost more men killed and wounded, he wrote: "what a bloody show this is. We had another man killed and two wounded, one rather badly. . . . I wouldn't mind so much if this was a pukka war, but our men are getting hit because a lot of bloody Annamites want to chuck the French out. I hope these French get a move on and take over the running of their own affairs." *Red Flash* 15 (February 1992): 6.

96. Kirby et al., *The War against Japan*, 5:302–303.

97. For some battalions, serious fighting ensued. See the Newsletters and Histories of 9/14 Punjab and the 2/8 Punjab regiments in the General Gracey Papers, files 5/5 and 5/12, for more details of the actions, as well as Dunn, *The First Indo-China War*, 257–259. As one battalion stated: "As far as the BN was concerned the shooting season for the Annamites [word used for the Vietminh by British and Indian troops] had opened." See also battalion history of the 9/14th Punjab, which stated: "it was an unsatisfactory sort of fighting. The enemy wore no uniform and usually did not carry arms visibly." Anonymous [John Booth], *Ninth Battalion Fourteenth Punjab Regiment* (Cardiff: Western Mail and Echo, 1948), 97.

98. See Dunn, *The First Indo-China War*, 236–237, and Dennis, *Troubled Days*, 64.

99. 100th Indian Infantry Brigade WO 172/7135, November 1945, NA.

100. This battalion was considered one of the best in the Burma campaign; at this point in the Indo-China campaign, it still had many of the veterans from Burma. See Daniel Marston, *The Phoenix from the Ashes: The Indian Army in the Burma Campaign* (Westport, CT: Praeger, 2003), for much more detail on the battlefield performance of this battalion.

101. This was a prewar Indianized regiment and performed well during the war. It was commanded at this point by an Indian officer, Lieutenant Colonel Chaudhuri.

102. Dunn, *The First Indo-China War*, 270–277; and 100th Indian Infantry Brigade, WO 172/7135, November 1945, NA.

103. 14/13th FFRifles November 1945, WO 172/7743, NA.

104. Dunn, *The First Indo-China War*, 280. This was not the first time that buildings were burned in retaliation by British and Indian troops. Members of the Bombay Sappers and Miners Company had destroyed huts after the killing of one of their men. See Dunn, 277. The issue with this is that although the Indian Army was an army that understood "minimum force," many within the 20th Indian Division were mistakenly viewing this campaign through the prism of conventional operations, due to the level of violence and the military organization and activities of the Vietminh. It must also be remembered that the burning of villages followed the doctrinal practice of "punitive expeditions" in the North-West Frontier Province over the previous eighty years. The British attempted to drop leaflets to inform the population, as they had done in the North-West Frontier Province. See letter from Gracey to Mountbatten, 9 November 1945, WO 203/4271, NA; and Dennis, *Troubled Days*, 174–175, for some of General Gracey's explanations for the destruction of houses and, potentially, villages.

105. 14/13th FFRifles, WO 172/7743, NA, November 1945, and 100 Indian Infantry Brigade, WO 172/7135, November 1945, NA.

106. Dunn, *The First Indo-China War*, 282. By the end of November, eighteen British and Indian soldiers had been killed and fifty-one wounded, along with nineteen Japanese killed and thirteen missing. It was estimated that close to four hundred Vietminh had been killed and more than four hundred had been captured by the 20th Indian Division; estimates from the French and Japanese were lacking. Dunn, 285.

107. Lieutenant Colonel Russell of 3/8th Gurkhas wrote, in a letter to his wife, "disarming the Japs is to start in a few days. . . . Unfortunately, the Japs I have had under my command are to be disarmed by the RAF. I wish we were doing it, as I can't

help liking the Jap Major who commands them, and I am sure he would prefer to be disarmed by us." *Red Flash* 15 (February 1992): 7.

108. See 100th Indian Infantry Brigade War Diary for the month of November 1945, as it lists "Jap Surrender Instr No 1" as well as other key tasks and operations for the brigade. WO 172/7135, November 1945, NA.

109. Gracey Papers, Gracey to Slim, Box 5/4, Liddell Hart Centre, 5 November 1945.

110. Auchinleck to Wavell, 13 November 1945, no. 1112, Auchinleck Papers, University of Manchester. He followed this with another letter on 20 November to G. E. B. Abell, private secretary to the viceroy, no. 1116, stating that the Government of India should be consulted before Indian troops were used in other areas. General Auchinleck and Wavell were under immense pressure due to the Indian National Army trials that were taking place in New Delhi and were aware of the potential additional pressure that would be applied to the Indian Army.

111. L/WS/1/1488, Auchinleck to the War Office, 15 November 1945, OIOC.

112. See both the battalion and brigade war diaries, WO 172/7135 and WO 172/7743, for more detail.

113. Dunn, *The First Indo-China War*, 311.

114. Interview with Indian Army officers, 1999–2007. It is also noted in W. E. H. Condon's regimental history *The Frontier Force Regiment* (Aldershot, UK: Gale & Polden, 1962): "As the concentration of surrendered Japanese troops increased, the men of the battalion [the 9/12th FFR] had naturally to come into closer contact with their late enemies, and had the opportunity to observe them closely. It is recorded that their discipline was first class, and they co-operated and carried out orders 100 percent. Never was there a cause for complaint, and the men grew to respect them and showed a tendency to fraternize" (512–513). The 9/14th Punjab Regiment's battalion history, while respecting the Japanese soldiers' discipline, still could not see them other than an enemy. As the battalion stated: "Many of them [surrendering Japanese soldiers], handing over their swords which were family heirlooms, were in tears but after what we had seen of them [in Burma] our hearts were closed to any pity for the Jap." Anonymous, *Ninth Battalion Fourteenth Punjab Regiment*, 99.

115. The battalion arrived in FIC in early October 1945. It was initially commanded by an Indian Commissioned Officer (ICO), Lt. Col. Hayaud Din, who had commanded the battalion during the heavy fighting in Burma in 1945. The battalion had served throughout the Burma campaigns of 1943–1945 with the 80th Indian Infantry Brigade. Upon the ending of the Burma campaign, the unit became the recce battalion for the division. During the first weeks of deployment to FIC, it served in the Cholon area of Saigon and participated in many clearing patrols of the area. In mid-October it was ordered to proceed to Cap St. Jacques to set up a series of internment camps for the Japanese POWs. See WO 172/7738, January to December 1945, as well as General Gracey Papers, file 4/26.

116. WO 172/7738, NA, 9/12 Frontier Force Regiment, December 1945.

117. See Dunn, *The First Indo-China War*, 314–316, for more details.

118. WO 172/7098, NA, 32nd Indian Infantry Brigade, NA, December 1945.

119. WO 172/7128, NA, 80th Indian Infantry Brigade, NA, December 1945.

120. WO 172/7738, NA, 9/12th FFR, December 1945, and also see Condon, *Frontier Force Regiment*, 509–513.

121. WO 172/7135, NA, 100th Indian Infantry Brigade, December 1945.

122. See General Gracey papers, File 4/16, 12 December 1945, Liddell Hart Centre. Also quoted in Dunn, *The First Indo-China War*, 325–326 and Dennis, *Troubled Days*, 177.

123. General Gracey papers, File 4/16, 12 December 1945, Liddell Hart Centre, Kings College London.

124. Interviews with officers from the 14/13th FFRifles. See Marston's *Phoenix from the Ashes* for more details on the 14/13th FFRifles and the "Sher Forces." See also WO 172/7743, December 1945, NA.

125. WO 172/10272 14/13th FFRifles February 1946, NA.

126. Dunn, *The First Indo-China War*, 334.

127. WO 172/7135, December 1945, NA.

128. See WO 172/7353 and WO 172/10060, NA for more details of the 16th Light Calvary.

129. 20th Indian Division HQ War Diary, WO 203/5995, February 1946, NA.

130. OIOC, L/MIL/17/5/4276, India Command Fortnightly Intelligence Reports, 1946, No. 2. 20 January 1946, BL.

131. Dunn, *The First Indo-China War*, 341. Hughes puts the figures at three thousand dead.

132. WO 172/7135, December 1945, NA.

133. Condon notes an interesting aspect of the withdrawal of the 9/12th FFR in *The Frontier Force Regiment*: "On 29th of March the battalion embarked at Cap St Jacques. . . . Many Japanese senior officers and men lined the route to say goodbye to the Battalion, and it was a curious, if not pathetic, scene to find the very men who had fought against us so bitterly, now so manifestly sorry to bid the Battalion farewell" (513).

134. Dunn, *The First Indo-China War*, 355–356.

135. Slim, *Defeat into Victory*, 532.

136. In the end, the 23rd, 26th, and 5th Indian divisions and supporting elements were deployed to the NEI.

137. Over six hundred soldiers and officers were killed in Java and Sumatra, compared to just over 40 in FIC. Kirby et al., *The War against Japan*, vol. 5, appendix 31, p. 544.

138. Kirby et al., 5:307.

139. There are numerous references to issues with Dutch colonial troops, especially the Ambonese. See Kirby et al., 5:339, and McMillan, *The British Occupation of Indonesia*, 86, as quick references to the issues.

140. See Dennis, *Troubled Days*, for an in-depth discussion of the higher-level decision making throughout the whole campaign, and the many back-and-forth debates and planning that occurred throughout this most difficult campaign.

141. Kirby et al., *The War against Japan*, 5:309–310 and Dennis, *Troubled Days*, 81.

142. Kirby et al., *The War against Japan*, 5:312; and see Lieutenant General

Christison's comments, "the one in East Java is tough and well led," in "Life and Times of General Sir Philip Christison," p. 178, Imperial War Museum.

143. Quoted in Kirby et al., *The War against Japan*, 5:311.

144. "Life and Times of General Sir Philip Christison," p. 175, Imperial War Museum.

145. This was part of the British Special Operation Executive that had been working in Southeast Asia throughout the war and had carried out sabotage and the raising of local guerrilla forces to oppose the Japanese occupations.

146. A battalion of British troops and supporting Royal Marine troops arrived in Batavia on 28 September to prepare for reinforcements coming behind.

147. See "Life and Times of General Sir Philip Christison," p. 176, Imperial War Museum; see also McMillan, *The British Occupation of Indonesia*, 16, for more details.

148. Kirby et al., *The War against Japan*, 5:314, and McMillan, *The British Occupation of Indonesia*, 19–20. The British Secretary of State for War, Mr. Lawson, specifically stated to Lieutenant General Christison, when they saw each other in Singapore, "that nothing should be done to suggest your troops are going to re-impose Dutch Colonial rule. You must not take sides." See "Life and Times of General Sir Philip Christison," p. 176, Imperial War Museum.

149. See Dennis, *Troubled Days*, 89–92, for details.

150. See Kirby et al., *The War against Japan*, vol. 5, appendix 24, for a full transcript of the radio message.

151. Kirby et al., *The War against Japan*, 5:315–316. Dennis deals with this issue in more detail. Mountbatten was asking the British Chiefs of Staff to support his push that the Dutch government needed to be clear in their aims in the NEI, that negotiations should begin between the Dutch and the Indonesian Republic. In the end, the Dutch became more set in their ways and responded that they would dictate what was needed in the NEI and that the British troops were there to maintain law and order until the Dutch forces arrived. There was much tension and the issue would not be resolved until British and Indian troops left later in the year. See Dennis, *Troubled Days*, 92–96.

152. Kirby et al., *The War against Japan*, 5:319.

153. "At first I ordered all troops not on duty to walk about and enter shops and pubs unarmed and there was much camaraderie." "Life and Times of General Sir Philip Christison," p. 180, Imperial War Museum; McMillan, *The British Occupation of Indonesia*, 20–21.

154. Kirby et al., *The War against Japan*, 5:321.

155. See War Diary of the Indian State Forces, 1st Patialas, WO 172/7827 October 1945, NA, and McMillan, *The British Occupation of Indonesia*, 22.

156. The KNIL recruited from two specific ethnic groups that were loyal and interested in seeing the return of the Netherlands to the islands. In the end, they had much to lose and wished to restore Indonesia to prewar policies.

157. McMillan, *The British Occupation of Indonesia*, 22–23.

158. Lieutenant General Christison reported seeing paperback books showing whites and Eurasians being tortured, dismembered, and killed; these were confirmed

by reports that came in each day. "Life and Times of General Sir Philip Christison," p. 180, Imperial War Museum.

159. Lord Pethick-Lawrence noted in a letter to Lord Wavell on 16 October 1945 that a second Indian Division was needed for Java and took priority over other areas, due to attitude of the Indonesian Nationalists. See *TOP*, VI, no. 145, Lord Pethick-Lawrence to Wavell, 16 October 1945. Lord Wavell, in responding to this request, highlighted significant concerns about the level of strain under which the Indian Army was operating due to the INA trials. He wrote: "I think it right to let you know privately that in my opinion loyalty and discipline of the Indian Army may be subjected to severe strain owing to the agitation about the INA demobilization. I think it is most important that we should not add further strain of commitments in the Netherlands East Indies or French Indo-China. I am sure you will appreciate this and do your best to resist employment of additional Indian Division in Java." Wavell to Pethwick-Lawrence, 17 October 1945, OIOC BL, L/WS/1/726; and *TOP*, VI, no. 148, p. 360.

160. See 1/16th Punjab Regiment, WO 172/7753, October 1945, NA.

161. See 3/3rd Gurkha Rifles, WO 172/7775, October-November 1945, and McMillan, *The British Occupation of Indonesia*, 23–24.

162. One Japanese officer, Major Kido, who worked heavily with the Gurkhas in Central Java, was actually recommended for a British decoration, the Distinguished Service Order (DSO), by General Christison. McMillan, *The British Occupation of Indonesia*, 30.

163. Kirby et al., *The War against Japan*, 5:321.

164. Doulton, *The Fighting Cock*, 246.

165. See 3/5th Gurkha Rifles, WO 172/7779, October-November 1945; and McMillan, *The British Occupation of Indonesia*, 25–26.

166. The battalion was specifically ordered to maintain law and order and not to take sides in any political matters. 3/10th Gurkha Rifles, WO 172/7792, November 1945; and McMillan, *The British Occupation of Indonesia*, 27.

167. Kirby et al., *The War against Japan*, 5:320.

168. McMillan, *The British Occupation of Indonesia*, 26.

169. 3/10th Gurkhas, November-December 1945; McMillan, *The British Occupation of Indonesia*, 27–28, and Kirby et al., *The War against Japan*, 5:336.

170. 3/10th Gurkhas, WO/172/7792 December 1945; and Kirby, *The War against Japan*, 5:337.

171. 49th Indian Infantry Brigade, WO 172/7108 December; and McMillan, *The British Occupation of Indonesia*, 28–29.

172. 49th Indian Infantry Brigade, WO 172/7108 December; and Kirby et al., *The War against Japan*, 5:338–339.

173. Kirby et al., *The War against Japan*, 5:339; and Dennis, *Troubled Days*, 189.

174. Kirby et al., *The War against Japan*, 5:321–322.

175. For more details regarding the conversation with Lieutenant General Christison, see "Life and Times of General Sir Philip Christison," p. 178, Imperial War Museum.

176. The dispatch of the 5th Indian Division caused much anger in New Delhi, as General Auchinleck was under more and more pressure not to use "Indian troops" in the NEI and FIC. He asked for the British 2nd Division to be sent, but Mountbatten overruled him, saying that the division was not ready and that he needed troops right away. See Dennis, *Troubled Days*, 121–123.

177. Brett-James, *Ball of Fire*, 451, and Kirby et al., *The War against Japan*, 5:322.

178. McMillan goes into some detail regarding Mallaby's background and friction with his second-in-command, Colonel Pugh. Brigadier Mallaby had spent most of the Second World War as a staff officer, serving as a major general as the Director of Military Operations at GHQ India. He dropped a rank to brigadier to command the 49th Brigade as it prepared for the final push against the Japanese. Colonel Pugh had a distinguished career as a commander during the Burma campaign, winning the DSO and Bar. He commanded the 33rd Indian Infantry Brigade in 1944 and 1945. It appears that, with the reshuffling of the commands at the end of the war, Pugh became the second in command and a colonel once again, with Mallaby as his commander. According to many sources, the two men were completely different, Mallaby "more relaxed" and Pugh "a bit of a fire eater." This apparently created significant friction, and the two men were barely speaking to each other by the time the brigade landed. See McMillan, *The British Occupation of Indonesia*, 33–34, for more details.

179. See 49th Indian Infantry Brigade, WO 172/7108; and McMillan, *The British Occupation of Indonesia*, 37.

180. Dennis, *Troubled Days*, 123.

181. McMillan, *The British Occupation of Indonesia*, 38–39.

182. Kirby et al., *The War against Japan*, 5:323.

183. See Kirby et al., *The War against Japan*, 5:323–324; Dennis, *Troubled Days*, 123–124; and McMillan, *The British Occupation of Indonesia*, 39–41, for more details. McMillan goes into detail about the disconnect between Brigadier Mallaby and Major General Hawthorn and the "glossing over" of the leaflets by the divisional historian, Lieutenant Colonel Doulton, in *The Fighting Cock*.

184. McMillan, *The British Occupation of Indonesia*, goes into some detail, stating that Mallaby did not reposition his forces to deal with a potential outbreak of violence and many officers did not understand why he did nothing to deal with a potential attack. See the comments in McMillan, *The British Occupation of Indonesia*, 41–44, especially the comments from the CO of 4/5th Mahratta Light Infantry.

185. McMillan, *The British Occupation of Indonesia*, gives quite a bit of detail of the fighting and the loss of life on pp. 43–45. See also the war diaries of 49th Indian Infantry Brigade for more details.

186. Doulton, *The Fighting Cock*, 255.

187. 5/6 Raj Rif, WO 172/7709 November, 1945.

188. Brett-James, *Ball of Fire*, 450.

189. See Kirby et al., *The War against Japan*, 5:324–325, Dennis, *Troubled Days*, 124; and McMillan, *The British Occupation of Indonesia*, 46–48.

190. See McMillan's very detailed and important analysis of this episode in *The British Occupation of Indonesia*, 48–50.

191. McMillan, *The British Occupation of Indonesia*, 51–52.

192. "Life and Times of General Sir Philip Christison," p. 185, Imperial War Museum.

193. Kirby et al., *The War against Japan*, 5:328.

194. Brett-James, *Ball of Fire*, 452.

195. The CO of the Dogra Machine Gun Battalion, Lt. Col. R. C. B. Bristow, noted this in his recollection of the arrival of the 5th Indian Division. See Bristow, *Memories of the British Raj: A Soldier in India* (London: Johnson, 1974), 139.

196. McMillan, *The British Occupation of Indonesia*, 55; Brett-James, *Ball of Fire*, 452–453; War Diaries of 9th Indian Infantry Brigade, WO 172/7085 and 123rd Indian Infantry Brigade, WO 172/7138.

197. Wavell to Pethick-Lawrence, 7 November 1945, OIOC, BL, L/WS/1/727; and *TOP*, VI, no. 198, p. 460.

198. Pethick-Lawrence to Wavell, OIOC, BL, L/WS/1/727; and *TOP*, VI, no. 206, pp. 474–475. Lord Wavell responded on 27 November to Lord Pethick-Lawrence, stating, "The INA trials have been embarrassing, but I think the use of Indian troops in Java and French Indo-China is more damaging in the long run because the case against it is, from the Indian point of view, almost a cast-iron one." Lord Wavell to Lord Pethick-Lawrence, 27 November 1945, *TOP*, VI, no. 246, p. 555.

199. Indonesians would refer to this as "Heroes' Day" from 1945 onward.

200. Doulton, *The Fighting Cock*, 265.

201. McMillan makes the point that the British did not bombard the city at will, as is claimed by some; this is confirmed in both the 5th Indian Division and the 13th Lancers war diaries. See also Brett-James, *The Fighting Cock*, 456–457; and "Life and Times of General Sir Philip Christison," p. 186, Imperial War Museum.

202. Lieutenant Colonel Bristow of the Dogra Machine Gun Battalion recalled that "clearing the town street by street was a slow and costly operation which last[ed] 19 days." Bristow, *Memories of the British Raj*, 139.

203. Dennis, *Troubled Days*, 126; McMillan, *The British Occupation of Indonesia*, 54–57; Kirby et al., *The War against Japan*, 5:333–336.

204. Kirby et al., *The War against Japan*, 5:336.

205. Brett-James, *Ball of Fire*, 463–465.

206. See Kirby et al., *The War against Japan*, 5:341, Dennis, *Troubled Days*, 190–191; and McMillan, *The British Occupation of Indonesia*, 61.

207. "Life and Times of General Sir Philip Christison," p. 188, IWM.

208. See Dennis and McMillan for an in-depth discussion of the many layers of negotiations, relations, and planning for Dutch Army troops to return to the NEI and their takeover of the British and Indian positions in Java and the NEI as a whole.

209. The 1/16th Punjabis described the mission as thus: "the main tasks at Buitzenborg were the maintenance of road communications up to the Poentijak Pass on the Bandoeng road, and the preservation of law and order in the surrounding country. During the following three months [February to May] frequent clashes with bands of extremists took place." Lawford, *Solah Punjab*, 235; see also WO 172/10280.

210. See 1st Patiala's, WO 172/10343 April 1946, as well as Doulton, *The Fighting Cock*, 294–299.

211. Kirby et al., *The War against Japan*, 5:342; McMillan, *The British Occupation of Indonesia*, 90–99.

212. Kirby et al., *The War against Japan*, 5:348.

213. Kirby et al., 5:374.

214. Kirby et al., 5:351.

215. Condon, *The Frontier Force Rifles*, 352. It must be noted that the battalion served with the 26th Indian Division in Burma, and had been on home leave since May, when it was called up again and shipped to Java in November 1945. Interestingly, the battalion was commended for its morale; this could easily have been otherwise, given that the men had been on home leave already.

216. Some of the key primary sources for this period are in the National Archives, UK. There are the two divisional war diaries, WO 172/7045 (1945) and WO 172/9893 (1946), as well as a report listed as WO 172/6160 "26th Indian Division in Sumatra."

217. Prasad listed it as: "(a) to reoccupy, with sufficient force, key areas, secure effective control, enforce the surrender and disarm the Japanese forces; (b) to render assistance to APWI." Prasad, *Post-War Occupation Forces*, 239. The 26th Indian Division report stated: "Full authority over Military and Civilians is to be exercised only in Key areas, and even in these areas Civilians will be dealt with through the Dutch Civil Administration." WO 172/6160, NA, p. 18.

218. The Division's 36th Brigade was diverted to Java: Prasad, *Post-War Occupation Forces*, 240.

219. See Kirby et al., *The War against Japan*, 5:355–357, plus map and McMillan, *The British Occupation of Indonesia*, 113–115.

220. The Netherlands Indies Civil Affairs (NICA) was attached to the divisional HQ and they were tasked with the civil administration outside the key three towns.

221. Quoted in McMillan, *The British Occupation of Indonesia*, 117.

222. See McMillan, 118–119, for a detailed description of the disappearance and killing of the brigade major and the Red Cross worker and the eventual reprisals by the 71st Indian Brigade.

223. Quoted in McMillan, *The British Occupation of Indonesia*, 118. See pp. 117–122 for more details of violence and the British reaction.

224. Kirby et al., *The War against Japan*, 5:359–360; and Prasad, *Post-War Occupation Forces*, 244.

225. Kirby et al., *The War Against Japan*, 5:360.

226. Prasad, *Post-War Occupation Forces*, 242.

227. Interestingly, the bodies were recovered by Japanese soldiers. Condon, *Frontier Force Rifles*, 209.

228. Quoted in McMillan, *The British Occupation of Indonesia*, 120.

229. Prasad, *Post-War Occupation Forces*, 242.

230. See McMillan, *The British Occupation of Indonesia*, 123–126, for more a detailed discussion.

231. McMillan, 134–137.

232. Kirby et al., *The War against Japan*, 5:363.

233. This section will only deal with the deployment and performance of the 268th

Indian Brigade and not the larger Commonwealth Occupation force, which included Australian and New Zealand forces as well as naval and air force representation.

234. The battalions inside the 268th were not all the same as in Burma. The 5/1st Punjab had been shifted over from the 26th Indian Division, 1/5th Mahratta Light Infantry had served in the Western Desert and the Italian campaigns, and the 2/5th Royal Gurkha Rifles had come from the 17th Indian Division.

235. Later retired as a full general. He had already commanded a brigade in battle, so this was not a tough choice for General Auchinleck.

236. For a much wider and more in-depth discussion of the initial planning and execution of the occupation of Japan, see the following monographs: *Reports of General MacArthur: MacArthur in Japan: The Occupation: Military Phase* (Washington, DC: Center of Military History, 1966); *The Far Eastern Commission: A Study in International Cooperation, 1945–1952* (Washington, DC: Department of State, 1954); Edwin Martin, *The Allied Occupation of Japan* (Stanford, CA: Stanford University Press, 1948); and Herbert Feis, *Contest over Japan* (New York: W. W. Norton, 1967).

237. Basic Initial Post-Surrender Directive to the Supreme Commander for the Allied Powers for the Occupation and Control of Japan, forwarded to SCAP on 8 November 1945, reproduced in Martin, *The Allied Occupation of Japan*, appendix C, p. 123.

238. Reproduced in Prasad, *Post-War Occupation Forces*, 16.

239. *MacArthur Report*, 64.

240. Thimayya had commanded a brigade in 1945 in Burma.

241. Bisheshwar Prasad, ed., *The Reconquest of Burma*, vol. 1 (Calcutta: Orient Longmans, 1958), 83–84. See WO 268/768 (BRINDIV); WO 268/769 (BRINDIV); WO 268/543 (268 BDE); WO 268/545 (5/1st Punjab); WO 268/547 (2/5th RGR) war diaries in the National Archives, UK, for a more detailed description of the mission.

242. All Commonwealth Forces were commended by SCAP.

243. For a wider understanding of the Indian Army in India during this period, see Marston, *The Indian Army*, for more detailed context.

244. Prasad, *Post-War Occupation Forces*, 164–165.

245. Doulton, *The Fighting Cock*, 302.

246. This quotation came from the 1/16th Punjabis, the longest-serving battalion in Java. Lawford, *Solah Punjab*, 236.

247. Patrick Davis, *Red Flash* 16 (March 1993): 10. He served in the 4/8th Gurkhas and commanded A Company, which arrived later in the campaign, during the summer of 1946. In one of his letters to his mother, which was published in the same *Red Flash* edition (p. 8), he discussed his concerns about the deployment. He stated: "We're still in Java. . . . We're all a little browned off to tell you the truth. . . . But I suppose someone has to be here. . . . We've have only had five killed in a month, which is very light, but not at all pleasant. One doesn't enjoy losing lives in such a dim and doubtful cause."

248. Bristow, *Memories of the British Raj*, 140.

249. See Marston, *The Indian Army*, for a deeper discussion of the issues faced by the Indian Army in India from 1945 to 1947.

250. Brett-James, *Ball of Fire*, 465.

Conclusion: The Last of Its Kind

1. A. E. Housman famously titled his paean to the British Expeditionary Force of 1914 "Epitaph on an Army of Mercenaries." The regular British Army of 1914 was a long-service, professional force that had long existed to garrison—and occasionally expand—empire. All its units were "British," but, in fact, with its mix of English, Scots, Welsh, and Irish, it was multiethnic, if not polyglot.

2. John Masters, *The Road Past Mandalay* (New York: Harper, 1961), 278.

Bibliography

Primary Sources

Unpublished

INDIA OFFICE PAPERS, BRITISH LIBRARY (OIOC, BL); PRINTED ARCHIVES
L/MIL/17
L/WS/1
L/WS/2

INDIA OFFICE PAPERS, BRITISH LIBRARY (OIOC, BL); ORAL ARCHIVES
MSS EUR T3 Field Marshal Sir Claude Auchinleck
MSS EUR T58 Lt. General Sir Reginald Savory

NATIONAL ARCHIVES, KEW (NA)
WO 32
WO 106
WO 171
WO 172
WO 203
WO 268
WO 305

IMPERIAL WAR MUSEUM (IWM)
Brigadier E. A. Ardene 97/7/1
Major General A. C. Curtis Papers
Brigadier H. K. Dimoline Papers
Lt. General Geoffrey Evans Papers
Lieut. Colonel W. L. Farrow 95/33/1
Lieut. Colonel John Hill 91/13/1
Major General A. W. Holsworthy 91/40/1
Major P. H. Gadsdon 78/6/2
Major H. C. Gay 88/48/1

Brigadier P. R. MacNamara 77/32/1
Brigadier L. R. Mizen 71/63/1
Major P. B. Poore
Major D. C. Purves 87/23/1
Major General J. K. Shepherd 99/69/1
Colonel G. R. Stevens 67/31/1
Lt. General Sir Francis Tuker 71/21
Broadcast Tapes of BBC (Mandalay)

NATIONAL ARMY MUSEUM (NAM)
Lieutenant Colonel A. J. F. Doulton
General Sir Robert Lockhart Papers
Major H. R. MacDwyer Papers
Major General L. E. Pert Papers
General Sir Reginald Savory Papers
Army in India Training Memoranda
Diary of Anthony Bickersteth (4/8th Gurkhas)
Diary of Lieut. Colonel John Hill
ODTAA: Diary of a Major in the 4/10th Gurkhas
Indian Military Intelligence Directorate "Japanese in Battle" 1943
Intelligence Notes from Burma 1943–1945 GHQ India
Southeast Asia Translation and Interrogation Centre Historical Bulletin no. 243
     and 245
7709–64–2 2/13th FFRifles "War History" Mss.
7711–232 "With the 4th Sikhs" (4/12th FFR) Lt Colonel I. A. J. Edwards-Stuart Mss.
7809–3 Major P. H. MacDwyer
8002–68 Colonel J. C. Cotton
8012–63 14/13th FFRifles Ts History
8303–110 IV and XXXIII Corps

LIDDELL HART CENTRE FOR MILITARY ARCHIVES, KING'S COLLEGE LONDON
General Sir Douglas Gracey Papers
Major General Woodburn Kirby Papers
Major General John Lethbridge Papers
Lt. General Sir Frank Messervy Papers

CHURCHILL ARCHIVES CENTER, CHURCHILL COLLEGE, CAMBRIDGE
General Sir Alexander Christison Papers
Ronald Lewin Papers
Brigadier Michael Roberts Papers
Field Marshal William Slim Papers

UNIVERSITY OF MANCHESTER
Field Marshal Sir Claude Auchinleck Papers

INTERVIEWS AND CORRESPONDENCE

5th Probyn's Horse; 7th Light Cavalry; 11th Prince Albert Victor's Own Cavalry (FF); Royal Indian Artillery; Royal Indian Engineers; KGO's Bengal Sappers and Miners; Bombay Sappers and Miners; 1st Punjab Regiment; 2nd Punjab Regiment; 3rd Madras Regiment; 4th Bombay Grenadiers; 6th Rajputana Rifles; 7th Rajput Regiment; 8th Punjab Regiment; 9th Jat Regiment; 10th Baluch Regiment; 11th Sikh Regiment; 12th Frontier Force Regiment; 13th Frontier Force Rifles; 14th Punjab Regiment; 16th Punjab Regiment; 17th Dogra Regiment; 18th Garhwal Rifles; Sikh Light Infantry; 4th Gurkha Rifles; 5th Royal Gurkha Rifles; 8th Gurkha Rifles; 10th Gurkha Rifles

Privately Published, Personal Diaries, Miscellaneous Manuscripts

Anonymous, History of 7/10th Baluch Regiment in Burma. Mss. 1945.

Anonymous, History of the 7th Light Cavalry in Burma. 2 volumes. 1944 and 1945.

Anonymous, "Probyn's Newsletter." 1944–1945.

Clarke, S. D. *Now or Never-The Story of the 4/3rd Madras in the Burma Campaign.* 1945.

Elliott, Sir Gerald. India a memoir. Mss 1960.

Kinloch, Major B. G. *A Subedar Remembers and Thirty Pieces of Silver.* 1991.

Murtough, V. I. "Recollections of my war." Mss 1970s.

Mylne, Major B. H., ed. *An Account of Operations in Burma Carried out by Probyn's Horse during February, March and April.* Privately published, 1945.

Roberts, Michael. Field diary dealing with operations in 1944.

Personal Accounts were found in the regimental newsletters of the 8th Gurkhas, *Red Flash*, copies seen 1992–2000 and *The Piffer* (the Journal of the Punjab Frontier Force Association), copies with personal accounts are from the 1990s.

Published

INDIAN ARMY AND GOVERNMENT

Demobilisation of the Indian Army. Simla: Government of India Press, 1947.

The Far Eastern Commission: A Study in International Cooperation, 1945–1952. Washington, DC: Department of State, 1954.

Mansergh, Nicholas, ed. *The Transfer of Power, 1942–1947,* 12 vols. London: HMSO, 1970–1983.

Post Surrender Tasks; Section E of the Report to the Combined Chiefs of Staff by the Supreme Allied Commander South-East Asia, 1943–1946. London: HMSO, 1969.

Reports of General McArthur. MacArthur in Japan: The Occupation: Military Phase. Washington, DC: Center of Military History, 1966.

JAPANESE MONOGRAPHS: US GOVERNMENT

Burma Operations Record: 15th Army Operations and Withdrawal to Northern Burma. Japanese Monograph 134. Tokyo: US Army HQ, 1957.

Burma Operations Record: 33rd Army Operations. Japanese Monograph 148, Tokyo: US Army HQ, 1957.

US GOVERNMENT

The Far Eastern Commission: A Study in International Cooperation, 1945–1952. Washington, DC: Department of State, 1954.

Reports of General McArthur: MacArthur in Japan: The Occupation: Military Phase. Washington, DC: Center of Military History, 1966.

MEMOIRS

Atkins, David. *The Forgotten Major.* Pulborough: Toat, 1989.

————. *The Reluctant Major.* Pulborough: Toat, 1986.

Bristow, R. C. B. *Memories of the British Raj: A Soldier in India.* London: Johnson, 1974.

Cooper, K. W. *The Little Men.* London: Hale, 1985.

Cooper, Raymond. *"B" Company, 9th Battalion the Border Regiment: One Man's War in Burma.* London: Dobson, 1978.

Coubrough, C. R. L. *Memories of a Perpetual Second Lieutenant.* York: Wilton 65, 1999.

Cubitt-Smith. *Yadgari or the Memories of the Raj.* Saxlingham, Norfolk: privately published, 1986.

Davis, Patrick. *A Child at Arms.* London: Hutchinson, 1970.

Evans, Geoffrey. *The Desert and Jungle.* London: Kimber, 1959.

Forteath, G. M. *Pipes, Kukris and Nips.* London: Pentland, 1992.

Fraser, David. *And We Shall Shock Them: The British Army in the Second World War.* London: Hodder and Stoughton, 1983.

Fraser, George MacDonald. *Quartered Safe Out Here.* London: Harvill, 1992.

Gilmore, Scott. *A Connecticut Yankee in the 8th Gurkha Rifles: A Burma Memoir.* Washington, DC: Brassey's, 1995.

Grounds, Tom. *Some Letters from Burma: Story of the 25th Dragoons at War.* Tunbridge Wells: Parapress, 1994.

Hastings, Robin. *An Undergraduate's War.* London: Bellhouse, 1997.

Hill, John. *China Dragons: A Rifle Company at War, Burma 1944–45.* London: Blandford, 1991.

Humphreys, Roy. *To Stop a Rising Sun: Reminiscences of Wartime in India and Burma.* Stroud: Alan Sutton, 1996.

Lowry, M. A. *An Infantry Company in Arakan and Kohima.* Aldershot, UK: Gale & Polden, 1950.

Lowry, Michael. *Fighting through to Kohima: A Memoir of War in India & Burma.* Yorkshire: Leo Cooper, 2003.

Masters, John. *The Road Past Mandalay.* New York: Harper, 1961.

Milne, Major B. H., ed. *An Account of Operations in Burma Carried Out by Probyn's Horse.* Privately published, 1945.

Mountbatten, Vice-Admiral Lord Louis, Earl of Burma. *Report to the Combined Chiefs of Staff by the Supreme Allied Commander South-East Asia 1943–1945.* London: His Majesty's Stationery Office, 1951.

Pickford, John. *Destination Rangoon.* Denbigh: Gee, 1989.

Prendergast, John. *Prender's Progress: A Soldier in India.* London: Cassell, 1979.

Rose, Angus. *Who Dies Fighting.* London: Jonathan Cape, 1944.

Rose, D. *Off the Record.* Stapelhurst: Spellmount, 1996.

Schlaefli, Robin. *Emergency Sahib*. London: Leach, 1992.

Sheil-Small, Denis. *Green Shadows: A Gurkha Story*. London: Kimber, 1982.

Slim, Field-Marshal Viscount William. *Defeat into Victory*. London: Cassell, 1956.

———. *Unofficial History*. New York: David McKay, 1959.

Smeeton, Miles. *A Change of Jungles*. London: Hart-Davis, 1962.

Wedemeyer, Albert. *Wedemeyer Reports! An Objective, Dispassionate Examination of World War II, Postwar Policies, and Grand Strategy*. New York: Henry Holt, 1958.

Ziegler, Philip, ed. *Personal Diary of Admiral the Lord Louis Mountbatten: Supreme Allied Commander, South-East Asian, 1943–1946*. London: Collins, 1988.

Secondary Sources

Allen, Louis. *Burma: The Longest War, 1941–1945*. London: Dent, 1984.

———. *The End of the War in Asia*. London: Hart-Davis MacGibbon, 1976.

———. *Sittang: The Last Battle*. New York: Ballantine, 1974.

Allport, Alan. *Browned-Off and Bloody-Minded: The British Soldier Goes To War, 1939–1945*. New Haven, CT: Yale University Press, 2015.

Anglim, Simon. *Orde Wingate and the British Army, 1922–1944*. London: Pickering & Chatto, 2010.

Bamford, Lieut. Colonel P. G. *1st King George V's Own Battalion: The Sikh Regiment*. Aldershot, UK: Gale & Polden, 1948.

Bandele, Biyi. *Burma Boy*. London: Jonathan Cape, 2007.

Barkawi, Tarak. "Culture and Combat in the Colonies: The Indian Army in the Second World War." *Journal of Contemporary History* 41, no. 2 (April 2006): 325–355.

———. *Soldiers of Empire*. Cambridge: Cambridge University Press, 2017.

Barua, Pradeep. *The Army Officer Corps and Military Modernisation in Later Colonial India*. Hull: University of Hull Press, 1999.

Bayly, Chris, and Tim Harper. *Forgotten Armies: The Fall of British Asia, 1941–1945*. London: Allen Lane, 2004.

Bidwell, Shelford. *The Chindit War: Stilwell, Wingate, and the Campaign in Burma, 1944*. New York: Macmillan, 1980.

Bond, Brian, ed. *British and Japanese Military Leadership in the Far Eastern War, 1941–1945*. London: Frank Cass, 2004.

Booth, John. *Ninth Battalion Fourteenth Punjab Regiment*. Cardiff: Western Mail and Echo, 1948.

Brett-James, Antony. *Ball of Fire: The Fifth Indian Division in the Second World War*. Aldershot, UK: Gale & Polden, 1951.

Brett-James, Antony, and Geoffrey Evans. *Imphal: A Flower on Lofty Heights*. London: Macmillan, 1962.

Bryant, Arthur. *Triumph in the West, 1943–1946*. New York: Doubleday, 1959.

Callahan, Raymond. *Burma, 1942–1945*. London: Davis-Poynter, 1978.

———. *Churchill and His Generals*. Lawrence: University Press of Kansas, 2007.

———. *The East India Company and Army Reform*. Cambridge, MA: Harvard University Press, 1972.

———. *Triumph at Imphal-Kohima: How the Indian Army Finally Stopped the Japanese Juggernaut.* Lawrence: University Press of Kansas, 2017.

Campbell, Arthur. *The Siege: A Story from Kohima.* London: Allen & Unwin, 1956.

Carfrae, Charles. *Chindit Column.* London: Kimber: 1985.

Chinh, Truong. *Primer for Revolt, The Communist Takeover in Viet-Nam: A Facsimile Edition of* The August Revolution *and* The Resistance Will Win. New York: Praeger, 1966.

Cohen, Stephen. *The Indian Army: Its Contribution to the Development of the Indian Nation.* Berkeley: University of California Press, 1971.

Colvin, John. *Not Ordinary Men: The Story of the Battle of Kohima.* London: Leo Cooper, 1995.

Condon, W. E. H. *The Frontier Force Regiment.* Aldershot, UK: Gale & Polden, 1962.

———. *The Frontier Force Rifles.* Aldershot, UK: Gale & Polden, 1953.

Connell, John. *Auchinleck.* London: Collins, 1959.

———. *Wavell: Supreme Commander 1941–1943.* London: Collins, 1969.

Cross, J. P. *Jungle Warfare: Experiences and Encounters.* London: Arms and Armour, 1989.

Danchev, Alex, and Daniel Todman, eds. *War Diaries, 1939–1945: Field Marshal Lord Alanbrooke.* London: Weidenfeld and Nicolson, 2001.

Dennis, Peter. *Troubled Days of Peace: Mountbatten and South East Asia Command, 1945–6.* Manchester: University of Manchester Press, 1987.

Donnison, F. S. V. *British Military Administration in the Far East, 1943–6.* London: Her Majesty's Stationery Office, 1956.

Doulton, A. J. F. *The Fighting Cock: Being the History of the 23rd Indian Division, 1942–1947.* Aldershot, UK: Gale & Polden, 1951.

Dunlop, Graham. *Military Economics, Culture and Logistics in the Burma Campaign, 1942–1945.* London: Routledge, 2009.

Dunn, Peter. *The First Indo-China War.* London: C. Hurst, 1985.

Ehrman, John. *Grand Strategy.* Vol. 6. London: HMSO, 1956.

Evans, Geoffrey. *Slim as Military Commander.* London: Batsford, 1969.

Feis, Herbert. *Contest over Japan.* New York: W. W. Norton, 1967.

Fraser, David. *Alanbrooke.* London: Collins, 1982.

Gaylor, John. *Sons of John Company.* Tunbridge Wells: Spellmount, 1992.

Gilbert, Martin, and Larry Arnn. *The Churchill Documents.* Vol. 20, *Normandy and beyond May-December 1944.* Hillsdale, MI: Hillsdale College Press, 2018.

———. *The Churchill Documents.* Vol. 21, *The Shadows of Victory January–July 1945.* Hillsdale, MI: Hillsdale College Press, 2018.

Grant, Ian Lyall. *Burma: The Turning Point: The Seven Battles on the Tiddim Road.* London: Zampi, 1993.

Hamid, Major General S. S. *So They Rode and Fought.* Tunbridge Wells, UK: Midas, 1983.

Hamilton, John A. L. *War Bush: 81st West African Division in Burma, 1943–1945.* Norwich: Michael Russell, 2001.

Hanley, Gerald. *Monsoon Victory.* London: Collins, 1946.

Hastings, Max. *Nemesis: The Battle for Japan.* London: Harper, 2007.

Haywood, A., and F. A. S. Clarke. *The History of the Royal West African Frontier Force.* Aldershot, UK: Gale & Polden, 1964.

Hickey, Michael. *The Unforgettable Army: Slim's XIVth Army in Burma.* London: Spellmount, 1992.

Hookway, J. D., ed. *M & R: A Regimental History of the Sikh Light Infantry.* Oxford: Oxford University Computer Services, 1999.

Hughes, Geraint. "A 'Post-War' War: The British Occupation of French-Indochina, September 1945–March 1946." *Small Wars & Insurgencies* 17, no. 3 (2006).

Jackson, Ashley. *The British Empire and the Second World War.* London: Hambledon, 2006.

Jeffreys, Alan. *Approach To Battle: Training The Indian Army during The Second World War.* Solihull, UK: Helion, 2017.

Jeffreys, Alan, and Patrick Rose, eds. *The Indian Army, 1939–1947.* Farnham, UK: Ashgate, 2012.

Karaka, D. F. *With the 14th Army.* Bombay: Thacker, 1944.

Khan, Yasmin. *The Raj at War: A People's History of India's Second World War.* London: Bodley Head, 2015.

King-Clark, R. *The Battle for Kohima, 1944: The Narrative of the 2nd Battaltion—the Manchester Regiment.* Cheshire: Fleur de Lys, 1995.

Kirby, S. Woodburn. *The War against Japan.* Vols. 1–5. London: Her Majesty's Stationery Office, 1957–1969.

Lawford, J. P. *Solah Punjab: The History of the 16th Punjab Regiment.* Aldershot, UK: Gale & Polden, 1967.

Lewin, Ronald. *Slim: The Standard Bearer.* London: Leo Cooper, 1976.

Lyman, Robert. *Slim: Master of War.* London: Constable, 2004.

Marston, Daniel. *The Indian Army and the End of the Raj.* Cambridge: Cambridge University Press, 2014.

———. *The Phoenix from the Ashes: The Indian Army in the Burma Campaign.* Westport, CT: Praeger, 2003.

Marston, Daniel, and Chandar Sundaram. eds. *Military History of India and South Asia.* Bloomington: Indiana University Press, 2007.

Martin, Edwin. *The Allied Occupation of Japan.* Stanford, CA: Stanford University Press, 1948.

Mason, Philip. *A Matter of Honour.* London: Cape, 1974.

———. *A Shaft of Sunlight.* London: Andre Deutsch, 1978.

Matthews, Geoffrey. *The Re-Conquest of Burma, 1943–1945.* Aldershot, UK: Gale & Polden, 1966.

Maule, Henry. *Spearhead General: The Epic Story of General Sir Frank Messervy.* London: Oldhams, 1961.

McKelvie, Roy. *The War in Burma.* London: Methuen, 1948.

McMillan, Richard. *The British Occupation of Indonesia, 1945–1946.* London: Routledge, 2005.

Menezes, S. L. *Fidelity & Honour: The Indian Army from the Seventeenth to the Twenty-First Century.* New Delhi: Viking, 1993.

Moreman, Timothy. *The Jungle, the Japanese and the British Commonwealth Armies at War, 1941–1945.* London: Frank Cass, 2005.

Moyse-Bartlett, H. *The King's African Rifles: A Study in the Military History of East and Central Africa, 1890–1945.* Aldershot, UK: Gale & Polden, 1956.

Neville, Peter. *Britain in Vietnam: Prelude to Disaster, 1945–6.* London: Routledge, 2007.

Owen, Frank. *The Campaign in Burma.* London: His Majesty's Stationery Office, 1946.

Palit, D. K. *Major General A. A. Rudra.* New Delhi: Reliance, 1997.

Perrett, Bryan. *Tank Tracks to Rangoon: The Story of British Armour in Burma.* London: Robert Hale, 1992.

Perry, F. W. *Commonwealth Armies: Manpower and Organisation in the Two World Wars.* Manchester: Manchester University Press, 1988.

Phillips, Barnaby. *Another Man's War: The Story of a Burma Boy in Britain's Forgotten African Army.* London, Oneworld, 2014.

Pocock, Tom. *Fighting General: The Public and Private Campaigns of General Sir Walter Walker.* London: Collins, 1973.

Prasad, Bisheshwar. *Official History of the Indian Armed Forces in the Second World War, 1939–1945. Expansion of the Armed Forces and Defence Organisation.* New Delhi: Historical Section (India & Pakistan), 1956.

———. *Post-War Occupation Forces: Japan and South-East Asia.* New Delhi: Orient Longmans, 1958.

———. *The Reconquest of Burma.* 2 vols. New Delhi: Orient Longmans, 1953.

Proudfoot, C. L. *We Lead: 7th Light Cavalry.* New Delhi: Lancer, 1991.

Qureshi, Major Mahommed Ibrahim. *The First Punjabis.* Aldershot, UK: Gale & Polden, 1958.

Raghavan, Srinath. *India's War: The Making of Modern South Asia, 1939–1945.* London: Allan Lane, 2016.

Reynolds, David. *In Command of History: Churchill Fighting and Writing the Second World War.* London: Random House, 2004.

Roberts, M. R. *Golden Arrow: The Story of the 7th Indian Division in the Second World War, 1939–1945.* Aldershot, UK: Gale & Polden, 1952.

Rooney, David. *Burma Victory: Imphal, Kohima and the Chindit Issue.* London: Arms and Armour, 1992.

Roy, Kaushik. *The Indian Army in the Two World Wars.* Leiden: Brill, 2012.

———. "Military Loyalty in the Colonial Context: A Case Study of the Indian Army during World War II." *Journal of Military History* 73 (April 2009).

———, ed. *War and Society in Colonial India.* New Delhi: Oxford University Press, 2006.

Sharma, Gautum. *Nationalisation of the Indian Army.* New Delhi: Allied, 1996.

Smith, Adrian. *Mountbatten: Apprentice Warlord.* London: I. B. Taurus, 2010.

Spector, Ronald. "After Hiroshima: Allied Military Occupations and the Fate of Japan's Empire, 1945–7." *Journal of Military History* 69, no. 4 (2005)."

Springhall, John. "Disaster in Surabaya: The Death of Brigadier Mallaby during the British Occupation of Java, 1945–6." *Journal of Imperial and Commonwealth History* 24, no. 3 (September 1996).

———. "Kicking Out the Vietminh: How Britain Allowed France to Reoccupy South Indo-China, 1945–6." *Journal of Contemporary History* 40, no. 1 (2005).

Streets, Heather. *Martial Races: The Military, Race, and Masculinity in the British Imperial Culture, 1857–1914*. Manchester: Manchester University Press, 2004.

Swinson, Arthur. *Four Samurai: A Quartet of Japanese Army Commanders in the Second World War*. London: Hutchinson, 1968.

———. *Kohima*. London: Cassell, 1966.

Thompson, Julian. *The Imperial War Museum Book of the War in Burma, 1942–1945*. London: Sidgwick and Jackson, 2002.

Trench, Charles Chenevix. *The Indian Army and the King's Enemies 1900–1947*. London: Thames and Hudson, 1988.

Turnbull, Patrick. *The Battle of the Box*. London: Ian Allen, 1979.

Warner, Philip. *Auchinleck: The Lonely Soldier*. London: Buchan & Enright, 1981.

Warren, Alan. *Burma 1942: The Road from Rangoon to Mandalay*. London: Continuum, 2011.

Yong, Tan Tai, *The Garrison State: Military, Government and Society in Colonial Punjab, 1849–1947*. New Delhi: Sage, 2005.

Ziegler, Philip. *Mountbatten: A Biography*. New York: Knopf, 1985.

Index